ARKLE

'The best book on Arkle.'
PADDY WOODS
Arkle's regular work rider

'Sean Magee's evocative tribute to Arkle is a "must-have" for all worshippers of great horses – an obit to die for.'
SIR PETER O'SULLEVAN CBE

'A splendid reassessment ... an affectionate but clear-headed portrait of a legend.'
ANDREW BAKER, *DAILY TELEGRAPH*

'All Arkle anoraks will relish this affectionate celebration ... a well-researched labour of love.'
RACING POST

'As the racehorse population swells through overproduction, so too do the annual additions to the racing library. In such a crowded field, head and shoulders above the rest, in literature as in life, stands *Arkle* by Sean Magee. Magee is a master of research ... He has unearthed much that has not been on display before.'
JOHN COBB, *THE INDEPENDENT*

'A feast for the eye as well as an enjoyable read.'
LEO POWELL, *IRISH FIELD*

'A story brilliantly told.'
IRISH NEWS

Arkle and Pat Taaffe before the 1965 Hennessy Gold Cup.

ARKLE

The Story of the World's Greatest Steeplechaser

50th Anniversary Edition

SEAN MAGEE

RACING POST

First published in 2005 by Highdown, an imprint of Raceform Ltd.
First published in paperback in 2009.

This revised and updated paperback edition published in 2014 by
Racing Post, Compton, Newbury, Berkshire, RG20 6NL

A catalogue record for this book is available from the British Library.

ISBN 978-1-909471-62-7

Designed by Tracey Scarlett
Printed and bound in the Czech Republic by Finidr

Cover photographs both by Gerry Cranham: *back*, Arkle before the 1964 Cheltenham Gold
Cup; *front*, Arkle at the final fence

www.racingpost.com/shop

Much of the pictorial material reproduced in this book has been gathered from private or informal
collections such as the Arkle Bar at Cheltenham racecourse, and it has not always been possible to
identify and credit the source. Omissions of the correct acknowledgement and copyright notice will
rectified in future editions if the publishers are notified. Sources of other illustrations are as follows:

Getty Images: 2, 77, 88, 138, 139, 142, 171

Alison Baker: 16

Racing Post: 18, 22, 29, 47, 84, 85. 87, 96. 103,
104, 110, 111, 119 (all), 128-9, 141. 146, 150,
151, 153, 156, 158-9, 162, 166, 184

Ordnance Survey © Crown Copyright 2002: 21

Bob Sutton: 30

Gerry Cranham: 35, 56 (lower), 57, 60 (both),
62 (top), 75, 97, 98, 99, 101 (both), 181

Empics: 43, 61, 86

Peter Biegel estate (courtesy of Mrs Anne
Hall): 55, 168

Essex Music: 66

A. J. Byles: 75, 89, 143, 148, 149

Bernard Parkin: 37, 80, 81, 179 (three b/w)

Illustrated London News: 100

Express Newspapers: 118

Observer: 134, 203

RaceTech: 135

Mrs Diana Winter: 165 (lower)

Tod Ramos: 180 (lower)

Christie's: 184

CONTENTS

Preface   6

'Do you know, I think we've got something there!'   8
Early years and early races

'The day Arkle became a god'   48
The 1964 Gold Cup

'The perfect, complete chaser'   68
The 1964-65 season

'Arkle for President'   92
The 1965-66 season

'He lost as a great horse should'   128
The final races

'An easy end'   158
Retirement, death and after

The racing record   188

Index   204

Acknowledgements   208

PREFACE

Late October, 2013. At the foot of a steeply inclined field in the northern part of County Dublin, a small group people are standing in the soft-falling rain. The focus of their attention is the headstone at the grave of a horse named – so the inscription informs them – Bright Cherry. As they linger there, getting wetter by the minute, over the hill gallop three young horses, who stare briefly at the group, as if seeking an explanation for this curious behaviour, then turn and skitter back over the skyline.

The young horses are not aware of it, but this place – Quarry Field at Malahow, near Naul – is a shrine, and the people are pilgrims. They have come to pay their respects to the mother of the horse whose name also appears on that headstone, 'Arkle 1957-1970, Horse of the Century' – and to see the rural idyll where the greatest of all steeplechasers spent his early years. They have already visited Ballymacoll Stud, where he was born, and from Malahow will go to Greenogue, where he was trained, and then to Bryanstown, where he retired and died.

The Arkle Pilgrimage – described on pages 186-7 of this book – provides yet more evidence of the hold which this extraordinary racehorse exerts so long after his racing career, and the trip came within a few months of the fiftieth anniversary of 'The day Arkle became a god' – his famous victory over Mill House in the 1964 Cheltenham Gold Cup. To mark that anniversary, this book – first published in 2005 and revised for paperback publication in 2009 – is now updated to the spring of 2014, with the addition of new material and several fresh photographs.

I saw him in the flesh only once, at Kempton Park on Boxing Day 1965, but can still feel the teenage thrill of being in his presence. Arkle – by then widely referred to as 'Himself' – was every bit as magnificent in real life as all those races on the telly and all those cuttings in my scrapbook had suggested, but no cathode-ray tube or photograph could ever have done justice to the corporeal reality of those ears. They were extraordinary – like animated radio masts scanning the crowd to pick up every nuance of the adoration – and to witness them at first hand was an awe-inspiring experience.

To be honest, I felt a little awkward about meeting him in person, as our relationship had not always been smooth. Having become an ardent Mill House fan as the Australian wicket-keeper Wally Grout began to lose his appeal, for most of 1964 I had refused to forgive Arkle for beating The Big Horse at Cheltenham. After that year's Hennessy and Massey-Ferguson I started to come round, and by the time I worked the wire of the transistor radio up my blazer arm before Father O'Halloran's religious instruction lesson on Gold Cup afternoon 1965, I was completely under Arkle's spell.

I have remained there ever since: still getting out my *Escalado* horse which Airfix paint has transformed into a bay carrying the colours of Anne, Duchess of Westminster (though the tassel fell off); still squirming when finding the scrapbook page where, next to the cutting headed 'ARKLE SCRAPES HOME IN PHOTO-FINISH',

I have written 'A headline rare indeed!!'; still relishing the moment when I walked into one of the vast betting halls at Sha Tin racetrack in Hong Kong to see the Susan Crawford portrait of Himself adorning the wall behind the counter; still remembering the moment when Tony Paley of the *Guardian* phoned to say he had a recording of the 1965 Gallaher Gold Cup – at last!; still finding excuses (compiling this book has been an excellent one) to track down those who knew Arkle well and talk about him.

Of course, the great horse has been extensively chronicled elsewhere, from Ivor Herbert's *Arkle: The story of a champion*, first published in 1966, to Anne Holland's *Arkle: The legend of 'Himself'*, published in 2013. Arkle has also been celebrated in two small picture books: *Arkle: A pictorial record of a great horse*, compiled by Howard Wright and published by Timeform in 1968, and *Arkle: The wonder horse* by John Richmond, also published in 1968. Videos dedicated to Himself include *Arkle: The legend*, directed by Nick O'Toole with music by The Chieftains, and *Arkle: Portrait of a legend*, sponsored by the *Irish Independent*. A bumper collection of the incomparable writing on Arkle by John Lawrence, later Lord Oaksey, is brought together in *Oaksey on Racing* (1991), while an exquisite account of Arkle's appeal can be found in Jamie Reid's *Days Like These: The education of a racing lover* (2003).

The idea of this book was born when readers of the *Racing Post*, in a poll concluded in February 2004, voted Arkle their favourite racehorse of all time. From a shortlist of ten, Arkle took 21.9 per cent of the vote, beating (in finishing order) Desert Orchid, Red Rum, Istabraq, Brigadier Gerard, One Man, Persian Punch, Dancing Brave, Sea Pigeon and Nijinsky. Arkle's victory was a remarkable tribute to the tenacity with which a horse who had been in his prime four decades earlier had maintained his position in the affection of racing fans.

Since the book was first published, that tenacity has constantly been brought home to me. A lady who phoned in to a radio programme on which I was promoting the book came over all tearful as she relived her own Arkle experience, and later sent me a card declaring that 'The flame still burns brightly.' Other correspondents wrote with their own reminiscences of Himself. One remarked how the book 'took me back to my schooldays, and watching my hero on an old black-and-white grainy TV'; another described how 'as I write, I'm looking at the Arkle Irish linen tea towel which is on display in my back room.' Arkle's effect on people, how he unlocks their emotions, remains one of the most remarkable themes of his story.

'Champions are made in heaven', said Tom Dreaper, and the magic of Arkle, the horse who became a god, really defies description. As Tommy Bracken, who peddled his poems round the bars of Dublin, wrote:

Indeed, the world seemed to cheer him,
Because his like they won't see again:
This horse called after a mountain
Is beyond the reach of a pen.

S.M.

'Do you know – I think
we've got something there!'

'Do you know – I think we've got something there!'

Early years and early races

'Arkle', wrote John Randall and Tony Morris in their book *A Century of Champions*, 'was a freak, an unrepeatably lucky shake of the genetic cocktail, the nearest thing the sport has ever seen to the perfect machine.'

The recipe for that cocktail was created late in 1955 by Mrs Mary Baker, a small-time breeder who kept a few mares on the family farm at Malahow, near Naul in the northern part of County Dublin. This is an area rich in the breeding of famous jumpers: Easter Hero, Golden Miller, Reynoldstown and Best Mate are just a few who first drew breath near here.

After ruminating where to send her mare Bright Cherry – in 1955 barren to the stallion Mustang – for mating the following year, Mrs Baker decided upon the sire Archive, who stood at a very reasonable fee down in County Kildare.

The offspring was born in April 1957, a month when – to put the event in historical perspective – Singapore was granted self-government from Britain (whose prime minister Harold Macmillan had been in 10 Downing Street for only three months), Tom Finney of Preston North End was voted Footballer of the Year, and 'Young Love' by Tab Hunter was finally knocked off the top of the pop charts, which it had occupied for seven weeks, by Lonnie Donegan's nasal rendition of 'Cumberland Gap'. The following month six European nations (but not the UK) signed the Rome Treaty to create the Common Market.

Bright Cherry's foal turned out to be a bay colt, somewhat ungainly and the sort likely to respond to an unhurried upbringing. He was given as long as he needed to mature, turned out with his dam at a very early age. On the day after his first birthday (actual, not official) he gashed a foreleg when getting caught on a strand of barbed wire while in pursuit of young fillies in the next field, and bore the scar for the rest of his life.

Late in the summer of 1958 he was gelded, and by the following spring the process of gently breaking him in was well under way, while he continued to be turned out in the fields day and night to strengthen and develop, with a view to his going to the sales as a three-year-old.

The landmarks in the bay's early life now started flicking by:

- *August 1960: bought by Anne, Duchess of Westminster*
- *late 1960 to mid 1961: easy living on the Duchess's estate in Cheshire*
- *summer 1961: trainer Tom Dreaper, given the choice of two of the Duchess's four-year-olds, chooses the bay gelding*
- *August 1961: arrives at Dreaper's yard at Kilsallaghan*
- *December 1961: runs his first race*
- *January 1962: wins for the first time, a hurdle race*
- *November 1962: wins first steeplechase*

Many of Arkle's admirers have observed that the horse was exceptionally fortunate in the human connections who steered his career. His breeder, his owner, his trainer, his trainer's staff and his regular jockey all knew that the key was patience, which surrounded him from the beginning and played a major part in making him what he became. As John Oaksey wrote: 'Throughout his life, in a world it takes all sorts to make, his selection of human beings was as unerring as his jumping.'

PREVIOUS SPREAD:
Greenogue.

				Phalaris
ARKLE bay colt, 1957	Archive bay 1941	Nearco	Pharos	Phalaris
				Scapa Flow
			Nogara	Havresac II
				Catnip
		Book Law	Buchan	Sunstar
				Hamoaze
			Popingaol	Dark Ronald
				Popinjay
	Bright Cherry chestnut 1944	Knight Of The Garter	Son-In-Law	Dark Ronald
				Mother-In-Law
			Castelline	Cyllene
				Cassine
		Greenogue Princess	My Prince	Marcovil
				Salvaich
			Cherry Branch II	Cerasus
				Lady Peace

Arkle's pedigree

While the achievements of some famous racehorses can be at least reasonably expected from their breeding, many seem to defy the prognosis of their pedigrees. Red Rum, famous for his feats in the 4½-mile Grand National, was sired by Quorum, a sprinter. On the Flat, where the genes seem to be weighed with more exactitude than in jump racing, an example of a hugely successful racehorse unfashionably bred was Brigadier Gerard, who won seventeen of his eighteen races between 1970

Bright Cherry winning the Raheny Chase at Baldoyle in September 1950, ridden by Pat Taaffe.

Bright Cherry's grave – bearing a suitable inscription – in the Quarry Field at Malahow.

and 1972 despite being a son of Queen's Hussar, who neither before siring that great horse nor afterwards ever produced anything remotely as good.

Arkle is another instance of a horse whose future exploits were hardly hinted at by his pedigree. His sire Archive registered not a single success as a racehorse in eleven outings between 1943 and 1945, his highest placing being runner-up in a £306 plate for maiden three-year-olds at Stockton in August 1944. Such lack of racecourse achievement was particularly frustrating for Archive's connections, for on breeding he should have been very good indeed. His sire Nearco was one of the greatest of all Italian horses – unbeaten (and unextended) in thirteen races in his native country plus the 1938 Grand Prix de Paris – and a hugely influential stallion. Archive's dam Book Law, owned and bred by Lord Astor, was a top-class and remarkably tough filly who in 1927 dead-heated for second in the One Thousand Guineas, was beaten a head in the Oaks and won the St Leger easily; her five other victories that season included the Coronation Stakes at Royal Ascot, Nassau Stakes at Goodwood and Jockey Club Stakes at Newmarket. In addition to Archive, her offspring included Rhodes Scholar, winner of the 1936 Eclipse Stakes.

Thus it was his breeding rather than any hint of racecourse prowess which qualified Archive to stand as a stallion at all, and his bargain-basement fee in 1956 of 48 guineas at the Loughtown Stud did not seem unreasonable, especially since his earlier progeny had included Lord Bicester's top-class chaser Mariner's Log, trained by Tom Dreaper to finish runner-up to Four Ten in the 1954 Gold Cup.

Bright Cherry, Arkle's dam, was far less well bred than Archive but had at least won. Born in 1944, she had been trained by Dreaper for Mrs Baker's late husband Henry, winning one hurdle and six chases between 1948 and 1951, and being placed on eleven occasions. She last raced as a seven-year-old in March 1951. The chestnut mare had further connections with Dreaper, for her dam Greenogue Princess (who came from and was named after the area where he established his yard) had been ridden by him in a point-to-point: it is a measure of his optimism in advance of this ride that he had a man stationed at the second last fence to catch Greenogue Princess should she fall and leg him back into the saddle – except that she did not fall, and they went on to win the race. To seal the links with Arkle's connections, Bright Cherry herself had been Pat Taaffe's first ride as a professional for the Dreaper yard at Leopardstown in January 1950.

Arkle's owner as well as his trainer and principal jockey could find family echoes in his pedigree. Bend Or, the great horse who won the Derby in 1880 for the first Duke of Westminster – grandfather of Anne, Duchess of Westminster's late husband – appears on both sides of the more extreme reaches of Arkle's breeding, as paternal great-great-great-great-great-grandsire of Archive and in the fifth generation of Bright Cherry's pedigree.

Birth

Bright Cherry's foal by Archive was safely delivered at 3.30 a.m. on Friday 19 April 1957 in one of the pair of ultra-spacious foaling boxes at the Ballymacoll Stud, County Meath.

Now the centre of the breeding and racing operation founded by Sir Michael Sobell and his son-in-law Lord Weinstock and made famous by such horses as Troy, Sun Princess, Pilsudski, Golan, North Light – the 2004 Derby winner foaled in 2001 in the very same box as Arkle – and Conduit, Ballymacoll Stud in 1957 was owned by Dorothy Paget, the vastly built, vastly rich and vastly eccentric lady who had owned five-times Gold Cup winner Golden Miller. Earlier in its life the stud had belonged to Boss Croker, the Irish-born New York politician at the heart of the Tammany Hall corruption scandal. There is no record of Dorothy Paget ever having visited Ballymacoll, and it was sold to Michael Sobell after her death in 1960.

The foaling box at Ballymacoll Stud in which Arkle was born. Between this and the adjacent box is the narrow room where the 'night man' sits up to observe the mares about to foal.

What granted the Ballymacoll Stud its signal place in racing history was the presence there of the stallion Straight Deal, Miss Paget's Derby winner in 1943 (when a substitute version of that Classic was run at Newmarket's July Course on account of the war). Straight Deal had failed to make much of a mark as a stallion breeding horses for the Flat, but by 1957 his fee was £98, low enough to make him a reasonable proposition for a small breeder such as Mrs Baker.

An entry in one of the ledger books which record all the matings and movements of the Bakers' mares reads: 'Bright Cherry went to Ballymacoll Stud to Straight Deal 28th March. April 19th Bright Cherry had bay colt foal by Archive. Bright Cherry last service to Straight Deal 22nd and 24th of June.'

The bay colt who tottered into the world that Friday morning was Bright Cherry's third foal, following fillies by Mustang born in 1952 and 1955, later named Cherry Tang and Cherry Bud. The latter proved a highly successful broodmare, her progeny including good chasers in the shape of Colebridge (whom Tom Dreaper's son Jim trained to win the Irish Grand National in 1974) and Vulture. After the successful delivery of the Archive foal, Bright Cherry proved barren to Straight Deal, and did not produce another foal until 1963, when after having been covered *au naturel* (as opposed to the controlled environment of the breeding shed) by Ballysway, she gave birth to a chestnut colt. Named Saval Beg, Arkle's first half-brother went into training with George Wells, and despite winning a maiden hurdle at Down Royal as a six-year-old in 1969 showed nothing of his distinguished relation's ability. Bright Cherry had two more foals (both by Escart III), Golden Sparkle in 1964 and Cherry Wine in 1966, but neither made any impact on the racecourse. Saval Beg's hurdle at Down Royal proved the only racecourse win for any of Arkle's siblings.

After foaling Cherry Wine, Bright Cherry continued barren, and was retired from stud in 1971. She died in July that year, and is buried in the Quarry Field at Malahow.

Archive, who never sired another horse remotely in the same league as Arkle, was put down in July 1960.

Three-year-old Arkle about to leave for the sales. By now he had undergone the first stages of breaking-in at the gentle hands of Mary Baker's daughter Alison, who recalled: 'He was very lanky – all legs – but right from the start you could tell that he loved people. He was very clever, the most intelligent horse I'd ever dealt with. The first time I put a saddle on him he went berserk, but the next time he was as quiet as a lamb, and he was like that throughout. He cottoned on amazingly quickly.'

Goff's Bloodstock Sales, 4 August 1960

The 74th Annual August Sales, held in the sales paddocks of the Royal Dublin Society at Ballsbridge in the first week of August 1960, was divided into two parts. On the first day, Wednesday, were offered 116 lots of yearlings; the second day, Thursday, offered a further 115 lots of 'Horse in Training, Likely 'Chasers, Untried and Unbroken Stock, etc.'. (An additional sale on the Saturday was of horses who had competed in that week's RDS Horse Show.)

Bright Cherry's still unnamed colt, who had been gelded as a yearling (as is almost invariably the case with young horses destined to become steeplechasers) was to be sold as lot 148. The fact that the top-priced yearling sold on the first day of the sale was a 700-guinea colt by Archive offered optimism that Mary Baker would get a good price for Bright Cherry's son, on whom she had placed a reserve of 500 guineas.

Once the bidding got under way in earnest that reserve price was soon reached and passed, and before long the gelding was knocked down to Tom Dreaper for 1,150 guineas, the best price the Bakers had ever received for one of the young horses bred at Malahow. Mary Baker's daughter Alison, watching the sale from the auctioneer's rostrum, went out to find Dreaper and discover who had bought the gelding for whom she had such a fond regard. He replied: 'The Duchess of Westminster'.

The catalogue for Goff's sale, which states of Lot 148 that 'This gelding has just been broken and driven in long reins, but not ridden.'

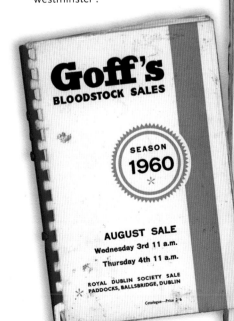

The Duchess

When Bright Cherry's gelding son was bought by Anne, Duchess of Westminster, she had been widowed from the 2nd Duke of Westminster for seven years.

The Duchess was born Anne Sullivan – she became widely known as 'Nancy' – in County Cork in April 1915, and from an early age was enthusiastic about horses. Sent to school in England, she made sure she was accompanied by her pony, and became a keen rider to hounds, both in England and Ireland, also developing a passion for racing – usually point-to-points or jumping meetings. She became the fourth wife of the 2nd Duke of Westminster, grandson of the 1st Duke and reputed to be the richest man in England, in 1947 (when she was thirty-one and her new husband sixty-seven). The Duke was nicknamed 'Bend Or' after the family's 1880

Anne, Duchess of Westminster with Arkle at Bryanstown in 1967.

Derby winner (who had himself been named after the Westminster coat of arms) and his bride was soon sharing his racing interests. The equine Bend Or was one of many fabled Westminster horses bred on the estate at Eaton Hall in Cheshire – the others included the mighty and unbeaten Ormonde, winner of the Triple Crown in 1886, and Flying Fox, who won the Triple Crown in 1899 (the year the 1st Duke died) – while the 2nd Duke himself had owned two Classic winners in Troutbeck (1906 St Leger) and Lambert Simnel (1941 Two Thousand Guineas).

The Duke died at their Scottish home in Sutherland in 1953, leaving the Duchess – who had no children – a life interest in the various estates. Widowed at the age of thirty-eight, she took an active part in managing the family's racing interests, and bred several good horses.

Her first well known horse as an owner was Sentina, who had won the National Hunt Chase at Cheltenham for another of Tom's owners in 1957. Sold to the Duchess, Sentina won the race again in 1958, and her next big win came with Cashel View in the Galway Hurdle in 1959, the year before she bought Arkle. (For her best known horses after Arkle, see page 174.)

Anne, Duchess of Westminster was as perfect an owner as any young horse could hope for, and the close relationship between her and Arkle is one of the most touching aspects of his story. She would regularly ride him around her Bryanstown estate, near Maynooth, during his summer holidays and after his retirement from racing, and when he was stretched out on the ground in his paddock would sit down with him for a bonding session. In an interview with Sue Mott in the *Daily Telegraph* in 2001 she recalled:

> *When he was out in the field and you shouted to him, he came galloping for his sugar. He knew one's voice. When I drove into the yard at Tom Dreaper's, he knew my voice. He'd go bang, bang, bang on the stable door. But I think he knew my car as well. He'd go thump, thump, thump – knowing there was a sugar lump.*

When she rode Arkle around her estate, 'He took great care of me. It was as if he knew who I was. He was a friend.'

As John Randall wrote in his *Racing Post* obituary after her death in 2003:

> *Nancy Westminster was a model owner. A countrywoman and a regular rider to hounds in Ireland in her youth, she understood horses and racing, and was prepared to give her colour-bearers plenty of time to realise their potential. Her wealth gave her an advantage over most other owners, but she always put the interests of her horses first, and the wisdom of that policy was reflected in the results she achieved.*

Cheshire – and Scotland

The bay gelding out of Bright Cherry was not the Duchess's only purchase at the Goff's sale. A few lots later she bought for 2,000 guineas another three-year-old, a handsome unbroken chestnut gelding by Flamenco named Bray Flame, who according to the catalogue 'has been well done since a foal and is expected to make a high-class chaser'. Bray Flame had been a winner in the show ring as a yearling in 1958, and earlier in the week of the sale had won the Hunters-in-Hand class at the Horse Show. No wonder he made the Duchess dig almost twice as deep into her pocket as the immature, unfurnished Bright Cherry gelding.

It was the Duchess's custom to bring her unbroken horses to the Westminster estate in Cheshire for completion of the breaking-in process and time to develop, and Bray Flame and the Bright Cherry gelding arrived there shortly after the sale, with the intention that they should remain a year or so before going into training.

The two young horses undertook the next stage of their education in the care of the Duchess's groom Bill Veal and looked after in the lap of equine luxury, but there was one thing of which the Bright Cherry gelding was in urgent need: a name.

Among the Westminster properties were several thousand acres of Sutherland, close to the most northerly part of north-west Scotland – in the region now formally known as Highland – and the name of the gelding's sire Archive triggered the idea of naming the horse after one of the magnificent mountains which rise above the estate. At 2,581 feet (787 metres), Arkle, some nineteen miles from Cape Wrath, is too low to be a Munro – 3,000 feet being the minimum height for that famous collection of Scottish peaks – but is none the less one of the glories of the area. The name Arkle may mean 'ark mountain' – from the Old Scandinavian *ork* (chest, ark) and *fjall* (mountain); or may mean 'whale mountain', with its first element deriving from Old Scandinavian *orc* (whale); or may mean neither. The Bright Cherry gelding's name was duly registered as Arkle, and notification of the registration published in the *Irish Racing Calendar* on 11 August 1961.(Anne Holland's 2013 profile of Arkle notes that Himself was not the only Westminster-owned horse named after that mountain. The 1st Duke's horse Arkle was born in 1894 and failed to win a race. He finished last in the 1897 Two Thousand Guineas.)

Study of the Ordnance Survey map will ring a couple of other bells with followers of racing, for Arkle was not the only Duchess of Westminster-owned horse to bear the name of a mountain in Sutherland.

A few miles north of Arkle the mountain is the long, pimply ridge of Foinaven, at 2,998 feet tantalisingly close to qualifying as a Munro. (The name probably means 'wart mountain', a sobriquet suggested by its undulating top.) Spelled as Foinavon, the name was given to a gelding by the great National Hunt sire Vulgan which Tom Dreaper bought on behalf of the Duchess as a three-year-old in 1961. Foinavon ran in twenty-two races in her colours, winning three, and at one point Pat Taaffe told

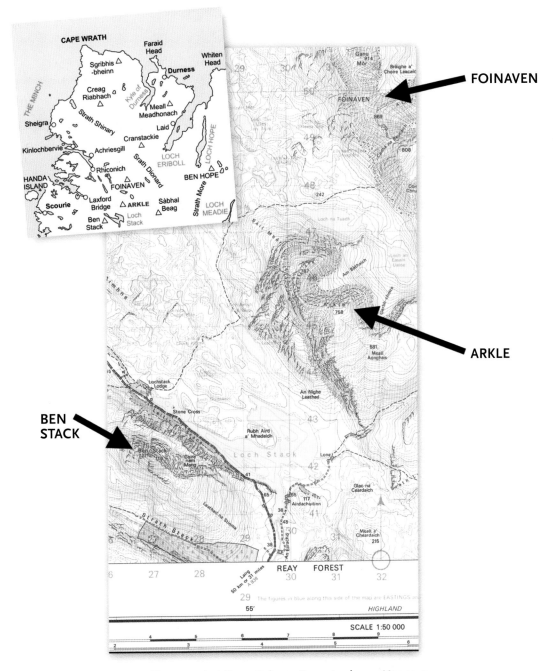

The mountain Arkle on Ordnance Survey Landranger Map no. 9,
'Cape Wrath, Durness and Scourie'. Ben Stack and Foinaven are also marked.

Arkle the mountain.

the Duchess that Foinavon would win a Grand National. But after a while the horse started showing himself not only devoid of the consistent level of ability which would make him a respectable member of the Dreaper academy, but of any sense of application whatsoever. Tom's wife Betty liked to recall the occasion at Baldoyle when Foinavon took a heavy fall on the far side, throwing Pat Taaffe well clear, and lay prostrate on the ground. The Dreapers, fearing the worst, rushed across to aid their stricken horse – and discovered Foinavon lying on the ground picking grass: he simply could not be bothered to get up. Pat Taaffe himself remarked that if Foinavon had been a man, 'he'd have spent his days, hands in pockets, whistling through his teeth, scuffling the dust.'

Taaffe's suggestion about the Grand National had come to look increasingly bizarre, and in 1965 the Duchess, frustrated by Foinavon's lack of commitment to his calling, sent the horse to the sales at Doncaster. Here he was bought by the Berkshire trainer John Kempton for his owner Cyril Watkins. Foinavon occasionally drifted into Arkle's orbit in later years, and in April 1967 made himself almost as famous as his former stable companion by winning the Grand National through the unusual tactic of getting so far behind that at the notorious twenty-third fence pile-up he was able to steer clear of trouble. He galloped home in glorious isolation at odds of 100-1 to prove Pat Taaffe right after all.

To the south west of Arkle is Ben Stack (2,365 feet), the name the Duchess gave to Arkle's contemporary who, trained by Tom Dreaper, won nine races, notably the Cotswold Chase (now the Racing Post Arkle Challenge Trophy) in 1963 and the National Hunt Two-Mile Champion Chase (now the Queen Mother Champion Chase) at Cheltenham in 1964, two days before Arkle won his first Gold Cup. Like his more distinguished stable companion, Ben Stack was a bay gelding with no white markings on his face or elsewhere on his coat, and – forgivably, for some people find that one bay horse looks much like another bay horse, and Ben Stack was usually ridden by Pat Taaffe in the famous black and yellow colours – many a less than vigilant picture editor has slapped an Arkle caption on a Ben Stack picture and got away with it. (A sombre association of the mountain Ben Stack is that it was here that Robin Cook, former foreign secretary and a passionate racing fan, was walking when he suffered a heart attack in August 2005, dying in an Inverness hospital a few hours later. An hour before his collapse he had sent a text message to his son Chris: 'Am on Ben Stack. View of Arkle and Foinaven can't be seen for mist. Weather foul. Wish you were here.')

Saval Beg, Arkle's half-brother born in 1963, was also named after a Highland mountain. Sabhal Beag has a 2,391-foot high peak, to the south east of Arkle.

By the summer of 1961 the Bright Cherry gelding had both a name and a decent education, and he and Bray Flame were ready to go into training.

The Duchess had her horses with two trainers in Ireland: Willie O'Grady, who had been Irish champion jockey in 1934 and 1935 before embarking on a training career at Ballynonty in County Tipperary which had brought him two victories in the Irish Grand National, and Tom Dreaper, who combined training with farming at Kilsallaghan, not far from Dublin airport. Dreaper was offered first choice, and travelled across to make his pick. Bray Flame was much the better looking horse, but Arkle's dam had been trained by Dreaper, and his granddam had brought him a point-to-point winner. There could really only be one choice, and it was Arkle who was soon on his way to County Dublin.

Bray Flame duly went to Willie O'Grady and made his racecourse debut when ridden by Pat Taaffe's brother Tos in a maiden hurdle at Leopardstown in early February 1962. 'Started slowly', records the *Irish Racing Calendar*, and he finished unplaced. The Duchess then changed his name to Brae Flame, but, afflicted by leg trouble, he never ran again.

Tom Dreaper

Born in 1898 into a farming family with a limited interest in racing, Tom Dreaper took up riding in point-to-points in his twenties, his first winner coming in 1923 on his own horse Dean Swift, and soon was one of the best riders 'between the flags' in Ireland. His first winner under Rules was at Navan in 1925 on a horse named Mattie's Dream – whose owner's name in the racecard was a fiction, as the horse belonged to the parish priest! In 1930 Dreaper's parents purchased a farm named Greenogue, near Ashbourne in County Meath, and the following year Tom took out a licence to train from there, while continuing to farm. (For most of his working life he considered himself a full-time farmer and part-time trainer.)

He had his first big break when taking in the horses of flour millionaire J. V. Rank after the intended trainer Bobby Power had been killed roadside in 1938 while changing a wheel on the way to the Dublin Horse Show, and his first great horse was Rank's chaser Prince Regent. Tom himself rode Prince Regent in his first three races in the 1939-40 season, winning one, and in 1942 Prince Regent won the Irish Grand National under 12 stone 7 pounds. It was not until wartime restrictions on racing had been lifted that Prince Regent could show his true worth by competing in England, and by then he was getting past his prime. None the less, he won the 1946 Gold Cup at the age of eleven, and three weeks later finished third in the Grand National under 12 stone 5 pounds. He was fourth in the 1947 National and won the Becher Chase at Aintree later that year. In all he won eighteen races, and it is a measure of his place in his trainer's affections that Tom Dreaper would not allow that Arkle might just be the better horse until Himself had won his third Gold Cup.

Prince Regent's victory in the 1942 Irish Grand National was the first of a remarkable ten in the race for Tom Dreaper, including an extraordinary seven winners in a row between 1960 and 1966, whose names form a rollcall of some of the great Dreaper chasers: Olympia, Fortria, Kerforo, Last Link, Arkle, Splash and Flyingbolt. His other Irish National winners were Shagreen in 1952 and the brilliant Royal Approach in 1954. (Royal Approach was owned by Lord Bicester, who did not take well to any criticism of his horses. In the Cheltenham unsaddling enclosure after Royal Approach had won the Cathcart Challenge Cup in 1954, the trainer Jack Anthony congratulated the owner, then added, 'But he's not much to look at, is he?' – to which Lord Bicester replied, 'When did you last look in a mirror?')

Tom Dreaper's wife Betty recalled how in 1956 her husband had returned from Leopardstown races to report that there would be a new horse and new owner coming to the yard.

'Good,' reacted Betty, 'I hope you liked the horse.'

'I haven't seen him.'

'Do you like the pedigree?'

'Not much, but I liked the look of the girl.'

'The girl' was Anne, Duchess of Westminster.

OPPOSITE

Tom Dreaper (on the right) with his head lad Paddy Murray.

24

Greenogue

The racing stable into which the young Arkle arrived in August 1961 was one of the most famous in the land. Tom Dreaper's principal rival as top Irish jumping trainer in the 1950s had been Vincent O'Brien, whose achievements with such horses as Cottage Rake (three consecutive Gold Cups, 1948-50) and Hatton's Grace (three consecutive Champion Hurdles, 1949-51) and the unique feat of winning three consecutive Grand Nationals with three different horses (Early Mist in 1953, Royal Tan in 1954 and Quare Times in 1955) were outstanding. (Early Mist had been trained by Dreaper until the death of his owner J. V. Rank in 1952.) From the late 1950s O'Brien had concentrated on the Flat, leaving Dreaper widely acknowledged as Ireland's leading jumps trainer. But even at the height of his career, Dreaper rarely had more than about thirty-five horses in his charge, quality being much more desirable for him than quantity.

The front yard at Greenogue. Box 7, Arkle's home for most of his working life, is second from the right.

Arkle initially evoked little excitement among the Greenogue lads. Head lad Paddy Murray (who died in 2005) described him as 'unfurnished – and he moved bad'; Paddy Woods – senior stable lad, work rider and jockey – remembers the new arrival as 'gangly'; and stable jockey Pat Taaffe memorably observed that 'you could have driven a wheelbarrow through his hind legs.' As a consequence there was no clamour among the lads to take charge of the Duchess's raw youngster, and he was assigned to sixteen-year-old Johnny Lumley, who had joined the stable only a few months before Arkle. As a new recruit Arkle spent his first couple of years in a box towards the rear of the yard before being moved towards the front gates and making box number 7 at Greenogue the most famous equine address in the racing world.

Arkle's name first appeared in *Horses in Training*, the annual list of racehorses in Britain and Ireland, in 1962. The stable star then was Fortria (no. 1 in the 1962 listing overleaf), who had already won four big races at Cheltenham: the Cotswold Chase in 1958, the Two-Mile Champion Chase in 1960 and again in 1961, and the inaugural Mackeson Gold Cup (run over two miles) in 1960; he had also won the Irish Grand National in 1961. Fortria was to win the Mackeson again in 1962, as well as finishing runner-up in the Gold Cup in both 1962 (to Mandarin) and 1963 (to Mill House).

Of the other horses listed in the T. W. Dreaper entry for 1962, Olympia (no. 5) had won the Irish Grand National in 1960, and the mare Kerforo (7) was to win that race in 1962, as well as the Thyestes Chase and Leopardstown Chase the same year. Mountcashel King (8) had won the Cotswold Chase in 1961. Last Link (15) was to win the Irish Grand National in 1963, Ben Stack (18) the Cotswold Chase in 1963 and the Two-Mile Champion Chase in 1964. Number 26, the four-year-old brown gelding by Vulgan out of Ecilace, became Foinavon.

Noteworthy additions in the 1963 *Horses in Training* include – as well as the now named Foinavon (16) – Splash (22), who would win the Irish Grand National in 1965; Dicky May (27), whose steeplechase victories included the Black and White Gold Cup at Ascot in 1966; Arkloin (24), an Archive gelding who would win the Totalisator Champion Novices' Chase (now the RSA Chase) at Cheltenham in 1965; and Owen's Sedge (28), who was owned by Hollywood actor Gregory Peck and would win the Leopardstown Chase for Tom Dreaper in 1963 (one of a sequence of seven consecutive winners of that race from Greenogue, including Arkle three times).

Greenogue was clearly a star-studded establishment, and one of the factors which characterised any Dreaper horse was his or her ability to jump efficiently and cleanly. In her book *Tom Dreaper and his Horses*, Bryony Fuller has described the trainer's teaching method:

> *The country around Greenogue is ditch country and the youngsters were*
> *introduced to jumping over open [i.e. natural] ditches. Tom had the*
> *young horse bridled and put on a cavesson [a form of noseband] with a*
> *long rope. He was led up to the edge of an open ditch where he was held*

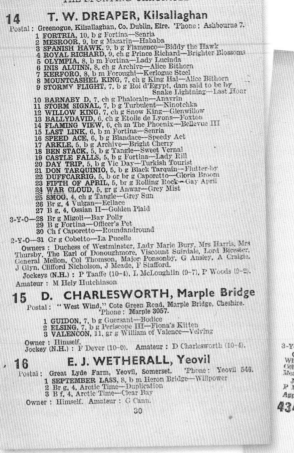

The Tom Dreaper entries in *Horses in Training*, 1962 and 1963.

and allowed to have a good look into and across the ditch. The man holding the horse threw the rope across the ditch to a couple of lads waiting in the landing field. The horse was encouraged to bring his hind legs up to his front legs and then made to jump the open ditch from a stand, using his hocks to produce propulsion. After he had repeated this a few times, the horse did it quite calmly and walked up to the edge, settled himself and took off.

The next stage in the horse's education was over baby bush fences where he was lunged around and around, jumping the fences slowly in each direction. Only when the horse was jumping open ditches and bush fences sensibly, using his hocks properly, was he ridden over fences.

At the same time as he was learning to jump, Arkle was engaged in regular exercise round the roads and up the gallops to remove, slowly but steadily, the tummy he had gained in the paddocks at Eaton Hall. By December 1961 he was, while far from fully fit, ready to race.

The first races

The first race for which the name Arkle appeared in the racecard was the Lough Ennel Plate for maidens (horses who had not won a race) ridden by amateurs at the now defunct course of Mullingar, County Westmeath, on Saturday 9 December 1961. Run over a distance of 2 miles 1 furlong 160 yards, this was 'bumper', a flat race run under Irish National Hunt Rules and used primarily for giving young horses racing experience without subjecting them to the additional complication of having to jump obstacles. (While long a feature of Irish jump racing, bumpers were not introduced to Britain until the 1980s.)

Arkle's first jockey was the Hon. Mark Hely-Hutchinson, twenty-seven-year-old second son of Lord Donoughmore (a major owner at the Dreaper yard, whose horses included Olympia). He had taken out a licence to ride as an amateur in 1958 and ridden his first winner the following year, fitting his race-riding in with his job with Guinness in Dublin. (He became managing director of Arthur Guinness in Ireland in 1975, and was later chief executive of the Bank of Ireland.) Hely-Hutchinson has described himself as 'very much an amateur's amateur – to me, all of the Dreaper horses felt like racing machines'. While his own modest assessment belies his record (which includes riding Olympia to win a good chase at Cheltenham in November 1960), among Arkle anoraks he has the distinction of being the only jockey to have ridden Himself in a race and never won on him.

For the Lough Ennel Plate, last event on a six-race programme and worth £133 to the winner, Hely-Hutchinson was able to claim a five-pound weight allowance, bringing Arkle's burden down to 11 stone 4 pounds from the 11st 9lb he had been allotted by the weight-for-age scale. As a debutant, there was little to recommend him to punters apart from the eminence of his stable, and he started 5-1 fourth favourite, behind co-favourites Lady Flame and Hal's Son (4-1), both of whom had run previously, and Kilspindie (9-2), who like Arkle was making his first racecourse appearance.

Arkle was not expected to win – the race was all part of building him towards a chasing career later – and the Dreapers were well satisfied with his performance in finishing third of the seventeen runners behind Lady Flame and Kilspindie, running on past beaten horses in the closing stages in going which Pat Taaffe, who had ridden earlier in the afternoon, described as 'like a ploughed field'. He finished nine lengths behind the winner, and paid 6s. 6d. for

Mark Hely-Hutchinson in 2004.

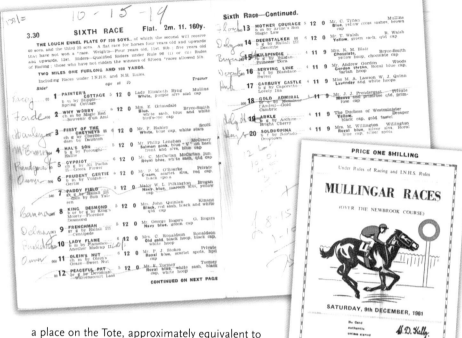

Arkle's name appears in a racecard for the first time: the Lough Ennel Plate at Mullingar on 9 December 1961.

a place on the Tote, approximately equivalent to odds of 13-8. (Irish Tote dividends were declared to a 2s. 6d. unit and included that stake.) Lady Flame never won another race, but wrote another footnote in racing history more than forty-six years later as third dam – that is, mother's mother's mother – of 2008 Grand National winner Comply Or Die.

Despite the desperate ground at Mullingar, Arkle came out of his first race so well that it was decided to give him another run two and a half weeks later, in another bumper for maidens, the two-mile Greystones Flat Race at Leopardstown, in the southern suburbs of Dublin, on St Stephen's Day (Boxing Day in Britain) 1961. Again Arkle was ridden by Mark Hely-Hutchinson, again he started at 5-1 (which made him third favourite), and again he ran encouragingly, finishing fourth of ten behind second favourite Artist's Treasure, favourite Glyndebourne, and the grey mare Flying Wild, who was to play a major role in one of Arkle's greatest occasions. At Leopardstown, Arkle – whom Hely-Hutchinson reported was much easier to keep up near the pace than at Mullingar – finished 8½ lengths behind the winner.

With two bumpers successfully if unspectacularly negotiated, it was time for Arkle to graduate to hurdles, and the chosen race was the Bective Novice Hurdle over three miles – the furthest he'd yet raced – at Navan, County Meath, on 20 January 1962. If the Dreaper yard had not expected him to return victorious from either of his earlier outings, there was even less expected in the heavy ground at Navan, as hot favourite for the race was the eight-year-old mare Kerforo, who was looking to extend a sequence of three consecutive wins, having landed chases at Thurles, Naas and Baldoyle since early November. Despite attracting a field of twenty-seven, the Navan novice hurdle looked a shoo-in for the mare (who although an experienced chaser had not won over hurdles and was therefore qualified for a novices' race), and it was no surprise that stable jockey Pat Taaffe chose to ride the even-money favourite rather than Arkle, a 20-1 chance having his first race over obstacles. The ride on the outsider went to Greenogue stable lad Liam McLoughlin.

In his autobiography *My Life and Arkle's*, Pat Taaffe wrote of his ride on Kerforo at Navan:

> We had just cleared the second flight from home and were concentrating on staying in touch with the leader Blunts Cross, ridden by Lord Patrick Beresford.
>
> It was at this moment that Arkle cruised past me. He overtook Blunts Cross pretty much the same way and came home to win, still on the bit. I was astonished. I had seen it happen and I still couldn't believe it.
>
> I walked back to the jockeys' room with Liam McLoughlin, Arkle's rider that day, and asked just how much he'd left at the end.
>
> 'He was just cantering', said Liam, the surprise in his voice matching my own. 'He had barely started to race. I just gave him a kick two flights out, that was all, and he began to fly.'
>
> That day at Navan ... gave us our first hint of things to come. But it would be wrong to say that we now recognised him as a future world-beater. No, he had done wonderfully well to beat Kerforo, the mare who would win the Irish Grand National before the year was out, but she had, after all, been giving him twelve pounds and in the mud at Navan every pound must have counted. So we looked upon him as an interesting prospect, but for the moment nothing more.

While far from carried away, Tom Dreaper took a more bullish view. Coming down from the stands after watching the stable ugly duckling come good, he turned to his wife and declared: 'Do you know, I think we've got something there!'

Arkle had won by 1½ lengths from Blunts Cross, with Kerforo another eight lengths back in third. Hardly earth-shattering, but he had started winning.

And he carried on winning. On 10 March he reverted from the three miles of the Navan race to two miles at Naas in County Kildare – a Mullingar meeting transferred from the Westmeath course on account of unraceable going – for the Rathconnel Handicap Hurdle. He won by four lengths from Soltest to record his second victory and three notable firsts: his first handicap, the first time he started favourite (at 2-1 in a field of ten) and the first time he was ridden in a race by Pat Taaffe.

But after those two consecutive victories, Arkle's 1961-62 season ended on a down beat with two defeats.

In the two-mile Balbriggan Handicap Hurdle at Baldoyle (like Mullingar, no longer a racecourse) he started 6-1 second favourite in a field of eighteen which included the Dreaper stable star Fortria, who in his previous race had finished runner-up to Mandarin in the Gold Cup at Cheltenham. Pat Taaffe rode Fortria and

Liam McLoughlin was on Arkle, but neither horse could get into the shake-up and both finished out of the frame. Liam McLoughlin reported that Arkle did not act easily round the tight bends of the seaside track, and was bumped when trying to improve his position. It was a mild disappointment but nothing worse, and the Balbriggan Hurdle was the only time Arkle finished out of the first four in his whole career.

There was one more outing that season, the two-mile New Handicap Hurdle at Fairyhouse, the racecourse closest to Greenogue. The field of nine runners included some interesting contenders, notably Quita Que, then a thirteen-year-old well past his prime but in his heyday a top-class performer who had finished runner-up in two consecutive Champion Hurdles (1956 and 1957) and won the Two-Mile Champion Chase at Cheltenham in 1959. Another five-year-old in the field was Ferry Boat, whom Arkle would encounter in major races later in his career. Pat Taaffe could not do the weight of 10 stone 5 pounds which Arkle had been allotted and rode the top weight Rainlough for his father Tom, with Liam McLoughlin again taking the ride on

Arkle. The race was won by 11-4 favourite Anthony, and Arkle, who started at 8-1, finished fourth – but he would never again be beaten in Ireland.

First working season finished and the future full of promise, Arkle was sent for his holidays to the Duchess's estate at Bryanstown for a lazy summer lyrically described by Ivor Herbert:

> All her horses go back there for the rest and unwinding which are such
> sweet settlers to a jumper's spirit, for the fresh grass to summerclean their
> taut, oat-crammed digestions, for the sun to warm their backs and the
> slow stroll across the turf to rest those twanging, hammered tendons in a
> jumper's legs.

The 1962-63 season, which would propel Arkle from obscurity to the *crème de la crème* of young steeplechasers, began with an outing in the Wee County Hurdle over 2 miles 216 yards at Dundalk. Pat Taaffe was back in the saddle for his second race ride on the young horse, and despite being unfancied in the betting (6-1 third favourite) Arkle won easily, finding a decisive turn of foot to scoot away and win by six lengths from Killykeen Star, with hot favourite Gosley third. The Wee County Hurdle instigated a sequence of nine consecutive victories which, but for once slipping up and once battling against an impossible weight, would have stretched to twenty-six.

A week later, on 17 October 1962, Arkle was out again. While Pat Taaffe had been easily able to do 11 stone 13 pounds in the Dundalk race, 10 stone 5 pounds in the two-mile President's Handicap Hurdle at Gowran Park proved a few pounds too light, and Dreaper insisted that his stable jockey should not put up overweight. So Paddy Woods, who rode Arkle in most of his home work throughout the horse's career and was a fine jockey in his own right, took the ride.

The race had attracted a strong field which included Owen's Sedge – soon to join the Dreaper stable in the ownership of Gregory Peck – and the doughty mare Height O' Fashion, who would dog Arkle's heels more than once in later races, and Arkle started 9-2 joint favourite with Ross Sea. Taking advantage of his light weight and little inconvenienced by misjudging the last hurdle – 'He flattened it!', says Paddy Woods – Arkle again found a decisive turn of foot and won by five lengths from the grey Silver Green, who had been a top-class hurdler and was then conceding Arkle twelve pounds.

Another decisive performance over hurdles. Arkle was ready to become what he had been bred to be: a steeplechaser.

OPPOSITE
The President's Hurdle at Gowran Park, 17 October 1962: Arkle and Paddy Woods well clear at the last. (Note the Duchess of Westminster's colours, officially registered in Ireland that year as 'Yellow, black cap with gold tassel' – colours which had belonged to the Westminster family for generations and had been carried by such famous horses as Ormonde and Bend Or. The black belt which completed the colours so familiar to British racegoers was not formally added to her Irish colours until 1963.)

Pat Taaffe

'God bless Mummy, God bless Daddy, and God bless Pat Taaffe.'

The Dreapers' young son Jim was right to include their stable jockey in his nightly prayers in the mid 1960s, for Pat Taaffe, one of the greatest jump jockeys Ireland ever produced, was an integral part of the Arkle story.

From the time Arkle took up chasing in November 1962, Taaffe rode him in every one of the twenty-six steeplechases he contested, forming a horse-jockey partnership on a par with Brown Jack and Steve Donoghue, Mill Reef and Geoff Lewis or Brigadier Gerard and Joe Mercer. In all, Pat rode Arkle in twenty-eight races, losing only four.

When Pat Taaffe was given the leg-up into Arkle's saddle at Naas in March 1962 before their first race together, he was thirty-one years old and had already been leading jump jockey in Ireland five times (1952-55 and 1961); he had been leading jockey, Flat or jumps, in 1952 and 1953.

Son of the trainer Tom Taaffe, who sent out 1958 Grand National winner Mr What, Pat was born in Rathcoole, County Dublin, in 1930, and honed his riding skills in the hunting field and through show jumping. His first point-to-point winner was Merry Coon at Bray in 1946 – when the jockey was a sixteen-year-old schoolboy – and he rode his first winner as an amateur under Rules on Ballincrona at Phoenix Park on Easter Sunday 1946. He became a professional jockey and joined Tom Dreaper in January 1950.

In August 1956 a fall at Kilbeggan left Taaffe with a fractured skull – and Dublin swirling with rumour that he had been killed – but he resumed race riding that November. Then another fall damaged a leg so badly that he told Dreaper that the trainer had better find another jockey for Greenogue horses in two big races coming up at Manchester. Dreaper's response was that 'If you don't ride them, we won't run them', so Taaffe rode both – and both won. Such faith was rewarded: by the time of the Arkle glory days Taaffe had won the Irish Grand National for the Dreaper stable on Royal Approach (1954) and Fortria (1961), as well as twice for other stables. He had also won the Grand National at Liverpool for the first time, not on a horse trained by Dreaper (who was never to win the race) but on Quare Times, third of three successive National winners for Vincent O'Brien.

The bond between Tom Dreaper and Pat Taaffe – echoed in the later relationship of O'Brien and Lester Piggott – was deep and long-lasting, and the trainer was fiercely loyal to his stable jockey. When the Hurst Park stewards once asked after a controversial race whether Dreaper was satisfied with the riding of Taaffe, the trainer replied: 'I have worse at home.'

OPPOSITE
Pat Taaffe and the Queen Mother at Sandown Park after the Gallaher Gold Cup, November 1965.

The early chases

Arkle's first run over steeplechase fences came not at some quiet country meeting in his native Ireland, but on one of the biggest days of the jumps season, Mackeson Gold Cup day at Cheltenham in mid-November. It was a mark of Tom Dreaper's confidence in his young horse that for his first run over the larger obstacles he was pitched in at the deep end. Racecourse rumour insisted that Arkle had been working exceptionally well, but such intelligence omitted the fact that he had taken a crashing fall when working over hurdles on the schooling ground of nearby trainer Dan Moore.

So positive had been the reports which preceded Arkle that he started 11-8 favourite (after having been as low as even money) in a field of twelve for the Honeybourne Chase over two and a half miles, opening race on the Cheltenham programme on Saturday 17 November 1962. Next in the market on 11-2 came Jomsviking, who had won his previous two races – both over hurdles – and like Arkle was running for the first time over fences. Third choice on 6-1 was Milo, who in his only previous chase had finished third in a strong-looking novice event at Newbury and was ridden by amateur jockey and later top trainer Ian Balding. Billy Bumps, trained by Paddy Sleator, was another Irish challenger, and Dargent came from the powerful Peter Cazalet stable and was running in the colours of the Queen Mother.

Both the opposition and the venue made this a stiff task for a first-time chaser, but Arkle hardly turned a hair in winning easily, initiating a notable double for the Dreaper yard: Fortria, ridden like his young stablemate by Pat Taaffe, won the Mackeson Gold Cup an hour and a quarter later to repeat his victory in the inaugural running two years earlier. Admittedly Arkle's task was made easier by the departure of main rival Jomsviking at the third fence and Dargent at the sixth, but after Pat Taaffe had eased his mount to the front three fences from home the result was never in doubt, and Arkle surged clear to win by twenty lengths and catch the eye, for the first time, of the British racing press. *The Times* wrote that Arkle

> *gave a demonstration of what schooling can achieve. The five-year-old*
> *jumped like an old hand, although without any experience of fences on*
> *the racecourse, to beat another well schooled Irish horse, Billy Bumps.*
> *Arkle, also [like Fortria] ridden quietly and with exquisite care by P.*
> *Taaffe, is a promising type.*

John Lawrence in *Horse and Hound* remarked that the chasing newcomer had 'jumped round like a seasoned veteran', adding that 'the fine big five-year-old was always cruising on a tight rein, and after disposing of Billy Bumps without difficulty down the hill, ran home to win in a style ominously reminiscent (from an English point of view) of Fortria himself in his younger days.'

For Brough Scott, then an aspiring young jockey and now a fixture in the Premier League of sports journalists, Arkle's first race in England was an epiphanic moment.

Over forty years later in 2004 he wrote in the *Sunday Telegraph*:

> *I remember exactly where I was when I first saw him: standing by the*
> *last fence at Cheltenham for the Honeybourne Novices' Chase on*
> *Saturday November 17, 1962, Arkle's first race over fences. I was a*
> *nineteen-year-old amateur already seriously affected by the racing bug*
> *and had no defence against the image in front of me. We had been*
> *warned the Irish thought this lean, greyhoundy, long-eared thing was a*
> *bit special, but what happened at the finish just took the breath away.*
> *There were decent horses against him, but Arkle just skipped the fence*
> *and sprinted twenty lengths clear as if he was another species altogether.*
> *Perhaps he was.*

**The second last fence
in the Honeybourne
Chase at Cheltenham,
17 November 1962: on
his way to winning his
first steeplechase,
Arkle (Pat Taaffe) goes
clear of Billy Bumps.**

After such a stylish start to his chasing career, Arkle did not race again for over
two months. The plan had always been to return to Cheltenham for the National
Hunt Festival meeting in March 1963 – then as now the high point of the jump
racing calendar – and the two-mile Milltown Chase at Leopardstown in February was
chosen as a prep race. The fiercest winter of recent memory had decimated the
racing programme in Britain between late December 1962 and early March 1963,
with only a solitary day at Ayr in early January punctuating a complete blank between
Uttoxeter on 22 December and Newbury on 8 March, just four days before the
Festival started. Consequently the big Leopardstown fixture in late February attracted
several English-trained horses desperate for a pre-Cheltenham run, notably the
chasers Frenchman's Cove and Carrickbeg in the Leopardstown Chase.

By the time of Arkle's race that afternoon the Greenogue stable was already in good heart. Owen's Sedge, who had finished well behind Arkle in the President's Hurdle the previous October and was now trained by Tom Dreaper for Gregory Peck, won the Leopardstown Chase easily (with Carrickbeg, soon to be narrowly beaten in the Grand National, third). Under the conditions of Milltown Chase race the now six-year-old Arkle was lumbered with 12 stone 11 pounds, the largest weight he carried in any race in his whole career. None the less, he started 1-2 favourite to demolish fourteen opponents and duly did so in a manner reminiscent of his Cheltenham victory, taking the lead three fences out and quickening away from the last to win very easily.

Next stop the Broadway Chase, run over three miles on the opening day of the 1963 National Hunt Meeting at Cheltenham. In view of the disruption to racing in Britain that winter, the Irish were expected to net a hatful of winners at the fixture, and after the favourite Honour Bound had won the opening hurdle for top British trainer Fred Rimell, the next four races all featured Irish-trained favourites: Scottish Memories, King Pin, Willow King and Osberstown Squire. All four were beaten, and the Cheltenham air bore the heavy whiff of burnt fingers as Arkle and Pat Taaffe made their way out for the sixth race of the day. Four consecutive reverses did not seem to have put punters off another Irish favourite, however, and the Dreaper horse started at 4-9, with Jomsviking second favourite at 11-2, then Billy Bumps on 100-7 and Border Flight and Brasher – who would feature in Arkle's later races – on 100-6. John Lawrence in *Horse and Hound* gave a graphic description of the race:

> Coming to the third last sandwiched between Brasher and Jomsviking, Arkle jumped it less well than either of his rivals and looked for a moment in grave danger of getting squeezed out.
>
> At the next fence, too, he gained no ground, and in front of me a partisan with an Irish air groaned – whether from heart or pocket or both I could not tell – 'Begod he's beat.' But the next ten seconds made him eat his words.
>
> Without a visible sign from Pat Taaffe, without the slightest apparent effort, Arkle was a dozen lengths clear. He simply shot from between the two English horses like a cherry stone from a schoolboy's fingers. It was done in less than 50 yards and neither of the others was stopping.

Other witnesses were similarly impressed. Tom Nickalls in the *Sporting Life* reported how after Arkle and Jomsviking had landed over the penultimate fence together, 'Taaffe let out a reef and Arkle seemed to slip into "overdrive", coming right away to win as he pleased.' The winning distance was twenty lengths from Jomsviking, with Brasher (ridden by Jimmy FitzGerald, later a top trainer) four lengths further back in third.

Two days later another six-year-old chaser of apparently limitless promise, a big horse named Mill House, won the Gold Cup, beating the Dreaper stable star Fortria

by a comfortable twelve lengths, and scarcely had he thundered past the winning post than racegoers started to debate what would happen when the two young champions went head to head. Mill House versus Arkle: that would be some race ...

But such a showdown would not take place until the following season, and meanwhile there were other considerations. With three steeplechase victories – two of them at Cheltenham – under his belt, Arkle needed more experience, and ran two more races during the 1962-63 season.

The first was at Fairyhouse on Easter Monday, 15 April, the day that Dreaper-trained Last Link, ridden by Paddy Woods, won the Irish Grand National – beating another Greenogue stalwart Willow King (Liam McLoughlin) into second place. (Stable jockey Pat Taaffe rode the top-weight Fortria, who fell. In the previous race, a handicap hurdle, he had ridden joint-favourite Foinavon. They were unplaced.)

Arkle faced just four opponents in the Power Gold Cup over 2¼ miles. He started 2-7 favourite, and won as any horse at such odds should, cruising home by three lengths from Willie Wagtail III.

Nor was he finished for the season. Having hardly broken sweat to win four chases on the trot, why not go to the big meeting at Punchestown and add another notch to the belt in the John Jameson Cup? Here Arkle faced only two other runners, and he had met them both before. Silver Green had been runner-up in the President's Hurdle at Gowran Park the previous October when giving him twelve pounds, and since then had won a valuable handicap hurdle at Liverpool and a novice chase at Navan before being brought down when warm favourite for the Mildmay Chase at the Liverpool Grand National meeting. Chelsea Set had finished third to Arkle in the Power Gold Cup, since when he had again come third in a chase at Naas and was now very much the outsider of three: at the off, the betting went 4-7 Arkle, 7-4 Silver Green, 100-7 Chelsea Set. Arkle sauntered round to win by fifteen lengths from Silver Green, with Chelsea Set a remote third.

Arkle's first term of steeplechasing thus ended with a record of five victories from five chases to follow two from two in early-season hurdles, posting an unblemished seven-race record for the 1962-63 season. Tom Dreaper's suggestion to his wife at Navan that 'I think we've got something there' was already thoroughly justified.

Arkle (Pat Taaffe) going clear of Silver Green (Alan Lillingston) to win the John Jameson Cup at Punchestown, 1 May 1963. (This photograph has been hand-coloured, with the black belt on Pat Taaffe's colours, not yet registered in Ireland, added erroneously.)

Arkle (T. P. Burns) wins the Donoughmore Plate at Navan.

After a lazy summer at Bryanstown, Arkle returned to Greenogue to begin work ahead of the new season. Six weeks or so of road work would bring him towards race fitness, then a routine in the fields across the road from the yard which typically would consist of a half-speed gallop of seven furlongs or a mile on Monday, a mile and a half at the same pace on Tuesday, walking and trotting around the fields on Wednesday and Thursday, then a mile and a half gallop again on Friday.

By the start of the 1963-64 season Arkle was no longer a novice chaser. He would be competing at the highest level with horses of significantly greater experience than previous opponents, and with a long and ambitious season ahead, Tom Dreaper opted for a fairly downbeat start to the term.

The Donoughmore Plate over 1 mile 6 furlongs at Navan on 9 October 1963 is the only race which Arkle ran on the Flat (as opposed to his two flat races under Irish National Hunt Rules, or 'bumpers'). He had won nine National Hunt races but was a maiden on the Flat, not having run under that code before. Ridden by T. P. Burns, who had been leading jockey (Flat and jumps combined) in 1954, 1955 and 1957 (the year he won the St Leger and Irish Derby on Ballymoss), Arkle won by five lengths from the three-year-old Descador. Burns later remembered:

> Going down the back towards the final turn we weren't travelling at all. He wasn't on the bridle and I could see the leaders beginning to get away from me. I kept telling myself not to panic. Even across the top we were still going nowhere. As we turned for home I had to get after him. Nothing happened for a few strides. Then Arkle clicked into gear. He had the lot of them beat in the next hundred yards. Thinking back on it, I believe the horse missed seeing a fence in front of him, something to get him fired up. If you remember, he always took a hold with Pat and I think it was the fences and the exhilaration of jumping at speed that turned Arkle on.

Fifteen days later Arkle carried top weight of 11 stone 13 pounds at Gowran Park in the 2½-mile Carey's Cottage Chase – named after a good chaser of the 1950s who had been trained by Pat Taaffe's father Tom. Conceding seventeen pounds to the second in the handicap, Silver Green, Arkle started at 4-7 in a field of ten and won smoothly, showing his characteristic turn of foot to beat Greatrakes by ten lengths.

With his return to chasing safely accomplished, sights were set on the biggest race of his career so far, and the first meeting – in the Hennessy Gold Cup at Newbury at the end of November – with the horse with whom his name would always be linked: Mill House.

Mill House

By the time of the 1963 Hennessy Gold Cup, most racing fans in Britain needed little convincing that there was a new champion in their midst in the massive shape of Mill House, like Arkle a six-year-old and like Arkle the product of Irish breeding – but unlike Arkle trained by then in England.

The story of Mill House touches that of Arkle very early on. Bred in County Kildare by the Lawlor family, who ran a hotel in Naas (Mill House's dam was named Nas Na Riogh – 'meeting place of the kings' – after the Gaelic name for the town), he received much of his infant education from none other than Pat Taaffe (who had ridden Nas Na Riogh in races). Mill House had been sent to Pat's father Tom for breaking in, and Pat was actively involved in the young horse's schooling. In his autobiography, he described how he had ridden Mill House over a low hurdle, and 'the surge of power was oceanic'. He continued:

> My schooling of Mill House moved from hurdles to fences and inevitably to the very best school of all, the hunting fields of Ireland. I hunted him with the Naas Harriers, the South County Dublin Harriers and the Kildare and he loved every minute of it. Nothing daunted him. If I put him at a gate, a wall or whatever, he would prick up his ears and go. No questions asked. And running free across the land, you can believe me he was something to fill the mind of a man.

Mill House and Willie Robinson power over the last fence to win the 1963 Gold Cup at Cheltenham.

Mill House went into training with Tom Taaffe. In his first race, a maiden hurdle at Naas in January 1961, he finished fourth, then won at the same course, ridden by Pat. He fell in a big novice hurdle at Punchestown in April 1961, but had caught the eye of bloodstock agent Jack Doyle and was soon sold to Bill Gollings, an advertising executive who had horses with Epsom trainer Syd Dale. In his first race for Dale, a four-year-old hurdle at Newbury in November 1961, Mill House fell at the first flight. He was unplaced in his next hurdle then won at Wincanton, after which his attention was turned to chasing: he fell at Hurst Park and won at

Cheltenham, and at the end of the season Gollings moved him to the Lambourn stable of Fulke Walwyn, one of the very best jumps trainers in Britain. Here his regular jockey would be Willie Robinson, who had ridden Paddy's Point to finish second to Hard Ridden in the 1958 Derby, and who was to become one of the extremely select band of jump jockeys to have won the Cheltenham Gold Cup, Champion Hurdle and Grand National. Willie soon received a letter from his friend Pat Taaffe informing him that he would be riding 'the best horse in Britain – and possibly the world.' (Before long Taaffe would be sending a note of revision: 'You are now up on the second best horse in the world.')

Mill House's first outing for Walwyn in November 1962 saw him win a handicap chase at Sandown Park off the very lenient weight of 10 stone 7 pounds. He was beaten at Kempton Park by King's Nephew, only to resume his winning ways at Sandown Park in December – and then his preparation for the Gold Cup fell foul of the weather as the big freeze-up tightened its grip. By Gold Cup day 1963 Mill House had not run for three months, but he started 7-2 favourite and turned in a memorable display of powerful galloping and rhythmic jumping to beat Fortria, flag-bearer of the Dreaper yard, by twelve lengths – a superlative performance for a six-year-old. Two days earlier Arkle had won the Broadway Chase, but it was Mill House who was being hailed as the new Golden Miller, potentially the greatest chaser of all time, a horse for whom the future offered limitless possibilities.

After Cheltenham, Mill House won the Mandarin Chase at Newbury and was then retired for the season, with racing fans already starting to salivate at the prospect of his first encounter with Arkle.

The connection between Arkle and the West African republic of Togo is not immediately apparent, but a portrait of Himself – clearly modelled on the pre-1963 Hennessy photo opposite – appeared on the 2-franc stamp issued there in 1985. This was part of a set entitled 'Les Chevaux de Course Celèbres' and included, in addition to the Arkle stamp, Allez France, Tingle Creek, Interco, Dawn Run, Seattle Slew, Nijinsky and Red Rum (who shared the 1,000-franc slot with Politician). According to philatelic experts there is no great significance in this parade of eminent horses appearing on Togolese stamps, as it is not unusual for small countries to have their stamps produced by outside agencies. Other sets produced for Togo included one marking the marriage of Prince Andrew and another celebrating the fiftieth anniversary of Donald Duck.

The 1963 Hennessy – and after

With little to connect the Mill House and Arkle form lines, the handicapper framing the weights for the 1963 Hennessy was faced with a conundrum. Mill House had won a Cheltenham Gold Cup against experienced and battle-hardened opposition while Arkle's form was more of an unknown quantity, and it occasioned little surprise that the Hennessy weights had 'The Big Horse' – as Mill House by then was widely known – conceding five pounds to his Irish-trained rival.

Arkle had had two races that season before the Hennessy while Mill House was making his first appearance, but few considered that The Big Horse would be short of peak fitness for such a test. His trainer Fulke Walwyn had already won the race three times: with Mandarin in 1957 and Taxidermist in 1958 (the first two years of the Hennessy, when it was run at Cheltenham) and Mandarin again at Newbury in 1961. He knew what was required. In a field of ten runners, Mill House went off a solid

Arkle and Pat Taaffe in the parade before the Hennessy Gold Cup, 30 November 1963.

Mill House
(no. 1) leads
John O' Groats
(13) and
Pappageno's
Cottage (5) over
the first fence in
the 1963
Hennessy Gold
Cup. Arkle is
taking off on
the extreme left.

15-8 favourite with Arkle well supported at 5-2. Duke Of York (8-1), Springbok (9-1) and Happy Spring (100-9) came next in the market. King's Nephew, who had beaten Mill House the previous season, was little fancied at 100-7.

The going was very soft, and while the form book describes the visibility as 'fair', that is not how Newbury racegoers or BBC television viewers remember the occasion. Much of the Hennessy seemed to be run in a mist which verged on fog, conditions which meant that the pivotal moment of the race was effectively lost in the murk. Mill House took an early lead, briefly ceded it to Solimyth, and then took up the running again towards the end of the long back straight on the first circuit. He maintained that lead with a seemingly effortless combination of gigantic stride and spring-heeled jumping.

Mill House was still in front and full of running as the field swung left-handed into the final straight, but Arkle, who had been quietly making ground from off the pace, was getting closer and closer. After the fourth last, the first in the straight, he was in Mill House's slipstream, and going into the third last, an open ditch, just a length behind and seemingly about to pounce. The television camera lingered on the fence, so exactly what happened to Arkle two strides beyond it has not been conclusively recorded. Some standing nearby claimed that Arkle put his foot in a hole. Whatever actually happened, it brought him almost to a standstill, and with Mill House resuming his relentless gallop, the race was gone beyond recall. As he struggled to recover his rhythm going to the second last Arkle was passed by Happy Spring, and although he was coming back at that horse close home, he could finish only third, 8¾ lengths behind Mill House.

The Dreaper camp was thrown into a gloom, but Betty Dreaper reported that the sombre mood did not last long:

> Tom never asked his jockey anything about a race the day of the race – he always waited until the next day. He said, 'Let him cool off and we'll get the true running.' Pat came down the next day to school and after the schooling was done they were going through the Calendar and Tom said, 'Will you beat Mill House next time, Pat?'
>
> 'Without a doubt,' says Pat.
>
> 'What makes you so sure?'
>
> 'Well,' says Pat, 'coming to the third last I gave him a kick, and I had no idea that he was going to accelerate like he did. If I'd sat quietly on him he'd have beaten Mill House, as he wouldn't have slipped when he landed.'

This was clearly a plausible excuse, but for many observers Mill House had scored a resounding victory and would never again be troubled by the upstart Irish challenger. After all, they reasoned, had Arkle gone in hot pursuit of Mill House after recovering from his mistake and rapidly reduced the distance between them? No, he had not – nor had he even managed to peg back Happy Spring for second place. In *Horse and Hound*, 'Audax' (John Lawrence) rhapsodised that Mill House 'was, to us, what Shakespeare must have been to Elizabethans on the first night of *Hamlet*, what Garbo sometimes was on the screen, Fonteyn on the Covent Garden stage, Caruso at La Scala, Matthews at Wembley, Bradman at the Oval.'

It was sad that so keenly anticipated a contest had hinged on one of the protagonists making a mistake – or perhaps suffering a wretched piece of bad luck – but a case could be made that Mill House's victory was less than conclusive. Arkle lived to fight again, and the rematch would be something to see.

Meanwhile there were other races to be run. Arkle got back into the winning habit in the three-mile Christmas Handicap Chase at Leopardstown on St Stephen's Day 1963 (seventy minutes after Mill House had galloped two very inferior opponents into the Kempton Park ground in the King George VI Chase). Conceding twenty-nine pounds to the good chaser Loving Record (who had won the Christmas Chase two years earlier) and more to four other opponents and starting at 4-7, Arkle duly won, but only after a struggle. The *Irish Field* wrote how

> *Arkle and Loving Record drew well clear of their opponents over the last*
> *three fences and engaged in a 'battle royal'.*
>   *The issue was very much in doubt, as Loving Record landed in front*
> *over the final fence, but on the run-in he wavered, and a very hard-*
> *pressed Arkle nabbed him in the last fifty yards. The margin of victory*
> *was two lengths, but this gives a very misleading impression of the*
> *closeness of the race.*

Plans to take on the top-class chaser Irish Imp, trained like Mill House by Fulke Walwyn, in the two-mile Knightsbridge Chase at Newbury on 18 January 1964 were scuppered by frost: the announcement of abandonment came just in time to prevent Arkle starting his journey from Kilsallaghan. But less than two weeks after that disappointment Arkle was back in racecourse action in the Thyestes Chase at Gowran Park. He again faced Loving Record, this time conceding thirty-one pounds, and, starting at 4-6, beat that horse into second place by twelve lengths. The mare Kerforo, who had been such a Dreaper favourite, was pulled up.

Arkle's final race before the 1964 Gold Cup was the three-mile Leopardstown Chase in mid-February. Starting at 4-7, he faced five opponents – including the grey mare Flying Wild, whom he had last encountered in his second bumper in December 1961, and who most recently had won the valuable Stone's Ginger Wine Chase at Sandown Park, beating Dormant, to whom she was conceding eighteen pounds. That she was now receiving twenty-six pounds from Arkle is some indication of how the Dreaper horse was drawing further and further away from his contemporaries – except one – in terms of form. The outsider Springtime Lad II fell early on and proceeded to make a nuisance of himself by attempting to bite or kick the surviving runners, but Pat Taaffe kept well clear of such an unlikely hazard, and the race came to the boil with Arkle and Flying Wild neck and neck at the second last – where the mare fell, leaving Arkle to cruise home unchallenged and win by twelve lengths from the rank outsider, 66-1 chance Greatrakes.

Arkle's victory was the middle leg of a Dreaper treble in three consecutive races at Leopardstown that afternoon. The race before, the Scalp Hurdle, had been won the five-year-old Flyingbolt, winning his fourth race in a row, from a strong field which included the mare Height O' Fashion and Winning Fair, who had won the 1963 Champion Hurdle. The race following Arkle's, the Milltown Chase, was won by the six-year-old Fort Leney, who before the end of the decade would be following in his stable companion's distinguished hoofprints at Cheltenham.

Arkle was clearly at the top of his form, and apparently unbeatable. So was Mill House, who had easily won his two races since the Hennessy. In the Gold Cup, something would have to give.

Anne, Duchess of Westminster leads in Arkle after the Thyestes Chase at Gowran Park.

'The day Arkle became a god'

'The day Arkle became a god'

The 1964 Gold Cup

The Gold Cup run at Cheltenham on 7 March 1964 remains one of the iconic events of modern racing history, a pivotal moment when the sport tilted from one era into another. This famous race was (and still is) celebrated on acres of newsprint, talked about in all the bars in Ireland and plenty in England, and – a true measure of its stature – celebrated in verse and song, in the rollicking ballad *Arkle*, delivered in suitably beer-stained manner by Dominic Behan, brother of the more famous Brendan. It has even played a central role in the 2005 version of *Days of Wine and Roses*.

But that status did not come out of the blue, the result of an unexpectedly brilliant performance which gave jump racing a new star. For it had been very clear since the previous year's National Hunt meeting at Cheltenham, when Arkle won the Broadway Chase and Mill House the Gold Cup, that in this pair the sport had not merely two young stars, but two closely matched horses who already seemed to be little short of proving the best of all time.

In those circumstances it is not surprising that the 1964 Gold Cup was preceded by a level of public expectation unparalleled in recent memory, nor that opinion divided along tribal lines. Mill House, though bred in Ireland and ridden by an Irishman, was trained in Lambourn, in deepest Berkshire, and thus was seen to be representing the home side. Arkle, Irish through and through in background and connections, was the challenger from across the water.

In his history of the Cheltenham Gold Cup, John Welcome caught the pre-race mood:

> The connections of Mill House were exuberantly confident. It seemed, oddly enough, as if the characteristics of the two nations were for once reversed. The taciturn English were loud and lavish in their pride and praise of Mill House, whereas the usually vociferous Irish were quiet and subdued, and content to await the outcome.

The 1964 Gold Cup was run on a Saturday, rather than the customary Thursday, for the first time in its history, after the racecourse board had changed the days of the meeting from the traditional Tuesday-Thursday to Thursday-Saturday. As it turned out, this shift allowed a much larger television audience to witness the great race than would have been the case had the usual schedule been continued, and undoubtedly contributed to the size and fervour of the nascent Arkle fan club. A measure of the excitement generated by the Gold Cup was that Cheltenham and the BBC gave permission for the sound broadcast of the race to be transmitted at the Market Rasen and Haydock Park meetings taking place the same day.

What else was happening in the first week of March 1964? Well, Cilla Black was on top of the pop charts with the Burt Bacharach song 'Anyone Who Had A Heart', and the Beatles had just returned from their first trip to the USA in order to start filming *A Hard Day's Night*.

The sporting world was still agog from the dethronement a few days earlier of world heavyweight boxing champion Sonny Liston by the noisy – and to some traditional tastes noisome – young challenger from Louisville, Kentucky, the future Muhammad Ali who was then plain Cassius Clay. ('Dethronement' is perhaps not the exact word, for Liston declined to get up off his seat and come out for the seventh round of the fight.) Clay's often repeated mantra was 'I am the greatest', and while both Mill House and Arkle were too well bred to be so brash and boastful, the Gold Cup would sort out which of them could make the same claim.

PREVIOUS SPREAD
The last fence in the 1964 Gold Cup: Arkle comes away from Mill House.

The build-up

Racing fans had long been stoking up the anticipation over the imminent clash between Mill House and Arkle, and as the race got nearer and nearer such parochial excitement proved contagious in the outside world. The issue of the *Radio Times* published two days before the race carried, facing an advert for the 'Parnall Spinwasher De Luxe with new "Selectromat" controls' (with the proud boast that 'Clever women prefer the top loading single tub'), a preview by John Lawrence. This described how 'two big brown horses' would be competing for 'the right to be called the greatest steeplechaser in Europe, if not in the world ... Those who tune in for the 1964 Gold Cup are in for a thrill they will not easily forget.'

In the print media, the racing specialists could scarcely contain their excitement. *Horse and Hound* had the same John Lawrence, writing as 'Audax', predicting:

> If all goes well, if these two young giants come to the last together, the Cheltenham crowd will surely get something no money can buy – a spectacle never excelled and very seldom equalled in the long, drama-studded annals of National Hunt racing.

Ratcheting up the anticipation early in the week, *The Times* deployed the historical perspective with the observation that 'Not since Golden Miller met Thomond II in 1935 has the Gold Cup raised such an exhilarating prospect as the contest expected between Mill House and Arkle on Saturday.'

The sense of anticipation was even more acute among those closest to the two protagonists. Neither Pat Taaffe nor Willie Robinson would hear of defeat when they joined BBC commentator Peter O'Sullevan at the Carlton Hotel in Cheltenham on the night before the race – an occasion which duly gave O'Sullevan a good story for his much-followed column in the *Daily Express* on Gold Cup morning:

> Willie Robinson will be taking a holiday at Pat Taaffe's expense after this afternoon's Gold Cup. At least, that is Pat's firm opinion.
>
> For over dinner in Cheltenham last night, the respective partners of the great protagonists, Mill House and Arkle, agreed that the rider of the winner (a bare 10 per cent of prize money comes to £800) would pay for 'an airline ticket to romantic places' for the loser.
>
> 'That Willie will be taking the trip all right,' affirmed Pat, indicating his four-years-younger and firm friend.
>
> But the quiet man, who'll be aboard 'the big horse', could find no ground for his adversary's assumption.
>
> By way of reply he sent for a timetable to learn the precise cost of a flight which he would inevitably be required to underwrite ...

Given the relentless cranking up of excitement over the weeks and months preceding the race, it was something of a miracle that Gold Cup day dawned with

The Cheltenham race programme in *The Times*, 7 March 1964.

both the principals fit and well, and it must have been a relief for readers of *The Times* to open their paper on the Saturday morning and see that the core of the big race was intact.

Four runners in other races that day were later to play supporting roles in the Arkle story. Sartorius, number 2 in the Spa Hurdle (which became the Stayers' Hurdle, and then, in 2005, the World Hurdle), finished last of the finishers behind Arkle in the 1966 Gold Cup. Big George, number 10 in the Spa Hurdle, was a remote fourth in the 1966 SGB Chase, the last race Arkle won. Freddie, who won the 1964 Foxhunters' easily at 1-3 and became one of the most popular chasers of the modern era and runner-up in both the 1965 and 1966 Grand Nationals, finished second to Arkle in the 1965 Hennessy (and last in the 1966 Hennessy behind Stalbridge Colonist and Arkle). Maigret, number 8 in the County Hurdle, finished third, a 'bad' distance behind the runner-up Arkle, in the 1966 King George, the last race that Himself ever ran.

The text which accompanied this programme in *The Times* gives the lie to any notion that rose-tinted nostalgia plays its part in describing the 1964 Gold Cup as the mostly keenly anticipated race of the modern age. 'Our Racing Correspondent' –

nothing so vulgar as naming names in the sports pages of 'The Thunderer' in those days – wrote:

> Mill House is taken to beat Arkle in the Gold Cup today in what should be one of the races of the century. These two great steeplechasers go to the post with full stable confidence behind each of them ... There is a prospect of a record crowd, and unless some incident intervenes, they are likely to see a race that they will not forget.

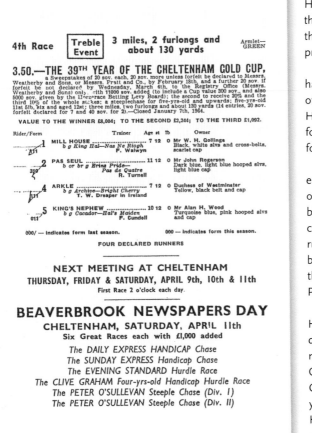

The correspondent's view that Mill House would shade it was repeated in the majority of other daily papers, and the *Sporting Life* likewise expressed a preference for Mill House.

A few days before the race there had been a real possibility that no other horse would oppose Mill House and Arkle, but in the event four (from an original entry of fourteen) were declared to run.

Arkle had been seen out six times earlier in the 1963-64 season, with only the third place in the Hennessy blotting his copybook. Mill House came to Cheltenham on a winning run of six races, not having been beaten since finishing runner-up in the Cottage Rake Chase at Kempton Park in November 1962.

The horse that had beaten Mill House at Kempton that November day was King's Nephew, who was now taking him on again at Cheltenham. Trained by Frank Cundell, the ten-year-old was three years senior to Arkle and Mill House, and was a high-class chaser. He came to Cheltenham fresh from winning the Great

The racecard for the 1964 Gold Cup. (It should be noted that whereas nowadays horses carrying the same weight would be listed in the racecard by alphabetical order of their names, in 1964 they were listed in alphabetical order of the owners' names – with the exception of any horse owned by the Queen, whose name always came first.)

Yorkshire Chase at Doncaster – then one of the biggest handicaps of the season – and had won two other races earlier in the season, the Hermitage Chase at Newbury and the Oatlands Chase at Kempton Park. He had also finished fifth in the Hennessy, nearly twenty-seven lengths behind the winner Mill House, and eighteen lengths behind Arkle. Good chaser as he was, and despite being ridden by three-times champion Stan Mellor (who was to play a leading role in a major Arkle moment in 1966), on form King's Nephew could hope for third place in the Gold Cup at best.

Pas Seul, the fourth runner, was taking part in his fifth Gold Cup. As a six-year-old in 1959, he was leading at the last fence when he fell heavily. In 1960 he won narrowly from Lochroe; in 1961 he finished runner-up to Saffron Tartan, beaten 1½ lengths; and in 1962 he started 9-4 favourite but could finish only fifth behind Mandarin. Perhaps the greatest single race of Pas Seul's distinguished career was the 1961 Whitbread Gold Cup at Sandown Park, where he was stopped in his tracks

'Four great chasers: Gold Cup runners, 7 Mar '64' by Peter Biegel. (Later in 1964, this picture became the first Christmas card for the charity which was to become the Injured Jockeys' Fund.)

by a falling horse at the Pond Fence three from home, yet recovered to beat that season's Grand National winner Nicolaus Silver, to whom he was conceding 21 pounds, an achievement described by one writer as 'probably the finest performance of any steeplechaser since the war'. Fred Winter, who rode Pas Seul only once, when winning a two-mile chase at Stratford immediately before that Whitbread, called him the best horse he had ever sat on. But he broke down in the Whitbread in April 1962 and missed the whole of the following season, returning to action in January 1964. He was now eleven years old and – although he had won one of his three races before the Gold Cup – a shadow of his former self.

So the four runners for the 1964 Gold Cup, which carried a first prize of £8,004, included two previous winners of the race.

Arkle's demeanour before the most important contest of his life was keen, fizzy, anxious to get on with it: he pricked his ears and bared his teeth. By contrast, Mill House was very calm and collected in the parade ring and moved to the start easily and – for such a large-framed horse – surprisingly gracefully, drawing the admiration of John Lawrence from *Horse and*

The pre-race parade: *above*, **Mill House and Willie Robinson;** *below*, **Arkle and Pat Taaffe.**

Hound, who remarked upon his 'extravagant, extended gait that would have done the High School in Vienna proud.'

Even the weather joined in the fun, alternating snow and sunshine on a cold spring day. One blizzard during the morning had briefly sent the stewards out onto the course to ascertain whether there was any threat to racing – it was decided that there was not – and while the runners were in the parade ring another snowstorm briefly obliterated Cleeve Hill, the glorious backdrop to Cheltenham racecourse. But that swirl of snow disappeared as quickly as it had arrived, and sunshine had returned as the runners inspected the first fence – a moment when, according to John Lawrence, 'the atmosphere was electric with a brand of suspense and fascination I never felt before on any British racecourse.'

Arkle and Pat Taaffe before the start.

The betting confirmed that this was essentially a two-horse race. Mill House was a strong favourite at a starting price of 8-13, with Arkle at 7-4. The other two runners attracted little support, King's Nephew starting at 20-1 and Pas Seul, who had been a well-fancied 6-1 chance when winning the 1960 race, the rank outsider at 50-1.

Having taken a good look at the first, the quartet circled at the 3 miles 2½ furlongs start, which in those days was located on a spur to the rear of the grandstand.

At 3.53, three minutes after the advertised post time, the starter plunged the handle down, the tapes rose, and the most keenly awaited steeplechase of modern times was under way.

The Gold Cup in its sporting and cultural context, as seen through the *Radio Times* listings for 7 March 1964. *Left:* The Grandstand schedule. (Rubin Carter, winner of the recorded 'Gillette Fight of the Week', was later immortalised in the Bob Dylan song 'Hurricane'.) *Right:* The Light Programme.

The race

An unusual account of a race which has been described in many ways over the years can be found in *Days of Wine and Roses*, Owen McCafferty's brilliant reworking for the stage of J. P. Miller's haunting depiction of alcoholism, best known through the Oscar-nominated film, released in 1962, starring Jack Lemmon and Lee Remick. In the Owen McCafferty version (first staged at the Donmar Warehouse in London in February 2005), Donal returns home to his wife Mona and baby son after seeing Arkle's victory. Donal is well lubricated, both emotionally and alcoholically, by his day at Cheltenham, and insists on treating his wife to a detailed description of the famous race:

> *Four runners – Arkle – Mill House – Pas Seul – and King's Nephew –*
> *Only four runners because Arkle and Mill House are a different class –*
> *The other two horses are top notch – But what prices are they? – Twenty*
> *to one and fifty to one – Not a prayer between them – It would've froze*
> *you solid today – The place is packed to the rafters – The Irish are*
> *hanging out of the woodwork – This is part of the importance of this –*
> *England's a great place – London, love it – Londoners, salt of the earth –*
> *The Irish are for Arkle – The English are for Mill House – This is a battle*
> *to the death – Before they go to the off the horses are parading around*
> *the paddock – You couldn't get moving for punters trying to see Arkle –*
> *You'd swear this horse knows it too – Once he hears the cheering it's as if*
> *he makes himself bigger – Then he holds his head up high – It's as if to*
> *say, Here I am, let the battle commence – This horse loves people, that's*
> *the only way I can describe it – This is another thing too that made you*
> *realise something special is going to happen here – Freezing – Ten*
> *minutes before the off it starts snowing – [Mona pours herself another*
> *drink] – Then just as the horses are making their way down to the start –*
> *It's like a gust of wind came and blew the snow away – And there was*
> *the sun – A clear blue sky – And a sun that lit the whole of Cheltenham*
> *– They're at the start – Twenty thousand punters – And four horses –*
> *They're under starter's orders and they're off – Twenty-one fences – Three*
> *miles two furlongs and a hundred and thirty yards – [He becomes*
> *animated, living the race] – All set off at a right clip – Mill House jumps*
> *the first in the lead – It's beautiful to see great horses move – It's poetry*
> *– All jumping like they were born for it – We're going downhill now –*
> *Mill House is ahead by about four lengths – You can see Pat Taaffe is*
> *trying to hold Arkle back – He's not having an easy ride – Doesn't want*
> *Arkle to go yet – Too early – Just hang in there – We're lying fourth but*
> *that's all right – Mill House and Pas Seul having a bit of a tussle – Good*
> *to watch but it's only the opening act – Mill House is jumping beautifully*
> *– Arkle still in fourth but starting to make up ground now – Pat Taaffe's*
> *just letting him go a bit – Just easing him forward – Into his stride now –*

The last fence: Arkle heads Mill House ... and scoots up the hill.

Clearing the fences like he had wings – Coming up to the seventeenth Pas Seul and King's Nephew are out of it now – Only ever there to make the numbers up – At the seventeenth Mill House and Arkle glide over the fence – Mill House is four lengths clear – Arkle's beginning to close – This is it – Time to make your move – Here we go boy –Arkle's closing all the time – They're rounding the home turn – Willie Robinson on Mill House has the whip out – We're there – Stride for stride – The whole of Cheltenham's busting open with noise – Arkle for Ireland – Mill House for England – Racing up to the last fence – Both of them still going great guns – Arkle on the stand side, Mill House on the far side – Arkle jumps a length ahead – We just got to keep going now – Just keep going – But Mill House makes one last attempt – Struggling to get up alongside Arkle – Arkle pulls away – The war's over – Arkle wins by five lengths – The greatest Gold Cup ever run – I was there to see it ...

The Times supplied a more sober description of the closing stages:

> *Crossing the water in the last circuit Mill House had established such a lead that everywhere in the crowd people were feeling and saying that it was not going to be a race. Taaffe, something of a worrier when on the ground, is a cool and endlessly patient man in the saddle. He made no attempt to make Arkle go with Mill House, but he made a significant move to halve the distance between the two horses as they turned to go uphill at the beginning of the last mile.*

At that point BBC television commentator Peter O'Sullevan – whose initially restrained calling of the race was now becoming ever more urgent, providing the perfect soundtrack to the momentous event taking place out on the course – cried that 'Irish voices in the stands are calling for Pat now!', and the jockey and his partner responded as if they had heard the encouragement from a mile away.

Back to *The Times*:

> *After that Taaffe approached no closer until they were coming to the third fence from home. But Mill House made a fine leap there to make*

Letting off steam.

perhaps half a length, and he set off for the corner about three lengths to the good. Then came the moment of truth. Taaffe, before our amazed gaze, gave away a second or two to turn Arkle slightly to the right, clear of Mill House's path, balanced him again, and went after the leader.

Mill House is not slow, but his lead disappeared in a flash. The two horses jumped level at the next fence [second last], and Arkle led by a length over the last. From there to the post he increased his superiority to five lengths.

At the last fence Mill House – on whom Willie Robinson had lost his whip between the last two – had parted the birch with one despairing lunge, and for a moment or two the momentum of that thrust had seemed about to push The Big Horse back into contention. But just as Mill House started to rally, so Arkle engaged yet another gear and sprinted up the hill, Pat Taaffe no more than tickling him with the whip. 'This is the champion!, cried Peter O'Sullevan, 'This is the best we've seen for a long time' – and all but the most diehard Mill House fanatics had to concede that he was right.

Pas Seul finished twenty-five lengths behind Mill House in third, and King's Nephew a remote fourth and last, but the official distances were of only academic interest, as was Arkle's winning time of 6 minutes 45.6 seconds, which beat the previous record for course and distance by four seconds. But lengths, minutes and seconds were redundant. Everyone knew that Arkle's true superiority went beyond any measure.

The reaction

After dismounting – by which time the result had been announced to the crowd at Lansdowne Road, Dublin, watching Ireland play Wales at rugby – Pat Taaffe declared Arkle 'the best horse I've ever ridden' and expressed confidence that they'd win the next year's Gold Cup. Mill House's connections were shell-shocked, not only by defeat but by its comprehensive nature. Brough Scott, then an Oxford undergraduate with a ride in the Cathcart Challenge Cup, two races after the Gold Cup, remembers:

> In the weighing room we couldn't believe what our eyes had told us. I remember poor Willie Robinson sitting on the bench just as shattered as if he had been taken out by the young Cassius Clay ... Willie had thought Mill House unbeatable. He was wrong.
> There was a sense of awe around the place which never left us whenever Arkle ran.

After the steam had cleared and the dust had settled, trainer Fulke Walwyn admitted to Clive Graham, Peter O'Sullevan's colleague on the *Daily Express*, that 'I can still hardly believe that any horse breathing could have done what Arkle did to him.'

The press displayed a similar sense of awe. In the *Sporting Life*, Tom Nickalls wrote:

> Not since Flying Fox won the Triple Crown in the last year of the last century has the House of Westminster had such a racehorse as Arkle proved himself on Saturday.
> The ease with which he beat Mill House – who, in defeat, was not disgraced – showed that Arkle is entitled to rank as high in the annals of steeplechasing as do Flying Fox and unbeaten Ormonde (another Westminster Triple Crown winner) in Flat racing history ...
> We have seen Irish jubilation in plenty at Cheltenham, but this time it broke all records in decibels.

Quintin Gilbey, reporting the race as 'Kettledrum' for the *Life*'s rival paper the *Sporting Chronicle*, struck a similar note:

> Amidst scenes of unprecedented enthusiasm – the cheering continued long after the jockeys had weighed in and the 'all right' had been announced – Irish-trained Arkle beat the English champion Mill House by five lengths in a never-to-be-forgotten race for the Cheltenham Gold Cup ...

The national newspapers echoed the rapture of the racing papers. John Hislop – later breeder of the great Brigadier Gerard – wrote in the Sunday's *News of the World* that the Gold Cup 'will go down as one of the greatest races of all time', while the following morning's *Times* echoed the trade papers in reporting the exultation of the

Cheltenham crowd: 'Exhilaration at the end of races is part of the National Hunt meeting, but never before has anything been seen like the elation on this occasion.' The following weekend John Lawrence in *Horse and Hound* showed that a few days' reflection had not served to diminish the magnitude of the occasion:

> *In more ways than one the 1964 Cheltenham Gold Cup defied belief. It was, for a start, almost unbelievable that the race should live up in full to such tremendous advance publicity – and to most of us in England it was quite unbelievable that, barring accidents, Mill House should be beaten by as much as five lengths. Yet both these wonders came to pass and, by achieving them, the Duchess of Westminster's Arkle proved himself beyond question the greatest steeplechaser seen in Europe since Prince Regent.*
>
> *With so much at stake, so much could have gone wrong – a single slip, a fall, a tiny error of judgement. Any of these might have left a nagging doubt in the mind – but none of them transpired. There can never have been a race more perfect in every way – or a triumph more complete.*

Attention switched to how Mill House might turn the tables in the future – if he did not have to make his own running, for example – but in their heart of hearts his supporters knew that The Big Horse would always be in the shadow of Arkle, and that the crown had changed hands in the most emphatic manner.

Some made even greater claims for this famous day. In Owen McCafferty's *Days of Wine and Roses*, Mona asks Donal, in boozy euphoria on his return from the racecourse, not to disturb their sleeping infant. But he is adamant:

> *It must be done – On this day never to be forgotten – March the seventh nineteen hundred and sixty-four – I must see the boy – So in years to come I can tell him that on the day Arkle became a god – I stood over his cot and whispered to him – Sleep the sleep of the gods, young man, for today we are all kings.*

The song

Stewball Was A Racehorse, according to the traditional song trilled by Peter, Paul and Mary, but not many real racehorses achieve such eminence that a song is written about them. The great Australian horse Phar Lap was one to reach that level of fame, and in recent years two famous jumpers have had their feats immortalised musically: triple Grand National winner Red Rum by Christopher, Robin, Alice and Ted; and Dawn Run, only horse ever to win both the Champion Hurdle and Gold Cup, by Foster and Allen. (The dirge which came to form the inevitable consequence of any victory by triple Gold Cup winner Best Mate, sung to the tune of 'Amazing Grace' and consisting of the two words 'Best Mate' repeated *ad nauseam*, does not qualify as a proper song.)

Arkle has earned his place in musical history through two recorded folksongs. 'Kempton Park' by Graeme Miles describes the 1965 King George VI Chase, when Arkle's victory was overshadowed by the death of the brilliant two-mile chaser Dunkirk (see page 109), but a much better-known musical incarnation of Himself is 'Arkle' by Dominic Behan, which tells the tale of the 1964 Gold Cup and was first issued as a single on the Marble Arch label in 1965.

A rollicking, up-tempo performance on which you can practically smell the Guinness, 'Arkle' records a great Irish victory largely through mockery of the condescending and snooty 'English racing gentlemen', whose horror at what is unfolding is given vivid expression in the song's climactic line:

'Look behind you, Willie Robinson, man what are you about?!'

Dominic Behan (1929-89) was the youngest of the four Behan brothers, of whom the most notable, and most notorious, was the oldest brother Brendan, as fabled for his drinking exploits as for his very popular plays: *Borstal Boy*, *The Hostage*, *The Quare Fellow*, etc. (Despite the claims of Kenneth Tynan in the 1960s, Brendan Behan was the first person to use the F-word on BBC television – on a live edition of *Panorama* in 1956. His speech was so slurred through drink that the transgression largely went unnoticed.) Dominic Behan was a notable writer of folk music – in addition to 'Arkle', his best known songs were 'Liverpool Lou' and 'The Patriot Game' – as well as drama, and while 'Arkle' did not make a mark on the higher reaches of the charts, the music and words have been anthologised in two collections. In *Ireland Sings: An anthology of modern and ancient Irish songs and ballads* (1965, new edition 1973), edited by Dominic Behan himself, the song carries the subtitle 'Mighty Millhouse' [*sic*], and is described in a note as telling the story of the 'Second battle of any real importance the Irish won on English soil.' The version printed in *New English Broadsides: Songs of our time from the English* [sic] *folk scene*, compiled by Nathan Joseph and Eric Winter and published in 1967, is musically truer to the recorded performance than that in *Ireland Sings*, and bears the intriguing gloss: 'Tune traditional, *Musselburgh Fair* – Dorian mode on D'.

Behan's original recording of the song can currently be found on the CDs *The Irish Folk Collection, volume 2*, and *Wild Irish Rose: Popular Irish ballads*, both issued in the USA by St Clair Records in 2001.

The introduction to *New English Broadsides* declares:

> Dominic Behan is often looked upon lightly as a typical wild Irishman and the youngest member of a wild and famous Irish family. He should not be dismissed so easily, for he has written a number of powerful songs. A few of them are lyrical and uncommitted, a few are directed against social and racial prejudice, but by far the greatest number of them are pro-Irish and anti-English.

That pro-Irish and anti-English stance is the key to why Arkle's demolition of Mill House so appealed to Behan. In revelling in the discomfiture of the defeated English and mocking their lame excuses, 'Arkle' is a proud and patriotic tribute to a great Irish triumph over the old enemy.

The leadsheet of 'Arkle' by Dominic Behan.

'Arkle' by Dominic Behan

It happened in the springtime of the year of sixty-four
When Englishmen were making pounds and fivers by the score.
He beat them on the hollows, he beat them on the jumps,
A pair of fancy fetlocks, well he showed them all the bumps.

He's English, he's English, English as you've seen,
A little bit of Arab stock and more from Stephen's Green.
Take a look at Mill House, throw out your chest with pride,
He's the greatest steeplechaser on the English countryside.

Then a quiet man called Dreaper living in the Emerald Isle
Said, 'That horse of yours called Mill House surely shows a bit of style.
'But I've a little fella, and Arkle is his name.
'Put your money where you put your mouth and then we'll play the game.'

Well the English racing gentlemen laughed till fit to burst.
'You've tried before, Tom Dreaper, and then you came off worst.
'If you think your horse can beat us, you're running short on brains.
'It's Mill House that you're talking of and not those beastly Danes.'

Arkle now is five to two, Mill House is money on.
They're off! – and dare believe I do, the champion has it won.
There are other horses in the race to test the great chap's might,
But dearie me! it's plain to see the rest are out of sight.

There are three more fences now to go, he leads by twenty lengths.
Brave Arkle's putting in a show – poor chap, he's all but spent!
Mill House sweeps on majestically, great glory in each stride.
He's the greatest horse undoubtedly within the whole world wide.

Two to go, still he comes, cutting down the lead,
He's beaten bar the shouting, he hasn't got the speed.
They're on the run up to the last – 'My God! can he hold out?
'Look behind you, Willie Robinson, man what are you about?!'

They're at the last and over, Pat Taaffe has more in hand.
He's passing England's Mill House, the finest in the land.
'My God, he has us beaten, what can we English say?
'The ground was wrong, the distance long, too early in the day.'

'The perfect, complete chaser'

'The perfect, complete chaser'

The 1964–65 season

Arkle's rout of Mill House in the 1964 Gold Cup powered his reputation to its cruising height and settled him at an altitude where for the next two and a half years he was, barring one entirely excusable blip, simply unbeatable. For the horse and his connections, life would never be the same again.

On the Sunday, the day after his Gold Cup triumph, he returned to Kilsallaghan by road and plane, and immediately had to start coming to terms with the consequences of his new-found fame. The country road which passes the stables had begun filling up with cars from an early hour, and Arkle arrived home into an almighty but entirely good-natured traffic jam, as people came from far and wide to salute the conquering hero. Betty Dreaper recalled how, then and thereafter, the horse revelled in the attention: 'Nobody enjoyed it more than he did. He adored it.'

But there was still work to be done, as Arkle was not finished racing for the season. On Easter Monday 1964, just over three weeks after Cheltenham, he went to nearby Fairyhouse for the Irish Grand National, which he won by a length and quarter from the tough mare Height O' Fashion, to whom he was conceding 2 stone 2 pounds.

While this may not have been his finest hour in terms of sheer performance, the 1964 Irish National has a special significance in the Arkle story, for the race conditions paid him the greatest compliment any sport can dispense to its best participants: the rules were changed to accommodate his transcendence. Henceforth any handicap race in which Arkle had been entered would be subject to a special procedure.

Arkle then spent the summer at Bryanstown, the Duchess of Westminster's Irish estate, where he spent a lazy time grazing with the cattle, receiving the attention of his doting owner and her friends, and generally unwinding. He returned to Greenogue in the early autumn to be prepared for the new season, in which the Hennessy Gold Cup would be an early target, with a second Gold Cup at Cheltenham the following March top of the agenda.

Thanks no doubt to the physical and mental benefits of a summer at grass, by the 1964-65 season the somewhat immature youngster of the previous term had filled out into a magnificent specimen. John Lawrence in *Horse and Hound* wrote of Arkle's appearance on Hennessy Day in early December, the first time he had seen the horse since the spring, that he 'not only looked a perfect picture of health and fitness (his coat carries a summer gleam and is so fine that it scarcely needs clipping) but had also put on weight and muscle since last season. Apart from his lovely, almost feminine head, the most notable thing about him is that great, deep chest in which so fabulous an engine lies concealed … He is bigger and stronger than ever before, and doubtless better, too. And until some flaw is revealed in Arkle's armoury, I for one will continue to believe that, in him, we are lucky enough to have seen the perfect, complete chaser.'

Yet it is sobering to reflect that as John Lawrence gazed in wonderment at Arkle in the Newbury parade ring, the great horse's career was already, in terms of races run, well past the halfway mark. Arkle had run nineteen races before the 1964 Cheltenham Gold Cup, and he would run only fifteen after it. Nobody was to know it, but there wasn't much time.

PREVIOUS SPREAD:
The first fence in the 1964 Hennessy Gold Cup at Newbury. Left to right: Arkle (Pat Taaffe), Mill House (Willie Robinson), Pappageno's Cottage (Tony Biddlecombe), John O'Groats (David Nicholson), Happy Spring (Steve Davenport), Vultrix (Stan Mellor), Ferry Boat (Tim Jones) and Hoodwinked (Pat Buckley); bringing up the rear is The Rip (Bill Rees).

Irish Grand National, 30 March 1964

Arkle ran in the Irish Grand National, in those days run over 3¼ miles and the most valuable steeplechase of the Irish season, just once, twenty-three days after his famous victory over Mill House at Cheltenham. He conceded two stone to the second highest weighted runner, the grey mare Flying Wild, in the first race in which the new 'A' and 'B' system of handicapping was used.

The Irish racing authorities had been concerned for some time that Arkle's huge superiority over every other chaser in the land made a nonsense of handicapping if he were entered for a race and then did not run, for the remaining runners would be competing at the originally allotted weights, down to a minimum specified for that race, and the differentials which are the essence of handicapping would be destroyed. (In those days the flexible 'long handicap' system with which modern racegoers are familiar, and which allows for weights to be raised if the top-weighted horse or horses do not run while preserving differentials among the lower-weighted runners, did not exist.)

The official report of the meeting of the Irish National Hunt Steeplechase Committee on 14 February 1964 declared:

The 1964 Irish Grand National: a tired Arkle comes home clear of Height O' Fashion.

The Stewards of the Irish National Hunt Steeplechase Committee using their powers under Rule 16 (xviii) have modified Rules 40 and 54 for the Irish Grand National, Fairyhouse, and have instructed the Handicapper that if in this race he allots a weight of 14lb or more below the top weight to the next horse in the handicap he shall prepare a second handicap, to be known as the 'B' handicap, for this race in which he shall exclude the horse originally allotted top weight.

Both handicaps will be published at the same time and declarations of forfeit and declarations of runners will apply to each handicap but should the horse allotted top weight be struck out or not declared a runner to the Registrar horses remaining in will carry the weights allotted in the 'B' handicap including any penalties which they may have incurred.

Unsurprisingly, Arkle was not mentioned by name, but his pre-eminence was certainly behind the change. There was historical precedent. Lottery, winner of the Grand Liverpool Steeplechase – which became the Grand National – in 1839, was, like Arkle, considered so much better than his contemporaries that the sport was becoming uncompetitive. A race at Horncastle in 1840 was described as 'open to all horses – except Mr Elmore's Lottery', while the conditions for a race at Finchley in 1842 stipulated: 'Lottery's entry fee £40, others £10'.

Arkle's first racecourse appearance in his native land since his famous victory over the Old Enemy drew a huge crowd to Fairyhouse on Easter Monday, and they were rewarded with a conclusive if unspectacular victory for the 1-2 favourite, who took the lead early in the straight and won by 1¼ lengths from Height O' Fashion, the tough and versatile mare whose previous outing had been when she ran unplaced in the Champion Hurdle.

It is clear from the photograph of the finish that conceding lumps of weight in a handicap on soft going has proved considerably more taxing than skipping away from Mill House at level weights in the Gold Cup, and after Fairyhouse, Arkle was ready for his summer rest.

Arkle, Pat Taaffe up, in the summer of 1964. He stood 16.2 hands high, and at race fitness his girth measurement was around 80 inches. It was often said that the depth of his ribcage indicated an unusually large heart. (Compare this portrait with that taken a year later, reproduced on page 91.)

Hennessy Gold Cup, Newbury, 5 December 1964

The new season dawned with Arkle's first major target the Hennessy Gold Cup at Newbury, the race which a year earlier had seen his first defeat in a steeplechase and now formed the 'rubber match' with Mill House.

Until the 1964 Hennessy, Mill House's large band of loyal supporters still clung to the hope that their hero might find a way to reverse Gold Cup placings with Arkle and return The Big Horse to his pedestal. There were so many ways in which that Cheltenham race could have been different, they reasoned: Willie Robinson had been forced to make the running and so played into Pat Taaffe's hands, he had dropped his whip at a crucial stage of the race, 'the ground was wrong, the distance long, too early in the day ...' Next time the tables would be turned!

Following defeat in the Gold Cup, Mill House had made one more appearance in the 1963-64 season, turning in a heroic effort in the Whitbread Gold Cup at Sandown Park. Lugging top weight of 12 stone 7 pounds, he led over the last fence but on the steep uphill run to the line was caught by Dormant, to whom he was conceding no less that three stone, and beaten half a length. (Two and a half years later, Dormant was unwittingly to become the blackest villain in the whole Arkle story.) Among those behind Mill House at Sandown Park was Pas Seul, who after Cheltenham had run in the Grand National, falling at the twelfth fence. (That year's National was won by Team Spirit, trained by Fulke Walwyn and ridden by Willie Robinson – some consolation for the Gold Cup defeat of Mill House.)

Mill House did not have a run in the 1964-65 season before the Hennessy, while Arkle warmed up for his first major target that term with an outing in the Carey's Cottage Handicap Chase at Gowran Park. Carrying twelve stone and conceding thirty-five pounds to just two rivals, Arkle started at 1-5 and won easily by five lengths from Greatrakes, with Gosley a remote third. Next stop Newbury.

The 1964 Hennessy Gold Cup: Arkle and Johnny Lumley in the paddock.

The betting market for the 1964 Hennessy suggested a very close contest. As well as the possible benefit of different tactics, there was an eight-pound turnaround in the weights: Arkle was now conceding three pounds to Mill House, whereas in the previous year's race he had received five. Arkle had beaten Mill House five lengths at Cheltenham, so a difference of three pounds could well bring them closer together, and might even turn the tables. From all over England came the sound of straws being clutched at.

In a field of nine, Arkle started at 5-4 (the last occasion in his career when he was sent off at odds against) and Mill House at 13-8. The Queen Mother's good chaser The Rip came next in the market at 8-1, and the rest of the field – which included Happy Spring, who had divided Mill House and Arkle the year before – on 20-1 or longer.

In the early stages of the race Mill House supporters could not believe their luck, for rather than sitting in behind the English horse and waiting to unleash his famous burst of speed towards the end of the race, Arkle immediately took on The Big Horse down Newbury's long back straight. Pat Taaffe's autobiography explains that it was a conscious decision to let Arkle have his way:

> On that day I rode Arkle the way I would ride no other horse. I let him dictate the tactics, absolutely confident that he would pick the right ones. So when he went to the front jumping alongside Mill House, I made no effort to check him. I am sure that he wanted to prove that he could outjump this king of jumpers and establish his own supremacy.
>
> He began by matching Mill House jump for jump. If Mill House put in a big one, Arkle would put in an even bigger.

The 1964 Hennessy Gold Cup: Arkle before the start.

The 1964
Hennessy: Arkle
and Pat Taaffe
emerge from the
gloom at the last.

Stirring stuff, but surely, reasoned the Mill House camp as they saw the race unfold on the first circuit, Arkle would burn himself out. On the contrary, it was Mill House who cracked, and as they left the back straight on the second circuit and negotiated the 'cross fence', five from home, Arkle started to pull effortlessly away. Mill House had no answer, and early in the straight his spluttering engine was running on vapours as Arkle strode home. At the second last Arkle hit the top of the fence and screwed on landing, but this did little to disrupt his progress, and he only needed to be ridden out to score a famous victory and end any lingering arguments about who – and remember that this was the age of Cassius Clay – was The Greatest. As Mill House weakened and plodded wearily home, he was passed by Ferry Boat, who finished second, ten lengths behind the winner, and then by The Rip, who made late headway to take third place, twenty-two lengths behind Arkle. Mill House, exhausted and emptied out, staggered over the line fourth, twenty-eight lengths behind Arkle. For all who had seen the horse in his Gold Cup-winning glory, it was a sad sight.

The finest contemporary chronicler of Arkle's feats was John Lawrence (now Lord Oaksey), whose combined experience as top-class amateur rider and top-class writer made him uniquely qualified to measure the horse's stature. The week after the Hennessy his *Horse and Hound* column yet again struck exactly the right note, and did so by reaching back to the very beginnings of the sport:

> *Since Messrs Blake and O'Callaghan set off to race from Buttevant*
> *Church to St Leger Steeple 212 years ago, thousands of men and women*

all over Great Britain and Ireland have worked and schemed and dreamed to produce the perfect chaser.

From time to time their dreams have been close to fulfilment. Perhaps, who knows, they were fulfilled. Cloister, Manifesto, Jerry M, Easter Hero, Golden Miller and Prince Regent – all these and other deathless names have kindled in men's hearts the self-same fire that burnt so bright at Newbury last Saturday afternoon.

Comparisons are pointless. All one can say without fear of contradiction is that no horse – certainly no seven-year-old – has ever looked more the complete, final, flawless answer than the Duchess of Westminster's Arkle.

The 1964 Hennessy: Anne, Duchess of Westminster leads in Arkle.

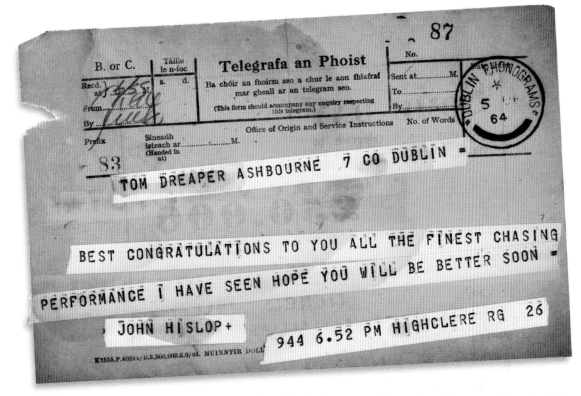

No. 87

Telegrafa an Phoist

TOM DREAPER ASHBOURNE 7 CO DUBLIN =

BEST CONGRATULATIONS TO YOU ALL THE FINEST CHASING PERFORMANCE I HAVE SEEN HOPE YOU WILL BE BETTER SOON =

JOHN HISLOP+

944 6.52 PM HIGHCLERE RG 26

John Hislop – racing journalist, leading amateur rider, and later the owner and breeder of the great miler Brigadier Gerard – sends a telegram of appreciation after the 1964 Hennessy. (Tom Dreaper had missed Newbury: he was in hospital with a viral infection.)

Massey-Ferguson Gold Cup, Cheltenham, 12 December 1964

After his conclusive victory in the Hennessy, Arkle remained in England – staying at the Duchess's Cheshire estate, where he was the subject of ceaseless attention from his admirers – and prepared to race again just one week after Newbury. The Massey-Ferguson Gold Cup at Cheltenham, another of the richly endowed sponsored jump races which were inaugurated in the wake of the Whitbread Gold Cup, the pioneer sponsored steeplechase first run in 1957, provided too good a prize to bypass.

Arkle's victory at Newbury added a three-pound penalty to the 12 stone 7 pounds he had inevitably been allotted in the original handicap, making him give weight to some extremely talented chasers. The grey mare Flying Wild, owned by Raymond Guest (who in 1962 had won his first Derby with Larkspur and would go on to own even more famous horses in the shape of Sir Ivor on the Flat and L'Escargot over jumps), had fallen in the Leopardstown Chase won by Arkle en route to the Gold Cup, but had finished runner-up in the previous year's Massey-Ferguson to Limeking (ridden by Pat Taaffe's brother Tos). In the Massey-Ferguson she was receiving thirty-two pounds from Arkle. The exceptionally

Arkle at the fifth fence in the Massey-Ferguson. A few years later Anne, Duchess of Westminster, having seen a photo of the Tom Dreaper-trained Fort Leney jumping a fence with his forelegs crossed, sent that horse's owner Colonel Sir John Thomson a copy of this picture, along with a postcard asking: 'Why do you suppose Tom teaches his horses to jump with their paws crossed?!!'

At the second last in the 1964 Massey-Ferguson: Arkle a length up, but Flying Wild about to pounce, and the weight about to tell.

promising seven-year-old Buona Notte, who had won the Totalisator Champion Novices' Chase at Cheltenham two days before Arkle beat Mill House in the Gold Cup, was receiving twenty-six pounds. Champion as he undoubtedly was, at the weights Arkle, with 12 stone 10 pounds, faced a very stiff task indeed, and his difficulties were compounded by other factors. The Massey-Ferguson was run over 2 miles 5 furlongs – significantly shorter than the distances at which Arkle had been excelling – and no matter how conclusive his Hennessy win may have appeared, to race again at the highest level a week later was asking a great deal of even the strongest constitution.

The betting reflected unease about Arkle's prospects – 8-11 Arkle, 4-1 Buona Notte, 8-1 Scottish Memories, 100-8 Flying Wild – and the doubters were proved right, but only after a performance of such heroic proportions that many experts consider it Arkle's finest hour. Having led for much of the race, he was still tanking along coming down the hill and led Flying Wild at the second last, but approaching the last the weight began to tell and, to the alarm of the huge crowd, Arkle gave way to Buona Notte and Flying Wild.

Buona Notte, ridden by Johnny Haine, blundered at the last, which threw the initiative to Tommy Carberry on Flying Wild, but Arkle was far from finished. Buona Notte recovered and set off in pursuit of the grey while Arkle struggled heroically against the weight anchoring him – and at the line Flying Wild had held on by a short head from Buona Notte, with Arkle, who was closing again close home, a mere length behind in third. Bloodied but unbowed.

'Arkle never surrendered in his life', wrote John Oaksey in his autobiography *Mince Pie for Starters*, 'and, of all his brilliant victories and against-the-odds defeats, that Massey-Ferguson Gold Cup was, for me, the bravest and the best.'

Betty Dreaper with Himself

For much of the 1964-65 season Tom Dreaper was unable to operate at full power due to illness, and the running of Greenogue was effectively controlled by his wife Betty.

Betty Dreaper was born Eva Elizabeth Russell in 1915, into a family devoted to hunting but with no special interest in racing. She married Tom Dreaper in St Patrick's Cathedral, Dublin, in June 1945, and immediately assumed at Greenogue the role of indispensable player in one of the greatest training operations jump racing in Ireland has ever seen.

Always more than happy to talk of the achievements and the character of the best horse ever to come under the Dreapers' charge, she particularly liked to recall Arkle's gentle demeanour at home. 'He loved life and he loved people, and if a horse likes both those things he makes it very nice and easy for the trainer.' A typical story was when her young daughter Valerie was playing with a tennis ball outside Arkle's box. 'The ball bounced in over the half door. She knew it was Arkle, so she opened the door and went in, looked round and ruffled round in the straw, but she couldn't find her ball. So she turned round and opened the door to go out, and something gave her a nudge in her shoulder. It was Arkle, and he dropped the ball at her foot.'

In 1979, four years after Tom's death, Betty Dreaper married Colonel Sir John Thomson, who had long had horses in the yard and who had himself been widowed, and a paddock near their Oxfordshire house provided a retirement home for several Dreaper veterans, notably Sir John's 1968 Gold Cup winner Fort Leney and the mean and mighty Flyingbolt. (See pages 116-17.)

When Betty Dreaper died in October 1993, her obituary in the *Sporting Life* described her as 'the unsung heroine' behind Arkle's career. No Arkleophile would disagree.

Cheltenham Gold Cup, 11 March 1965

Following his heroic defeat in the Massey-Ferguson Gold Cup in December 1964, Arkle had a well deserved rest, not reappearing until the end of February 1965, for the Leopardstown Chase, a handicap over three miles. Of his eight rivals the main danger appeared to be Scottish Memories, a good chaser who had finished two lengths behind Arkle in the Massey-Ferguson and was now two pounds better off in the handicap, receiving thirty-five pounds. If handicapping meant anything this would be a close race, and so it proved. The Irish *Sunday Independent* described a memorable finish:

> Arkle never failed to thrill the crowd, and as he jumped those last three fences making light of the welter burden of 12 stone 7 pounds, with Scottish Memories, receiving two and a half stone, in hot pursuit, the crowd really rose to him.
>
> At each jump he gained ground, but Frank Carroll on Scottish Memories kept stealing a bit back on the flat to take the last less than three lengths in arrears.
>
> And what a climax on the run-in! Scottish Memories challenged strongly on the inside. Gradually he closed the gap until only a length

Leopardstown Chase, 1965: Arkle (Pat Taaffe) grinds out a hard-fought victory over Scottish Memories (Frank Carroll).

Arkle and Mill House on the first circuit of the 1965 Gold Cup.

divided them halfway to the post. Arkle, however, would not give in, and
as Taaffe shook him up the great bay allowed his rival no further inroads.

In the 1965 Gold Cup – which following course realignment was run over a distance of 3 miles 2 furlongs 76 yards, 54 yards shorter than in 1964 – he faced three opponents, as he had the previous year.

Since his Hennessy humiliation Mill House had not been taking it easy. In mid January he returned to Newbury and was put through the wringer to scrape home by a head from old rival Dormant in the Mandarin Chase. He then went to Sandown Park in February, and again had to dig deep to beat Ferry Boat a length and a half. He was winning races the hard way, and nothing seriously suggested that he could beat Arkle on their fourth meeting: Arkle started 30-100 favourite for the 1965 Gold Cup, Mill House 100-30, and their two opponents Caduval and Stoney Crossing at 33-1 and 100-1 respectively.

While he had no chance of winning, Stoney Crossing was an interesting contender. His owner and Gold Cup jockey was the cavalier Australian rider Bill Roycroft, a famous three-day-eventer who competed in five Olympic Games and won Badminton in 1960 on the ex-stock pony Our Solo. Later in 1965 Roycroft rode three separate horses in the main Badminton event, finishing second on Eldorado and sixth on Stoney Crossing himself. (The third horse failed to complete.) Stoney Crossing had won steeplechases in his native Australia, but his participation in the Gold Cup was essentially a sporting endeavour on the part of his remarkably versatile and durable owner, who was fifty-one years old at the time.

The race needs little describing. Arkle allowed Mill House to accompany him part of the way round, and then left him for dead on the home turn – 'Like a sports car!, enthused BBC commentator Peter O'Sullevan – jumped the last brilliantly and strode home for a facile victory. Mill House finished twenty lengths behind, Stoney Crossing a further thirty lengths away third, and Caduval a distant last.

Arkle was indisputably in a class of his own, on a completely separate level from any other chaser in training, and, in the opinion of many experts, from any other chaser in history. When asked what the future might hold for his charge, Tom Dreaper was only half joking when replying: 'The Duchess could ride him in the Newmarket Town Plate!'

'Arkle and Mill House in the 1965 Cheltenham Gold Cup' by Lionel Edwards.

The 1965 Gold Cup: Arkle on his own at the last fence.

By now Arkle's fame had spread across the Atlantic, and thirteen days after the Gold Cup, the *Sporting Life* reported that the Duchess had received an invitation for Himself to run in the American Grand National and the Temple Gwathmey Steeplechase at Aqueduct, New York, the following October. James Mills, a member of the National Steeplechase and Hunt Association of America, declared: 'We would be delighted if the great Arkle could be flown over to compete for these two very valuable races later this year.' Although Arkle's connections declined the invitation, this was not the last time that a clash between Arkle and the cream of American chasers was mooted.

Meanwhile, Arkle bypassed the Irish Grand National – won in his absence by stable companion Splash – and headed for the Whitbread Gold Cup at Sandown Park.

Whitbread Gold Cup, Sandown Park, 24 April 1965

In the Whitbread Gold Cup, traditionally the last big race of the jumps season, Arkle faced six opponents. They included Willow King, once at Greenogue and now trained by Derek Ancil in Oxfordshire, and Brasher, who two weeks earlier had won the Scottish Grand National at Bogside (a race in which Arkle's young and highly promising stable companion Fort Leney had been pulled up when warm favourite).

Arkle was giving lumps of weight away all round – two and a half stone to Brasher and Over Court, more than that to Willow King, Rough Tweed, Persian Signal and Sign Post – but started hot favourite at 4-9. After leading until the sixteenth fence he briefly let Brasher take up the running, then reasserted at the third of the Railway Fences – last of the spectacular sequence of jumps down Sandown's back straight – and made the best of his way home. Brasher stuck to his task doggedly and was only a couple of lengths down at the last, but Pat Taaffe touched the accelerator and Arkle effortlessly skipped up the hill to win by five lengths.

Another £8,230 – the largest single prize Arkle ever won – in the bank.

BELOW

The 1965 Whitbread – an exuberant Arkle at the first.

OPPOSITE PAGE

The 1965 Whitbread – snapshots by racegoer Tony Byles.

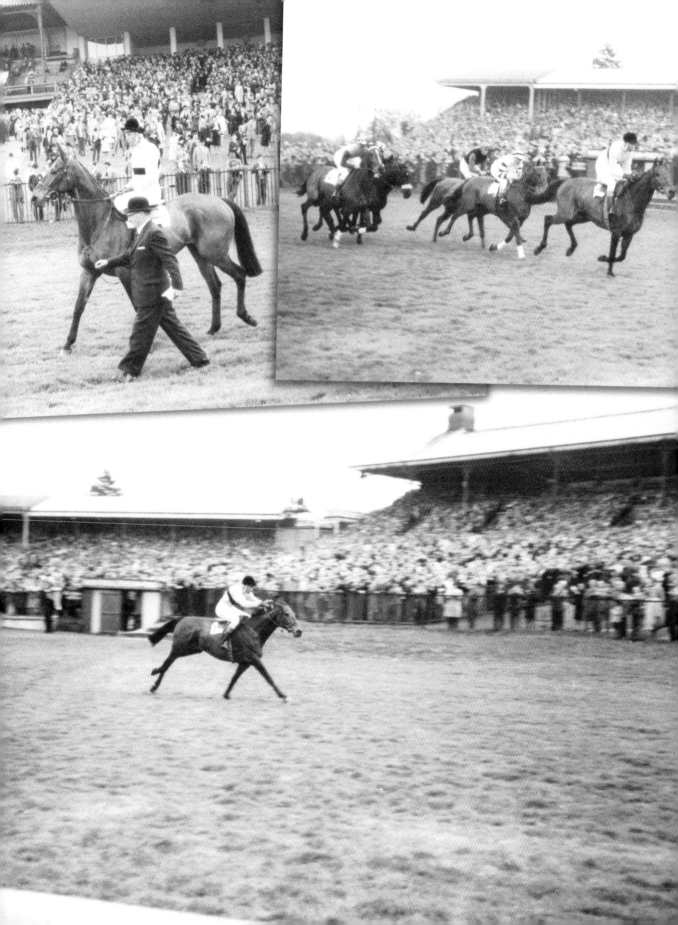

Summer holidays

Bryanstown, the Duchess of Westminster's Irish estate near Maynooth, was a second home to Arkle throughout his racing career and a retirement home after that career was over. Here he would laze and graze, often accompanied by other livestock, and was frequently ridden round the estate by the Duchess.

Arkle on his summer holidays at Bryanstown.

But by the summer of 1965 Arkle was beyond dispute an Irish national hero whose ardent followers demanded the occasional public appearance, and in August that year he was invited to parade at the Dublin Horse Show, biggest date in the Irish equestrian calendar.

The original plan was for Himself to be ridden over a few exhibition jumps in the Ballsbridge arena, but he had returned from his Whitbread Gold Cup victory with some heat in his off-fore fetlock joint, so that idea was vetoed and Arkle simply paraded. Alison Baker, daughter of his breeder Mary Baker, recalls how before he entered the ring an announcement was made to the effect that the crowd should not applaud, lest the great horse take fright. Arkle and Pat Taaffe duly came in and made one sedate circuit of the arena, but the crowd's emotion could not be contained, and despite themselves started to applaud – at which point Arkle pricked up his ears, picked up his feet and strutted proudly round, an early instance of the playing to the gallery which otherwise sensible and hardened observers insist was a genuine characteristic of the horse.

Arkle and Pat Taaffe in spring 1965. (Compare with the portrait on page 74.)

'Arkle for President'

'Arkle for President'

The 1965-66 season

When concentrating on Arkle, we should not forget what an *annus mirabilis* 1965 was for European racing in general. That year Flat racing saw, all too briefly, Arkle's parallel in the shape of Sea-Bird, who had his first race as a three-year-old (the Prix Greffulhe) in early April, and his last (the Prix de l'Arc de Triomphe) in early October; in between those two bookends he won the Prix Lupin, the Derby, and the Grand Prix de Saint-Cloud, and was widely hailed as the best Flat racehorse of the twentieth century.

If Sea-Bird was a meteor, Arkle was the North Star, steady in his luminescence, and his fame was rapidly spreading beyond the confines of the racing world. He began the 1965-66 season feted as the best steeplechaser in the history of the sport and a horse enjoying unprecedented superiority over his contemporaries; he ended it as a major personality in his own right, on a level associated with what a few years later would come to be called a 'megastar', or more recently an 'A-list' celebrity.

The non-racing pages of the newspapers had first started paying attention to Arkle in the immediate wake of his first Gold Cup victory. In 1964 the photographer David Bailey published his *Box of Pin-Ups* (a book which controversially included the Kray twins), and soon afterwards in the London *Evening Standard* the columnist Angus McGill gave his own list of twelve pin-ups: Maria Callas; Picasso; Margot Fonteyn; Nubar Gulbenkian; Yuri Gagarin; Jackie Kennedy; actress Vivien Leigh; a Beatle; Charles Wilson, of 'Great Train Robbery' notoriety; the bullfighter El Cordobes – and Arkle. The citation read: 'The world's greatest steeplechaser, magnificent, unbeatable, one of the great aristocrats of our time. Anyone misguided enough to complain that horses aren't people is not a true-born Englishman.'

Arkle's 1965-66 campaign consisted of just five races, all of which he won. He was at the height of his powers as well as of his fame, and in his first race of the term, the Gallaher Gold Cup at Sandown Park, produced probably the greatest individual performance of his life. The few strides which took him whooshing past Mill House – to whom he was conceding sixteen pounds – on the final bend provided the defining moment of his whole career, an exhibition of sheer class unparalleled in jump racing history.

For many years it proved impossible, despite the efforts of throngs of devotees, to locate any recording of that race with which to wow a younger generation, and it was accepted among the brotherhood of Arkle anoraks that the crucial seconds would live on only in their collective memory. Then a few years ago a grainy copy was unearthed – minus the commentary – and after it had been broadcast in Ireland, video-cassette recordings started circulating among aficionados, who would gather in a darkened room and close the curtains, like believers about to hear Mass from a recusant priest during the Elizabethan persecution, before slotting the cassette into the machine. To their relief and joy, the recording – with the commentary replaced by lilting Irish folk music – proved that the first and only sighting, marinated in decades of nostalgia, had been correctly remembered. That day Arkle had been simply unbelievable.

There was never really a parallel moment during the rest of his season. The 1965 Hennessy was straightforward enough, the King George VI Chase clouded by the death of Dunkirk, the Leopardstown Chase something of a slog in desperate ground, and the 1966 Gold Cup a stroll in the Cotswolds against the weakest opposition that Arkle ever faced in a major steeplechase.

Arkle had become much more than a mere racehorse, and when towards the end of 1965 the words 'ARKLE FOR PRESIDENT' were scrawled in large letters on a Dublin wall, it seemed like a perfectly rational proposition.

PREVIOUS SPREAD
Paddy Woods steers Arkle out of the yard. Betty and Tom Dreaper look on.

Gallaher Gold Cup, Sandown Park, 6 November 1965

The tobacco company Gallaher had first sponsored the three-mile handicap chase at Sandown Park's early November meeting in 1964, when the Senior Service Trophy was won by 33-1 outsider John O' Groats, by a neck from the Queen Mother's popular gelding The Rip, with the Dreaper-trained favourite Fort Leney only fifth. (Both John O' Groats and The Rip had next run four weeks later in the Hennessy Gold Cup. The Rip finished third, twenty-two lengths behind Arkle – who was conceding him thirty-three pounds – and John O' Groats was pulled up.) In 1965 the race became the Gallaher Gold Cup, with a first prize of £5,165.

On paper the Gallaher appeared to be a serious test for Arkle, for among his six rivals was Mill House, to whom he was asked to concede sixteen pounds: Arkle carried 12 stone 7 pounds (as he invariably did in handicaps by now), Mill House 11 stone 5 pounds. Arkle had beaten Mill House by twenty lengths at level weights in the Gold Cup the previous March and the weight concession would surely make a major difference to the chances of The Big Horse. Furthermore, reports from Lambourn suggested that Mill House was somewhere near his best again, and he had had two previous runs before the Gallaher – second to the brilliant two-mile chaser Dunkirk at Ascot and a bloodless victory over single opponent Crobeg at Sandown – whereas Arkle would be having his first run of the season and might not be 100 per cent fit.

Five days before the race, Arkle and Pat Taaffe had had a racecourse workout at Leopardstown. The *Daily Express*, describing the occasion as 'the oddest race of his career', reported how Arkle was intended to jump five fences with stable companion Throughway (ridden by Sean Barker), who spoiled the

Arkle reads up his Gallaher Gold Cup chances over the shoulder of head lad Paddy Murray.

plan by falling at the first and continuing riderless in pursuit of his distinguished colleague. Another Greenogue horse Reay Forest, ridden by Paddy Woods, was waiting after the fifth fence and joined in for the finish. Arkle 'won' by a length.

In the Gallaher Gold Cup, Pat Taaffe rode Arkle as usual, but Mill House's regular rider Willie Robinson was injured: David Nicholson, then a leading jump jockey and later champion trainer, came in for a memorable spare ride.

Not all the other runners were simply cannon fodder, certain to be shot to pieces by the big two. In addition to The Rip and John O'Groats, who had fought out that tight finish a year earlier, there was Rondetto, like Arkle having his first run of the season. Rondetto, who had finished runner-up to Mill House in a Wincanton hurdle four years earlier, had won the Stones Ginger Wine Chase at Sandown and the

Arkle with Pat Taaffe in the parade ring.

National Hunt Handicap Chase at the Cheltenham Festival earlier in 1965 and was fast becoming a staple of the best handicap chases: later in his career he would win the 1967 Hennessy, by a head from Stalbridge Colonist, as well as finishing third in both the 1968 Scottish Grand National and the 1969 Grand National. In the Gallaher, Rondetto was getting twenty-six pounds from Arkle. Making up the seven-runner field were two rank outsiders, Lira and Candy.

The headline on the front page of the *Sporting Life* on the morning of the Gallaher Gold Cup – famously captured in the photograph of Himself reading the paper over the shoulder of head lad Paddy Murray – was 'ARKLE LOOKS UNBEATABLE BAR MISHAP', and the betting market reflected that view, with starting prices reading 4-9 Arkle, 7-2 Mill House, 9-1 Rondetto, 20 The Rip, 33 John O' Groats, 100-1 Lira and Candy.

Sandown Park was bathed in autumnal sunshine as the runners went round the old paddock – now the pre-parade ring at the Esher course – in an atmosphere of excitement and anticipation unknown since the 1964 Gold Cup. For while Arkle did indeed look unbeatable from most perspectives, if Mill House really *were* back to his best, a weight difference of sixteen pounds must bring them closer together than in the 1964 Hennessy or 1965 Gold Cup. So far the pair had met four times and the score was 3-1 in Arkle's favour, but died-in-the-wool Mill House fans – and there were still a good few of this endangered species around – knew that if ever their hero was to get his revenge for earlier humiliation, it would be today.

It is a measure of how Arkle and Mill House had captivated jump racing fans over the last two years that as the runners left the parade ring, some racegoers started applauding – an action unheard of before a race on a British racecourse at the time. The applause grew as the runners made their way down the Rhododendron Walk and out onto the course, and swelled to a crescendo of clapping and cheering as they turned and cantered back past the stands to the 3 miles 118 yard start, located on the downhill stretch of the course beyond the winning post.

This is how a famous race was described in *Horse and Hound* by John Lawrence:

Led by Candy over the first two fences, Mill House brushed him imperiously aside down the Railway straight – and each succeeding giant leap drew a roar of appreciation from the crowded stands and rails.

Some lengths behind him Arkle had, unusually for him, settled calmly in Pat Taaffe's hands. But clearly there's a compass in his handsome head for, swinging round towards the Pond, he suddenly decided it was time to go.

I can't remember a more obvious display of understanding in a racehorse. No one had told Arkle the distance of the Gallaher Gold Cup, but he knew Sandown – and would tolerate no leader up the well-remembered hill.

Sweeping over the open ditch before the stands, he and Mill House were cheered again and realising that this was not, after all, the end, Arkle settled once more, saving his strength and letting his rival draw ahead.

This, of course, is hindsight. At the time, as Mill House stormed majestically down the Railway straight, recalling with every stride the

days of his supremacy, there seemed, to us in the stands, a very real chance that he would win.

David Nicholson's orders were to press on from the water and, obeying them superbly, he gained a length at each of the three close fences. Was Pat Taaffe waiting, or had he, perhaps, seen the spectre of defeat? We could not tell – but the answer was not long delayed.

For now, round the final bend, without coming off the bit, without, apparently, the slightest encouragement, Arkle unsheathed his sword. It flashed once, brilliant in the sunshine, and, before the Pond, for the fourth and surely the last time, poor, brave Mill House saw destiny sweep by.

I doubt if he has ever run a better race. No other living horse could have done more and, in that moment, sympathy and sadness mingled with our admiration for his conqueror.

Now, with two fences left, there was only one horse at Sandown.

Going to the last, Arkle was still, almost literally, running away. Landing over it Pat Taaffe just shook the reins and, unbelievably, he quickened. I seriously doubt whether the 300 yards of the run-in has ever been covered much faster – and certainly no winner ever came home, on this or any other course, to a greater, more rapturous welcome.

As Arkle swept up the hill, Rondetto passed Mill House on the run-in to claim second place, twenty lengths behind the winner, who, completely unruffled by the race, returned to a thunderous ovation in the winner's enclosure. (Rondetto and Mill House, supporting actors to Arkle's lead, were also accorded a generous reception.)

ABOVE
Arkle and Pat Taaffe at the last.

OPPOSITE PAGE

TOP
A hero's welcome. The Duchess leads Arkle in; Johnny Lumley follows.

BOTTOM
The winner's enclosure: Arkle and the Duchess.

Arkle's win rewrote more than one entry in the record books. The time of the race, 5 minutes 59 seconds, smashed the previous course record, set by Mill House in the Gainsborough Chase the previous February, by *seventeen seconds* and was thirty-five seconds under the average time for the distance. And the £5,165 first prize took his career winnings to £50,214, beating the previous record for a jumper, the £46,676 earned by Mandarin.

The Gallaher Gold Cup was more than an astonishing horse race. It was one of the great racing occasions, as the press was quick to relay. 'Hotspur' in the *Daily Telegraph* wrote of the 'tumultuous reception', while Tom Nickalls in the *Sporting Life* described the race as 'a spectacle which I shall never forget' and Arkle's reception afterwards as 'the greatest ovation I have ever heard on a racecourse'. The weekly *Sporting Life Guide* wrote: 'There never was such a day and no one present will ever forget the experience,' while the *Daily Express* came over all lyrical: 'As an example of a great, genuine horse at the height of his powers it was unforgettable ... a piece of Old England in the crisp, almost salty sunshine, at its best.' Topping even that, Quintin Gilbey in the *Sporting Chronicle* wrote:

> *Races may come and go, but the Gallaher Gold Cup of 1965 will be talked about as long as the men and women of this country take pleasure from the spectacle of great horses battling it out over fences on a winter's day.*

Hennessy Gold Cup, Newbury, 27 November 1965

Three weeks after Sandown Park, Arkle returned to Newbury for his third Hennessy Gold Cup. The weights for the race had been published before the Gallaher Gold Cup, so nothing could be done by the handicapper to give the comparative minnows more of a chance against the champion, and he faced just seven opponents, making this the smallest field yet in nine runnings of the Hennessy.

In the absence of Mill House, the only conceivable danger was the great Scottish-trained (though Irish-bred) horse Freddie, who had won the Foxhunters' at Cheltenham in 1964, two races before Arkle beat Mill House in their famous Gold Cup, and who became one of the few hunter chasers to make the transition successfully to top-class steeplechasing. Carrying 11 stone 10 pounds and starting warm favourite, he had been narrowly beaten by Jay Trump in a grinding finish to the 1965 Grand National, and had finished fourth in both his earlier races in the 1965-66 season, at Carlisle and Wetherby. Among Freddie's opponents in the Wetherby race had been Brasher, the 1965 Scottish Grand National winner who had finished second to Arkle in the 1965 Whitbread and was now reopposing in the Hennessy.

Despite conceding thirty-two pounds to Freddie and thirty-five pounds to Brasher, Arkle started at 1-6, the shortest price of his career so far. Freddie was on 9-1, Wayward Queen (who had won at Windsor nine days earlier) on 20-1, and Brasher one of three horses on 25-1. Since the presence of Arkle in the field comprehensively killed the Hennessy as a betting medium, there was, unusually for the time, a second market on the race. The customary each-way betting was replaced with 'Special Place Betting' without the favourite, allowing punters to back a horse to come second or third to Arkle (or win outright, though that was not considered remotely likely). This market, which was officially recorded in the form book (see

Brasher leads from Arkle on the first circuit.

page 200), had Freddie at 1-2, Wayward Queen at 4-5, Brasher, Happy Arthur and John O' Groats at 3-1, Norther at 6-1, Game Purston at 100-8, and 'Arkle in proportion'. (The *Sporting Life* stated that 'not a great deal of business was transacted' on the Special Place Betting.)

Arkle duly won from Freddie (ridden by Pat McCarron) and Brasher (Jimmy FitzGerald), and the report in the *Sporting Chronicle* by Quintin Gilbey captured how Arkle was increasingly enthralling the racing public:

> Arkle once again gladdened our hearts without lining our pockets by putting up a glorious display of jumping to win the Hennessy Gold Cup for the second year running and be accorded a reception fitting for a hero.
>
> Heavy rain during the night and forenoon had slowed down the going, jockeys told me, so there was no prospect of Arkle breaking yet another record, and in the circumstance his time of 6 min. 48 sec. was fast.
>
> Perfect specimen of the steeplechase horse that he is, Arkle would not be so far superior to the other horses if he did not derive such pleasure from humbling his opponents.
>
> There is something of the extrovert in the composition of all great athletes, and from the moment he is stripped in the paddock till he is led out of the winning enclosure to the accompaniment of a further burst of cheering and clapping of hands, Arkle is fully aware that he is the centre of attention, and he loves every moment of it.
>
> There is an old saying: 'When a horse cocks his ears he's happy, but when he lays them back beware.' And throughout the parade Arkle's ears were forward and in his eye a gleam of pleasurable anticipation.

A tired Arkle at the last.

He jumps every fence with obvious enjoyment, though he never loses sight of the fact that racing is a deadly serious business, and although I have seen him jump upwards of a hundred fences I have never seen him take a liberty, not even when he is twenty lengths clear, with the race in his pocket.

Arkle is not only the perfect specimen of the steeplechase horse, but he is also blessed with an abnormal intelligence which is reflected in that lovely shaped head and honest expression.

Standing within a few feet of him as Pat Taaffe removed his saddle, one could not doubt that this wonder horse knew exactly what all the fuss was about and was as proud as a peacock that he was the cynosure of all eyes. Freddie also looked pleased with himself, and it may well be that he thought he had won. He was the best part of twenty-five lengths behind Arkle and Brasher entering the straight, but poor Brasher was so exhausted landing over the last fence that Freddie was able to run him out of second place.

By this time Arkle was on his way back to the paddock, so the chances are that Freddie never saw him.

The only chance any of Arkle's opponents possessed of making a race of it with him was to set a cracking pace and FitzGerald on Brasher did just that, and Freddie was close up with them followed by Wayward Queen over the first half dozen fences.

As the race progressed, however, Brasher and Arkle began to draw further and further ahead, and to our amazement the Scottish Grand National winner outjumped his famous opponent at several fences.

Arkle was content to let Brasher lead him in the same way as he had permitted Mill House to do at Sandown, but at the sixth fence from home Arkle put in a magnificent jump to take the lead.

'This is it, it's all over', we said to ourselves, but it was nothing of the sort as to his undying credit Brasher had another go at him at the next fence, and actually regained the lead, racing neck and neck with him into the straight.

At the first fence in the straight, however, the great-hearted Brasher began to falter and Arkle strode away.

But the excitement was not quite over as Arkle made what for him was an untidy jump at the third from home, the fence which had cost him the race two years ago …

Having demonstrated, as one spectator put it, that he was human, Arkle popped over the last two fences in the approved Arkle style to beat Freddie by fifteen lengths.

If ever a horse deserved to finish second that horse was Brasher, who took on Arkle from flagfall, and jumped fence after fence with him in the same stride as Mill House had done three weeks earlier.

But no horse can live indefinitely with this super chaser and there comes a time when, with the limbs aching with fatigue, there is no more breath to keep the machine in action.

This happened to Brasher at much the same spot as it had happened to Mill House, and he was deprived of the second place he so richly deserved by a horse who had 'never been at the races' while Brasher was waging that do-or-die battle for supremacy with the greatest horse of all time.

Easily as he won in terms of distance, Arkle at the end of the Hennessy was tired in a way that he had clearly not been at Sandown Park. After the last fence Pat Taaffe had had to give him two slaps of the whip down his shoulder to keep him up to his work, and afterwards the jockey insisted that he had ridden a bad race: 'If Arkle had been beaten that day it would have been entirely my fault. I was wrong to go on pushing after I'd passed Brasher.'

The 1965 Hennessy had been another stirring performance by Arkle, but one which raised a fresh worry. As Tom Nickalls put it in his *Sporting Life* report of the Newbury race: 'Arkle still reigns supreme – but there really does seem to be every reason now to wonder what can be done about him. He is going to spoil every race for which he starts.' Whether you could agree with such a view, of course, depends on quite what you mean by 'spoil', but there was no doubt that Arkle was rendering races uncompetitive. How could his horizons be widened beyond the top steeplechases on the park courses of Britain and Ireland? The Duchess had long remained adamant that he would never be entered in the Grand National – the risk of injury would be too great – but there were always valuable overseas races. The US invitation had not been taken up, but a real possibility was the Grand Steeplechase de Paris at Auteuil, famously won by Fred Winter on the bitless Mandarin in 1962: under the conditions of that race Arkle would carry only 10 stone 1 pound, which would have made him think he was running loose. When the idea was put to Tom Dreaper by *Sporting Life* journalist Len Scott after the 1965 Hennessy, the trainer thought it an idea worthy of serious consideration.

Meanwhile another big race in England was approaching.

The Duchess leads Arkle in.

King George VI Chase, Kempton Park, 27 December 1965

Six of the eight race meetings scheduled for Boxing Day 1965 were lost to the weather (five to frost, one to flooding); only Kempton Park, where the feature race was the King George VI Chase, and Newton Abbot survived.

Before the first race at Kempton Park on there was a parade of old champions (a common feature of big race meetings nowadays but highly innovative then). The procession of venerable chasers was led by Mandarin, behind whom came Pas Seul (who had once crossed swords with Arkle), Kilmore, Nicolaus Silver, Saffron Tartan, Halloween (accompanied by his pony friend Peggy), Taxidermist and Blessington Esquire.

By contrast, only four went to post for the 'King George', after the Cheltenham Gold Cup steeplechasing's most prestigious race for three-mile chasers. Of Arkle's three rivals, one was the not-a-snowball's-chance-in-Hell runner Arctic Ocean and another was Dormant, who had beaten Mill House in the 1964 Whitbread when in receipt of forty-two pounds and who in his last race had run third at Kempton behind future Gold Cup winner What A Myth. But the fourth member of the quartet who went to post for the King George attracted a huge amount of attention.

Dunkirk, like Arkle, was five days from his (official) ninth birthday. Trained by Peter Cazalet and owned by Colonel Bill Whitbread (the moving force behind the Whitbread Gold Cup), Dunkirk was as spectacular and speedy a two-mile chaser as any seen in the modern age. The first time jockey Dave Dick rode the horse, Dunkirk turned in a characteristically exhilarating display which elicited from that cavalier rider a single-word comment in the winner's enclosure: 'Blimey!' By Boxing Day 1965, Dunkirk had won eight chases, including the National Hunt Two-Mile Champion Chase at the 1965 Cheltenham Festival and, immediately before his trip to Kempton, the Mackeson Gold Cup (then run over two miles). Now ridden by Bill Rees, he was a horse at the top of his form, but it was clear that he was essentially a two-miler, and even round the flat and comparatively tight Kempton Park circuit was

The 1965 King George: Arkle and Pat Taaffe in full flight.

highly unlikely to stay the three miles of the King George. His taking on Arkle was testament to the sporting character of his owner.

The *Sporting Life* on Boxing Day morning summed up the race:

> It is no matter that Arkle is the nearest thing to a racing certainty. Thousands will thrill to see him gallop and jump his three rivals into the ground in the King George. It is a privilege to see such a champion walk over but at least he now has Dunkirk, an opponent who is capable of making him put his best foot forward for at least the first two miles of the trip.
>
> Dunkirk, the champion at this distance, must be in front to show at his best so until his stamina gives out it should be a treat to see some electrifying jumping.
>
> Perhaps we are taking it too much for granted that Dunkirk's stamina will be found wanting but he appears to have had quite enough at the end of two and a half miles the only time he attempted it.
>
> But should the hot pace cause Arkle to make a blunder Dunkirk may then reap the full reward of his owner's bold policy ...

Arkle varied between 1-6 and 1-8 in the betting ring before returning a starting price of 1-7 (his shortest price yet, after 1-6 in the Hennessy); Dunkirk started at 7-1, Dormant at 25-1, and Arctic Ocean at 100-1.

Again, Quintin Gilbey in the *Sporting Chronicle* provides the report:

> With the raising of the tapes Dunkirk was in top gear in the space of a few strides, and with Arkle content to drop his bit and amble along with the lesser lights, Dunkirk, having jumped the first three fences at a greater speed than most horses can jump hurdles, had opened up a lead of 200 yards.
>
> A gasp of astonishment went up from the tightly-packed stand as no one had thought that a horse could treat the mighty Arkle with such disrespect. Doubts were expressed whether even Arkle could give away so much start, and a race which had appeared one-sided had become a real thrill.
>
> Passing the stands, both horses were given an ovation, the underdog Dunkirk for his audacity, and Arkle for what everyone hoped he would accomplish in the second half of the race.
>
> Over the water, and Arkle, with no apparent effort, began to reduce the distance between him and the leader hand over fist to the accompaniment of more cheers, which reached a crescendo as Arkle took the lead a couple of strides before reaching the fifth fence from home, which is incidentally a plain fence.
>
> Arkle's sudden appearance, looking twice as fresh and going twice as fast as Dunkirk, was something that the tiring Dunkirk had not expected

and, in desperation, he gathered his remaining strength for a tremendous leap in a do-or-die endeavour to regain the lead.

But it was a hurried and ill-timed effort, and before the cheers for Arkle had died down Dunkirk was lying motionless, while all that could be seen of Bill Rees was his yellow cap.

The fence at which the catastrophe occurred is one of the farthest from the stand, and to many of those present it was just another fall. Binoculars were still focused on Arkle, now alone in his splendour, and it was not until he had passed the post and the cheers had died down that thoughts were turned to Bill Rees and Dunkirk.

We saw Rees lifted into the ambulance, but there was no sign of Dunkirk, and it was not until Arkle had been led out of the unsaddling enclosure, where he had, as always, enjoyed the adulation bestowed upon him, that we heard that Dunkirk had broken his neck and died instantly, and that Bill Rees had broken his thigh.

A post-mortem on Dunkirk was immediately carried out, and trainer Peter Cazalet informed the press: 'The vet tells me Dunkirk had a congestion of blood in the lungs as he approached the fence. This caused him to fall and he broke his neck.'

It was a sad end to a great horse, and understandably cast a gloom over Arkle's victory: he had won by a distance from Dormant ('never near to challenge', read the form book report), with Arctic Ocean ('always in rear') a further distance behind in third. (Four years later Roy Pettit, who was Dormant's trainer at the time of the 1965 King George, revealed in the *Sun* newspaper that before the race he had given his horse a tonic which contained caffeine – but he was still beaten out of sight by Arkle.)

In mid-January 1966 the front page of the *Sporting Life* carried a story which, had it concerned any horse but Arkle, would have been better dated 1 April: Tom Dreaper had announced that Arkle would be entered for the Champion Hurdle – then run the day before the Gold Cup. The major bookmakers were quick off the mark, Ladbrokes quoting Arkle at 1-3 for the Gold Cup, 4-5 for the Champion Hurdle, 5-4 the double, with William Hill going even money for the hurdle. But scarcely had Arkle fans started drooling at the prospect of their hero attempting such an unheard-of double than the idea was shelved. The Champion Hurdle's two miles was well short of Arkle's preferred distance range, reasoned the Duchess, and the risk of his undergoing a tough race just twenty-four hours before the Gold Cup was too great.

And the following month saw renewed speculation that Arkle might seek fresh worlds to conquer by running in the Grand Steeplechase de Paris in June 1966, where he could face Bon Nouvel, then the chasing sensation of America and winner of the 1965 Temple Gwathmey, one of the Aqueduct races to which Arkle had been invited.

Arkle himself, unaware of what was or was not being planned for him, set about enjoying a short break at home.

'Kempton Park' by Graeme Miles

The death of Dunkirk was the subject of the song 'Kempton Park' by the Wearside folk singer Graeme Miles. It was included on his album *Songs of Sport and Play*, originally issued in 1977 on the Folktrax label and now available on CD as Folktrax 227 (see www.folktrax.org).

It's of a chaser I will tell and Dunkirk he was named,
The pride of Cazalet's stable, and none were better trained.
In his last three races, he'd won them every one.
He had the speed, the class and form to take the champions on.

It was the day of the King George Chase and Kempton was full and packed,
For Arkle's name was on the card and as favourite he was backed.
But Dunkirk too was running, aye and fancied by a few
Who said he'd said he'd take great Arkle's crown before his days were
   through.

And when the race got under way Dunkirk it was that led,
Making all the running he slowly forged ahead.
Neat and crisp he took his jumps till the pace began to tell,
As Arkle quickened up his stride, Pat Taaffe was riding well.

The champion now began to show that famous turn of speed,
Taking up the challenge now he threatened Dunkirk's lead.
Inch by inch he closed the gap with every bounding stride,
Until five jumps away from home they were running side by side.

But Dunkirk never made that jump, nor did he make it home,
For with a heavy thud he crashed, leaving Arkle on his own.
Dormant lagged too far behind to take the champion on,
Though he made a desperate challenge then, his chance had long since gone.

Though Arkle's hollow victory was given warm applause,
All the eyes of Kempton Park were turned back up the course,
Where the brave and gallant Dunkirk, the heir to Arkle's crown,
Was lying dead with a shattered neck upon the frozen ground.

Arkle at home

Arkle may have become the most famous racehorse in Ireland, and for many admirers the greatest steeplechaser in history, but his domestic routine at Kilsallaghan did not, for the most part, differ in any significant detail from that of any other horse in training there. He was a magnet for visitors, and a constant stream of admirers would turn up at the stables and ask for a glimpse of their hero, or a few tail hairs, or the opportunity to stroke him or have their photo taken in his presence. It was one thing for the Dreapers to accommodate a crowd wishing to pay homage after a big race victory – as had understandably been the case after the first Gold Cup – but another to cater for random visitors. (On one occasion Betty Dreaper, asked on Irish television about how people could visit Arkle, jokingly suggested that they would be announcing a schedule of visiting hours, as with a hospital ward. The next day several carloads of fans arrived at Greenogue asking about when these visiting hours would be.) In the circumstances, the Dreaper family was extraordinarily compliant with the desires of Arkle's fans: no request for a small child to sit on his back would be turned down.

Any training stable exists on routine, but Arkle's routine was markedly different from that of a top racehorse in a large yard in Lambourn or Newmarket. He spent little time each day outside his box, and in his hours of confinement would be entertained by a constant stream of activity in the yard. Betty Dreaper told Ivor Herbert that the Greenogue horses were not short on entertainment: 'With traffic passing in front of them, pigeons roosting on their backs, dogs, children, and lads playing football in the yard and handball against the stable walls, they've no opportunity for boredom.' In addition, throughout Arkle's glory years Greenogue remained a working farm, and Arkle – along with other horses in training there – would undertake his share of farm work, which included regularly rounding up the sheep.

Much attention was paid to Arkle's diet when it was revealed that every day two pints of Guinness (and at least two eggs) were added to his regular diet of oats.

Fortifying a racehorse in training with beer was by no means a novel idea – Mandarin had been very partial to stout, and was sent two bottles a day by Whitbread throughout his long retirement – but Arkle's intake of Guinness seemed especially appropriate: the nation's horse training on the national drink.

Leopardstown Chase, 1 March 1966

With sights now firmly set on a third Gold Cup, a third Leopardstown Chase in mid-February seemed ideally timed for Arkle's next racecourse appearance. But it had been an exceptionally wet winter in Ireland: the Leopardstown programme scheduled for Saturday 19 February was postponed, and it was not until Tuesday 1 March that Arkle was seen at the Dublin course for what – though nobody suspected it at the time – would be his last race in his native land.

On the first occasion when the invalid Mary Baker was able to get to a racecourse to see the famous horse she had bred, Arkle faced just three rivals in the Leopardstown Chase: his stable companion Splash (ridden by Paddy Woods), who had won the Irish Grand National the previous year; Packed Home, who earlier in the season had won the Kerry National at Listowel and on his last outing had beaten Splash in a valuable chase at Fairyhouse; and the mare Height O' Fashion, runner-up to Arkle in the 1964 Irish Grand National and a regular opponent of his, now ridden by J. P. Sullivan. Arkle, carrying 12 stone 7 pounds, conceded three stone to all three.

Among the throng pressed ten-deep around the Leopardstown paddock was the correspondent from the *Irish Field*:

> Arkle 'sends' people – he really does. The moment he appeared in the parade ring before the race there was a terrific outburst of clapping, and something about the tilt of his head and the proud way he carried himself conveys the message that he was pleased.
>
> The first time he passed round a man beside me solemnly raised his hat (I nearly forgave him for pushing his way in and not apologising when he stood on my foot), a pixyish lady bowed to the horse – I'd swear she did – and a small boy with a ruler and a lunch box sticking out of his duffel pocket said 'Hello, Arkle' at every round.

Ostensibly unbeatable despite the huge weight concession in heavy going, Arkle started at 1-5, with the rest of the starting prices reading 7-1 Splash, 10-1 Packed Home, 100-8 Height O' Fashion.

Charles Benson of the *Daily Express*, visiting Leopardstown to see Irish hopefuls for Cheltenham put through their final racecourse paces, had a near-sensation to report:

> Arkle, the mighty, unbeatable Arkle, sniffed the scent of defeat yesterday for only the third time in his chasing career.
>
> He held on to a photo-finish neck lead over the gallant little mare, Height O' Fashion, in the Leopardstown Chase.
>
> And once again that oldest of racing adages that weight can bring any two horses together was proved true.

THE IRISH TIMES

SATURDAY, FEB. 19, 1966

AGREED CANDIDATE

This afternoon a horse is running in a race at Leopardstown. The bookmakers are expected to ask punters to stake six pounds in the hope of winning one, if he wins. The stake is £3,000 added, but only four horses may be running against him; and one of these is a stable-companion. To all his four opponents, this horse gives three stone in weight. His name is Arkle. Nobody expects him to be beaten. Nobody — except the owners of his rivals — wants him to be beaten. He is most unlikely to be beaten. The race, indeed, unless the Furies are abroad, is likely to take the form of a p r o c e s s i o n. The competitive element — the only point in racing — will be largely absent. And yet this race will attract an abnormal crowd of spectators. Unless the weather is even worse than usual, very much worse than usual, record c r o w d s will go to Leopardstown to watch what everyone expects to be a formality. How can it be accounted for?

The answer is the glamour of success and personality. This horse is very close to the heart of the nation. He has again and again confirmed his supremacy over all rivals in Britain. Every time he appears on an English racecourse, he raises the morale at home. He is so emphatically the best. And more than this: he looks the best. He even looks as if he knew he was the best. Not with the swagger and air of self-glory which characterises, say, Mr. Cassius Clay; but with the dignity, the look of supreme self-assurance that marks President de Gaulle. No groom would dare to say "Hi" to this magnificent creature. And yet, we are told of moving acts of condescension by the horse. He has lowered himself — with utmost dignity — to accommodate the groom who was saddling him. The truly great unbend in private in just this courteous way.

The tragic moment will come if Arkle ever falls from grace. There is always the element of unhappy chance — but it is too terrible even to contemplate. And then there is age — the universal enemy. Champions can never be champions forever. In the ordinary course, Arkle should remain at near his peak — he is there at present — for two more years at least. His only possible rival in the foreseeable future seems to be a stable-companion, Flyingbolt. Some would match these horses. And if it happened, there is no racecourse that would accommodate the crowd. If Flyingbolt continues to improve, it should be done. Otherwise there will be a tantalising "if" that will vex racing enthusiasts for generations. Perhaps next year . . . Whichever loses might never recover from the effort. Mill House, who once beat Arkle, does not seem to be the same horse since he was trounced in the next encounter. For the present, it suffices that we have a champion. And the enthusiasm, merely to see him, shows what hero-worshippers we all are at heart.

Another record for Arkle — the first racehorse to be compared with President de Gaulle, in a leader in the *Irish Times* on the day when the 1966 Leopardstown Chase should have been run.

Those of us accustomed to witnessing the ritual slaughter of his English rivals expected to see the great horse deal equally summarily with his three rivals.

And so it seemed likely when Arkle, who had made the running at his own carefully dictated pace, accelerated going into the second-last fence before the final turn, and quickly put four lengths between himself and his two nearest pursuers.

The locals thought so, too, as they cheered the champ the moment he cleared the final fence.

But strange things happen on the long, uphill Leopardstown run-in. Pat Taaffe quickly went for his whip and waved it encouragingly at first, threateningly strides later as Height O' Fashion steadily reduced the gap.

The danger seemed only fleeting, but Height O' Fashion, making the most of her unusually light weight, surged steadily on in the cloying mud and Pat Taaffe had to ride out Arkle to ensure victory only a stride or so off the post.

It was a photo-finish, but the verdict was clear – a neck in favour of the champion.

Splash was third, fifteen lengths behind the mare.

Despite the narrowness of the margin, beating Height O' Fashion at a weight difference of three stone in boggy going was a top-notch achievement, and the explanation that Tom Dreaper had had difficulty getting enough work into Arkle on the saturated home gallops over the previous few weeks was largely unnecessary. Pat Taaffe was not perturbed: 'This is the first time Arkle ever won in a photo-finish. I was never really worried because he jumped brilliantly all the time, though he never could reach peak acceleration in the gluey conditions. After clearing the second last I thought we would win by a fair margin, but then I realised that Height O' Fashion was coming up strongly behind and I had to put my mount under pressure.'

Arkle came out of his tough race fit and well, and thoughts turned to Cheltenham.

The 1966
Leopardstown
Chase: Arkle the
centre of attention
in the paddock,
and going out
under Pat Taaffe.

Flyingbolt

By the beginning of 1966 there was one stable companion at Greenogue who seemed destined to become a real rival for Arkle, in ability if not in popularity.

Flyingbolt, a tall, white-faced chestnut by the 1946 Derby winner Airborne and unlike most Dreaper horses bred in England, was two years Arkle's junior and joined the stable – where, like Arkle, he was assigned to the care of Johnny Lumley – in 1962.

After educational runs in two Flat races and a bumper in 1963, he started to show exceptional ability over hurdles, winning four consecutive races in the 1963-64 season including the important Scalp Hurdle at Leopardstown (the race before Arkle won his first Leopardstown Chase) and the first division of the Gloucestershire Hurdle (nowadays the Supreme Novices') at Cheltenham. The following season he began his chasing career and won all his five races, including the Cotswold Chase (now Arkle Trophy) at Cheltenham. By the time of the 1966 Cheltenham Festival he had added another four big prizes to his chasing haul: the Carey's Cottage Chase at Gowran Park, the Black and White Gold Cup at Ascot, the Massey-Fergsuon Chase at Cheltenham and the Thyestes Chase at Gowran Park. Such victories sent him shooting up the handicap, and when the weights for the 1966 Irish Grand National were published he was rated only four pounds behind Arkle, who was still considered way in front of every other chaser.

Flyingbolt and Pat Taaffe winning the National Hunt Two-Mile Champion Chase at Cheltenham, 15 March 1966.

Flyingbolt's finest hour spanned two days – the first two days of the 1966 Cheltenham Festival. On the Tuesday he won the National Hunt Two-Mile Champion Chase by an effortless fifteen lengths, starting at 1-5 ('canter', said the form book), and the following day ran third behind Salmon Spray and Sempervivum in the Champion Hurdle, beaten 3¾ lengths by the winner, having raced too wide for much of the race and having made a serious error four hurdles out. Though defeated, to have come so very close to pulling off that double was a remarkable achievement.

During the summer of 1966 – by which time Flyingbolt had added the Irish Grand National to his haul – speculation was rampant about what would happen in the event of the two Dreaper stars meeting each other in a race. Pat Taaffe was convinced that the older horse would win: 'Flyingbolt was a front runner. Arkle would have been able to sit on his tail and beat him for speed.' In his autobiography, Taaffe remembered riding Arkle in an explosive schooling session, when Flyingbolt, ridden by Paddy Woods, and Himself seemed to be staging their own private race:

> They took the next four fences, neck and neck, flat out as though their lives depended on the outcome. While Paddy and I just held on to them for dear life and waited for the fires to die down. Well, they cleared them all right, but it was a bit too close for comfort. And Mr Dreaper never allowed them to be schooled together again.

What kept Flyingbolt well behind Arkle in the popularity stakes was his demeanour. While Arkle was famously as gentle as a lamb – polite, accommodating, gracious, kind to children – Flyingbolt was a brute. Pat Taaffe wrote: 'A small child could walk into Arkle's box in absolute safety. No child, no man would ever willingly step into Flyingbolt's ... at least, not twice. He'd kick the eye out of your head.' (The present author remembered Taaffe's words when meeting twenty-one-year-old Flyingbolt over the gate of an Oxfordshire paddock in 1980. But age had mellowed the mean and moody horse – quietly spending his old age in that field with another Dreaper stalwart, 1968 Gold Cup winner Fort Leney – and no blood was shed.)

Flyingbolt, once handicapped within two pounds of Arkle, is the forgotten horse of modern jump racing – to the extent that in the *Racing Post* readers' vote for their favourite racehorse in 2004 he did not appear in the top 100. Unpleasant as he might occasionally have been to those around him, he deserved better.

ABOVE
Oxfordshire, 1980: Flyingbolt, aged twenty-one, with wary admirer. Beyond Flyingbolt is Fort Leney.

BELOW
Arkle (Paddy Woods) and Flyingbolt (Liam McLoughlin) lead the Dreaper string.

Cheltenham Gold Cup, 17 March 1966

Since the Gold Cup was first run in 1924, only two horses had won the race three times.

Golden Miller, owned by Dorothy Paget (at whose Ballymacoll Stud Arkle had been born), notched up a remarkable sequence of five consecutive victories between 1932 and 1936, and might well have won a sixth in 1937 had not that year's meeting been lost to the weather. He was runner-up to Morse Code in the 1938 race. Golden Miller's feat of winning the Gold Cup and Grand National in the same year – 1934 – has never been matched. The other triple Gold Cup winner was Cottage Rake, trained by the young Vincent O'Brien, in 1948, 1949 and 1950.

Arkle's attempt to follow in the distinguished hoofprints of Golden Miller and Cottage Rake produced, but for one extraordinary moment, the dullest race of his chasing career. With Mill House sidelined with tendon trouble, the opposition

Giles cartoon in the *Daily Express*, 17 March 1966. The 1966 Gold Cup was run while the general election campaign was in full swing, causing confusion to Granny (who on the day would have won just one shilling for her ten bob on Arkle). Polling day was 31 March, and the Labour party led by Harold Wilson secured a 96-seat overall majority to consolidate its grip on power.

"Ten shillings to win—Arkle."

looked very weak for steeplechasing's elite race, even allowing for the fact that the unbeatable Arkle had scared away all decent competition. Only four took him on. Dormant, remote runner-up in the King George, had meanwhile run fourth at Windsor behind Oedipe and Anglo (who would win the 1966 Grand National), and unseated his jockey in the Gainsborough Chase at Sandown Park. Snaigow was a promising young chaser who had won his last two races, both at Newbury. Hunch had run at Cheltenham two days earlier, finishing unplaced ('always behind', according to the form book) behind Gregory Peck's gelding Different Class in the Totalisator Champion Novices' Chase. The outsider of the quintet was Sartorius, an eleven-year-old whose only previous run that season had seen him finish last in a handicap hurdle at Kempton Park five days before the Gold Cup. Arkle would win, but there was decent place money for the others to scrap over: £2,306 for second, £1,113 for third, £516 10s. for fourth.

On St Patrick's Day, a sprig of shamrock was lodged in the browband of Arkle's bridle, and with divine backing thus assured he started at 1-10, by a considerable margin the shortest priced favourite in Gold Cup history, before or since. Snaigow went off at 100-7, Dormant 20-1, Hunch 33-1 and Sartorius 50-1, having opened at a more realistic 200-1.

The BBC commentaries of Peter (now Sir Peter) O'Sullevan provided the indelible soundtrack of Arkle's career for television viewers, and in the 1966 Gold Cup he called how Dormant made the early running, with Arkle taking over the lead at the eighth fence, at the top of the hill on the first circuit. He then described Arkle's stately progress as he led the field into the straight, with another whole circuit to go:

The eleventh fence ...

... then Arkle scoots clear at the final bend ...

... and over the last.

Johnny Lumley
brings the
unperturbed
Arkle back ...

Ears pricked, having a look here at the crowds on his right, Arkle, as he comes up to the next ... Dormant second, Snaigow third, Sartorius and then Hunch ... Another complete circuit ... [as Arkle comes to the fence in front of the stands] ... **OHHHHHHH!** *And he barely took off at that one! ... He just looked at it and ignored it, and how he got the other side ...Well, you should have heard the gasp from the crowd here! It looked as though he wasn't going to jump at all. He just ignored the fence completely, and how he got the other side's a mystery ... This is an open ditch – and he jumped THAT one! ... Arkle from Dormant, Snaigow, Sartorius and Hunch ...*

The cardiac unit at Cheltenham General Hospital went on full alert, but Arkle, completely unfazed by ploughing through that eleventh fence, went on his merry way, cruising round another circuit and coming right away to win by thirty lengths from Dormant, with Snaigow another ten lengths back in third and Sartorius fourth. Hunch had been tailed off when falling three fences out and sustaining fatal injuries.

Arkle's non-jump was the big story the following morning, a popular line being that the horse had clearly benefited from the protection of Ireland's patron saint at his moment of crisis. The *Daily Sketch*, with a photo of the famous blunder under the headline 'ARKLE – JUST PROVING THERE IS SUCH A THING AS A RACING CERTAINTY', wrote:

If St Patrick himself had been in the saddle, he couldn't have diminished the adoration of Arkle.

The thousands at Cheltenham – sprouting shamrock flown over with the compliments of the Lord Mayor of Dublin – and the mesmerised millions in front of the television never doubted that Arkle could give the other four a couple of fences start and still win his third Gold Cup.

And so he did. Galloping home again with that consuming grace and the air of knowing his own supremacy that arouses strange emotions in the dourest racegoer. Sure, say the Irish, the sight of him would make a man with marble legs dance with delight.

Pat Taaffe, ever imperturbable, said: 'I knew he wouldn't fall. Arkle can always find a fifth leg.'

The post-Gold Cup plan had again been the Whitbread Gold Cup rather than the Irish Grand National, and in Arkle's absence his stablemate Flyingbolt won the Fairyhouse race by two lengths from Height O' Fashion, to whom he was conceding forty pounds. Relating this form to that of the Leopardstown Chase six weeks earlier put Flyingbolt very close to Arkle, a proximity confirmed by the weights for the Whitbread Gold Cup: Arkle on 12 stone (then the maximum weight for that race), Flyingbolt just four pounds less.

But plans to go for a second Whitbread were abandoned on the day before the race when it became clear that the going would be very soft, and Arkle was wound down before starting his summer holiday at Bryanstown.

... to a relieved
Duchess.

Adulation

While Arkle lazed around in his usual paddock, back at Kilsallaghan letters from his fans were piling up. He had started receiving a significant amount of mail in the wake of the first Gold Cup win in 1964, and by the summer of 1966 it was pouring in, often accompanied by sugar lumps or other sweetmeats, or a ten-shilling note with the suggestion that it be spent on carrots for him, or a request for a photograph.

Every week one of the Duchess's secretaries was dispatched from Bryanstown to make the short trip to Greenogue, where she would help Betty Dreaper deal with the mail, the level of which reached a noticeable swelling on Arkle's official birthday (1 January), actual birthday (19 April) and St Patrick's Day. Letters came from all over the world. Some bore helpful suggestions: for example, 'I note he was born on the 19th April (Primrose Day) and I hope someone will place a little

Guinness Group Sales (Ireland) Ltd.
ST. JAMES'S GATE DUBLIN 8. TELEPHONE DUBLIN 56701 · TELEX DUBLIN 5138 · TELEGRAMS 'GUINNESS' DUBLIN.

9th February, 1966.

Dear Mrs. Dreaper,

I feel it is a great lack of courtesy on our part not to supply you with the Guinness for Arkle, Flying Bolt and the other leading steeplechasers in your stables which apparently benefit greatly from our product. I am therefore arranging with Findlater's of O'Connell Street that your weekly order for Guinness should be charged to our account during the training period, which I think you indicated is from December to April. I think you also said that the quantity would be of the order of 10 dozen bottles per week.

I need hardly say how much we appreciate the very kind and pleasant publicity we have had from the association of Guinness with Arkle and your other horses and this is our way of saying 'thank you'.

Yours sincerely,

(Guy Jackson)

(G. P. Jackson)
Managing Director

Mrs. Dreaper,
Greenogue,
Kilsallaghan,
Co. Meath.

MK

Directors : A. H. Hughes, G. P. Jackson

Time for a
Guinness —
courtesy of the
brewery, and
served up by
Paddy Murray.

bunch of primroses in his stable on that day for many happy returns (from me).' Some letters had a mild sting in the tail, such as the one which included a photograph of a painting of Arkle with the Duchess – though the lady in the painting bore more of a resemblance to Gracie Fields than the former Nancy Sullivan – and asked whether the Dreapers would like to purchase the original for fifty guineas. The envelope was annotated by Betty for the secretary to draft a letter: 'NO, THANK YOU!'

This was a more innocent age than a later time, when Red Rum's manure would be available for purchase as a tasteful souvenir, or Desert Orchid fans keep up with their hero through a telephone 'hotline', or a range of Best Mate merchandise be sold (for charity) to an eager public, or supporters of Kauto Star or Denman wrap themselves in scarves in their hero's racing colours. But none the less there was

Public appearances in 1965. Arkle (with Pat Taaffe, Tom Dreaper and the Duchess) at the Dublin Horse Show ...

commercial advantage to be gained from any link with the great horse. The managing director of Guinness Group Sales (Ireland) Ltd wrote to acknowledge 'the very kind and pleasant publicity we have had from the association of Guinness with Arkle' and committed to a gratis delivery to the stable of 120 bottles per week.

Arkle was in demand for public appearances. His visit to the Dublin Horse Show in 1965 had been a huge success, and the same year he appeared at the Tolka Park stadium in Dublin as part of a fund-raiser for the local athletic club in Kilsallaghan.

This was arranged by Paddy Woods: 'The Duchess gave her permission, and I drove Arkle down in the box. I got Pat to come down and ride him round the pitch a few times, and we raised enough money to build a clubhouse – which of course we named the Arkle Pavilion.'

In May 1966, Arkle could not make it to the Anglo-American Sporting Club dinner at the London Hilton in honour of Himself, Pat Taaffe and Tom Dreaper – but another sporting icon could, in the shape of boxer Muhammad Ali.

By now Arkle's fame had crossed continents. The Australian racing community was intrigued to learn that Des Lake, a top Aussie jockey then riding for trainer Paddy Prendergast in Ireland, had given the opinion that Arkle would certainly win the Melbourne Cup, Australia's most famous Flat race, carrying ten stone. In January 1966 the *San Francisco Chronicle* carried a column by 'Our Fearless Correspondent' Charles McCabe:

> *I always like being nice to a horse on his way up. For one thing you may meet him socially on his way down. For another, as the nuns never tire of telling their girls in the Sacred Heart convents, you can never tell who he will marry.*
>
> *But the Irish jumping champion Arkle, it may be argued, is carrying things a bit far. It makes one wonder about that old sales manager's aphorism that nothing succeeds like success. He's too much, almost.*

... and fund-raising for the Kilsallaghan athletic club at Tolka Park.

Arkle, poor dear, ain't never going to marry anyone. On account of he is not what the horse trade calls with consummate delicacy 'an entire'. When a youth he had his maleness removed, in the interests of nervous stability, or placidity, or something. ...

There can only be one explanation for this extraordinary horse, and it obviously ain't sex. It must be all that Guinness's stout.

Closer to home, a young Irishman named Terry Wogan had written in an Irish magazine:

I often think that it's great thing that we have racehorses in this country, otherwise we'd never win anything at all. I'll admit that we are glorious in defeat; why wouldn't we? We've had lots of practice. But Arkle actually wins, and wins, and wins. It's a pity we can't decorate him for all the money he brings into the country, as Queen Elizabeth did with the Beatles.

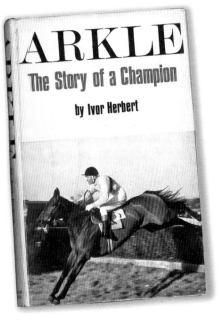

Arkle's image adorned playing cards, table mats, countless commemorative plates, paintings, figurines and sculptures (many of which actually looked like him). Ivor Herbert's book *Arkle: The story of a champion* was first published in the early autumn of 1966 and reached the bestseller list, and at about the same time the Anglo-American Chewing Gum Company of Halifax included Arkle as number 33 in its 66-card series 'The Horse'. The description on the back of the card stated: 'It is anyone's guess as to how long this success will last ...'

'He lost as a great horse should'

'He lost as a great horse should'

The final races

The 1966-67 season opened with Arkle on the crest of a wave. He had not lost since December 1964, his every race seemed to confirm that there was no chink in his armour, and at the age of nine he was physically at his prime. Talk of emulating – or even beating – Golden Miller's record of five consecutive Gold Cups had long since ceased being fanciful and was now routine: it was surely only a matter of his surviving fit and well and carrying on racing.

His position in the pantheon of sporting legends was secure, not to be compromised even when on 30 July 1966, while he was picking at the Bryanstown grass, the England football team beat West Germany to win the World Cup and induct another eleven heroes into the sporting Hall of Fame. When towards the end of 1966 *TV Times* magazine staged a poll among its readers for the most popular personality of 1966, the result was: third, The Beatles (who had issued the LP *Revolver* that year); second, Bobby Moore, captain of England's World Cup-winning team; first … Arkle.

Arkle's career had raised the profile of jump racing, initially through his famous races against Mill House but by now through the sheer excellence of his racing performance as well as (and very few horses can have this claimed of them with a straight face) the force of his personality. Everyone loved Arkle, as everyone loved the Queen Mother and Terry Biddlecombe and would later love Red Rum and Desert Orchid and Kauto Star. His races were front-page news. People flocked to watch him in action, and many would return to the racecourse when he was not racing. In later business-speak, Arkle increased the customer base of jump racing.

Take the case of Nicholas Clee, who as a nine-year-old in short trousers was taken by his cousin and his cousin's girlfriend to watch the 1966 King George VI Chase at Kempton Park:

*I had ridden a horse once in my life, I had spent no time with
horses, but I could tell, as Arkle appeared in front of the stands
before the race, that this was the animal at the centre of the day's
events: in his deportment, in his alertness, in what one can sum up
only as his presence, he stood out from the rest.*

That sight sparked in little Nicholas an interest in racing which was
to prove lifelong – to the extent that in 2009 he wrote the definitive
book about Arkle's fabled ancestor, the great eighteenth-century
racehorse Eclipse. There are countless other examples of dyed-in-the-
wool racing fans who were initially drawn to the sport by witnessing,
either on television or in person, the magic of Arkle in his prime.

But fame often draws into its eddy the streetwise with an eye for
the main chance. In 1928 the Irish government had set up a committee,
which included W. B. Yeats, to advise on redesigning Irish coinage to
reflect the natural products of the country, and a horse – an Irish
hunter – was featured on the half-crown (2s. 6d., or 12½ pence) coin,
remaining there for the succeeding decades. At the height of Arkle's
fame a wily operator acquired 100 freshly minted Irish half crowns and
took them to England, where he sold them for 10s. each – four times
face value – as medallions officially minted in celebration of Himself.

Celebration would soon turn to commemoration, for Arkle's
1966-67 season came to resemble one of those truncated upright stone
pillars seen in graveyards: a tall and stately monument cut off halfway
up, to signify that things come out of the blue.

If there is one song on *Revolver* whose title could describe the next
episode of the Arkle story, it is the last track: 'Tomorrow Never Knows'.

PREVIOUS SPREAD
The 1966 Hennessy: Arkle leads Stalbridge Colonist at the last.

Hennessy Gold Cup, Newbury, 26 November 1966

During the summer of 1966 the idea of taking Arkle to Auteuil to run in the Grand Steeplechase de Paris was dropped. Tom Dreaper insisted that the horse needed a proper close-season rest if he was to keep appearing in the top races in England and Ireland, and with a fourth Gold Cup in March 1967 topping the agenda, the Grand Steeple, run over 4 miles and half a furlong in June, would not fit easily into his schedule.

For the fourth year running the Hennessy Gold Cup would be Arkle's principal pre-Christmas target, and this time there was to be no preliminary outing before Newbury – which, given that the previous season he had not raced after the Gold Cup, meant that come Hennessy day he would not have run for over eight months. Two weeks before the race Arkle cut himself while schooling over the Kilsallaghan fences – not badly, but the injury was enough for him to miss a week's serious work at a crucial point in his training programme.

There were six runners in the 1966 Hennessy, and only two of Arkle's opponents were carrying more than the minimum 10 stone against his 12 stone 7 pounds.

Freddie, runner-up to Arkle in the 1965 race and twice runner-up in the Grand National, had incurred a seven-pound penalty for winning the Gallaher Gold Cup three weeks earlier and now carried 10 stone 7 pounds, while What A Myth, trained by Ryan Price and ridden by Paul Kelleway, was on 10 stone 2 pounds: he had won six valuable chases the previous season – notably taking advantage of the absence of Arkle to land the Whitbread – and had suffered only one defeat, when falling at second Becher's in the Grand National.

Like all great stars, Arkle did his bit for charity. *Child '66*, issued in December that year, announced that Anne, Duchess of Westminster would donate a proportion of his season's winnings to UNICEF, who declared that 'This gesture has prompted the Irish committee of UNICEF to adopt him as their mascot.'

Of the other three runners, two had finished behind Freddie at Sandown Park – Kellsboro Wood runner-up and Master Mascus fifth – and the Hennessy sextet was completed by outsider Stalbridge Colonist, trained by Ken Cundell at Compton and ridden by Stan Mellor, three times champion jump jockey.

Two years younger than Arkle, the grey Stalbridge Colonist had won eleven races (two hurdles, nine steeplechases) in the 1965-66 season, including six chases in a row. Over the summer he had run three times in France – a faller and second at Auteuil, then a faller again at Enghien – after which he was temporarily stranded on the Continent by a ban on horses travelling on account of an outbreak of swamp fever. On his most recent outing, he had run inexplicably badly when tailed off early on behind Dreaper-trained Dicky May in the valuable Black and White Gold Cup at Ascot.

Arkle's starting price of 4-6 – the longest he had been for any race since starting at 8-11 for the Leopardstown Chase in February 1965 – reflected that this was going to be no cakewalk. He was conceding large amounts of weight to some high-class rivals (one of whom – What A Myth – would be winning a Cheltenham Gold Cup before the decade was out), and he was probably not at the very peak of his fitness. What A Myth, who had won his only previous race of the season at Huntingdon, was second favourite at 7-2, Freddie 13-2, and the rest of the betting went 10-1 Master Mascus, 22-1 Kellsboro Wood, 25-1 Stalbridge Colonist. The market suggested that Arkle was there to be shot at, though it did not correctly identify the most likely assailant.

Until the last fence the race seemed fairly straightforward. Arkle led throughout the first circuit, jumping with exuberance, with Freddie and Kellsboro Wood keeping reasonably close attention, and he continued to lead up the straight and down the far side. Then Freddie started to fade, leaving Kellsboro Wood as Arkle's most persistent challenger early in the straight, with Stalbridge Colonist making steady headway. Kellsboro Wood's effort petered out, leaving the grey as the only visible danger, and on the run to the second last the Hennessy reached boiling point.

Landing over the second last, Arkle was greeted by an exultant roar from the crowd – hundreds of whom lined the course in a manner which these days would have Health and Safety reaching for the smelling salts – but still Stan Mellor, riding a brilliant tactical race on the lightly weighted Stalbridge Colonist, bided his time. Then, going to the last fence snug in Arkle's slipstream and still full of running, he suddenly pulled the grey to the right and roared Stalbridge Colonist into his challenge. Cue Peter O'Sullevan:

> *They're coming up to the last fence now and it's Arkle the leader, and a great crowd at the fence now waiting to part as he comes to jump it ... Arkle 12 stone 7 the leader from Stalbridge Colonist ... Arkle comes to it and he jumps it clear of Stalbridge Colonist second ... And Stalbridge Colonist putting in a great challenge and it's Stalbridge Colonist on the stands side, Arkle on the far side ... Here's where the weight is going to*

tell ...And its Stalbridge Colonist going away from Arkle now ... As they battle up to the line ... Arkle is going to be beaten ... It's Stalbridge Colonist from Arkle and What A Myth putting in a great finish but Stalbridge Colonist is the winner at the line, Arkle is second, third is What A Myth ...

Stalbridge Colonist had won a superlative race by half a length, with the fast-finishing What A Myth a length and a half behind in third.

Hugh McIlvanney of the *Observer*, the Arkle of modern sports journalists, struck a mildly elegiac note in his Newbury report:

Two years of magnificent processions came to an end here today, when the great Arkle was beaten for the first time since December 1964. It was, however, a minimal defeat, that left him as the hero of a superb contest, and still surely the finest steeplechaser ever seen on a racecourse.

Weight was Arkle's real conqueror in the Hennessy Gold Cup, although nothing should detract from the

Front page news in the *Observer*.

CHRIS HARTLEY

Arkle loses to outsider

The 25-1 outsider Stalbridge Colonist (left) overtaking the champion steeplechaser Arkle to win the Hennessy Gold Cup by half a length at Newbury yesterday. It was Arkle's first defeat since December 1964.

The official
photo-finish
picture.

*splendid victory of Stalbridge Colonist, a seven-year-old grey who was
brought with a beautifully timed challenge at the last fence, to surge
ahead in front of the roaring stands and win by half a length ...*

*Taaffe said later that when Stalbridge Colonist jumped faster at the
last, and headed him two strides from the fence, he felt that Arkle might
be left trailing. But his mount refused to yield, and in a finish that would
not have disgraced a flat race, he showed again that he has the heart to
match his phenomenal talent.*

*Afterwards Arkle was given the same excited acclamation that has
greeted his victories. He was cheered out of the unsaddling enclosure, a
champion who had lost a battle, but had been in no danger of losing his
title.*

But it was not only the thirty-five pound weight concession which beat Arkle. In
an interview for the video *Arkle: The legend*, Stan Mellor gave a fascinating insight
into the part which riding tactics had played in outgunning Arkle in the closing
stages: 'No way did I want to take him on, and I didn't want [Pat Taaffe] to think we
were any danger at all. I was lucky in the way that no other horse was good enough
to take Arkle on, and him just go away from me altogether. It worked out just as we
hoped it would. Arkle jumped the second last going very well and clear, and I was
four or five lengths behind him, and *directly* behind him – the whole idea.' As Pat
Taaffe glanced fleetingly round, Mellor appeared to be labouring – 'I tried to make it
difficult for him to see me' – and then, as Arkle's jockey settled down to concentrate
on the last fence, 'As soon as he turned to look at the last – *Bang*! we went! We used
this turn of foot which Stalbridge Colonist had and went into the last like a rocket.'
The momentum of Stalbridge Colonist's jump had propelled him alongside Arkle

then given him half a length advantage, which despite a valiant rally by the Irish horse he maintained to the winning post.

Arkle returned to the unsaddling enclosure looking little the worse for the race and Peter O'Sullevan hailed 'a magnificent, noble effort', though its true magnitude would become obvious only over the next eighteen months. For Stalbridge Colonist was beaten three quarters of a length when runner-up in the 1967 Cheltenham Gold Cup, and a length and a neck when third in the same race the following year. That is, the grey very nearly won two Gold Cups, and he had beaten a less than fully fit Arkle half a length when receiving thirty-five pounds. You think back to Brough Scott's comment on watching Arkle win his first race at Cheltenham 'as if he was another species altogether. Perhaps he was.'

Arkle's run in the Hennessy had been of such magnitude that it was even the subject of a leading article in *The Times* on the following Monday, under the heading 'When A Loss Is As Good As A Win':

> *The defeat of Arkle at Newbury races dented a legend, but did not destroy it. The champion steeplechaser was finally headed more by the handicapper's slide rule than by a genuine challenger for the title ... It may be small consolation to disgruntled punters to know that the champion's defeat in this manner was no bad thing for steeplechasing ... Now trainers may feel less deterred from pitting their own stars against the not altogether invincible Arkle.*

Years after this famous defeat, a bizarre rumour started circulating among those searching every nook and cranny for a new angle on Arkle that on Hennessy day 1966 Pat Taaffe had not been on top form as he was suffering from a bout of piles. Where this curious idea came from is obscure, and study of the race video shows the great man riding with all his customary gusto. But if the story is correct and Taaffe had indeed been enduring such discomfort, he would have done well not to ask for treatment from a nurse in Newry, who two days after the race wrote to Tom Dreaper and enclosed with her letter slips from three local betting shops. She started by expressing sympathy for the Newbury defeat of Arkle, 'the noblest and greatest of them all', and went on: 'Why were you all so trusting? Why oh why did it happen? May he arise from this temporary defeat and beat them all hollow again.' So far, so heartfelt an Arkle fan letter. Then she came to her point:

> *His defeat was an even greater blow than my own loss. A nurse, getting over a three years' illness, I staked my savings of £45 on him, never dreaming such a thing could happen to him.*
>
> *Could you tell me, is there any way of regaining this loss, which I cannot afford to lose now – please? I thought you could help me.*

Presumably she had included the betting slips as documentary evidence of her dilemma, but Betty Dreaper in her reply refrained from the obvious suggestion of how to recoup the losses – back Himself next time out – and politely declined to make good her losses.

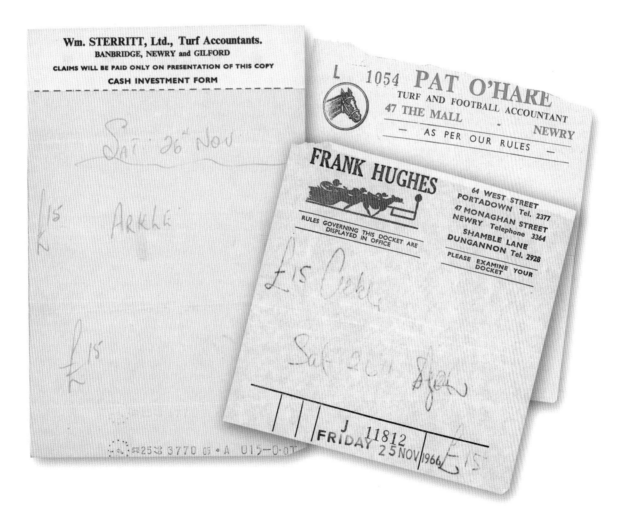

SGB Handicap Chase, Ascot, 14 December 1966

'God help them next time he runs' had been Pat Taaffe's post-Hennessy comment, and that next time proved not the King George VI Chase on Boxing Day, as had been widely expected, but the three-mile SGB Handicap Chase at Ascot, two and a half weeks after the Hennessy and eleven days before Christmas. The decision to run again so soon was taken once it became clear that Arkle had suffered no ill effects whatsoever from his Newbury exertions. Three days before the Ascot race, Tom MacGinty in the Irish *Sunday Independent* reported:

> *The very fact that Arkle runs again so soon after the Hennessy Gold Cup indicates how well he is. Schooled over four fences on Friday morning he gave every satisfaction, and now that he has had the benefit of an outing, he must be a confident choice to resume his winning way.*

The 1966 SGB Chase: Arkle's rivals keep a respectful distance first time round ...

Jumping at Ascot was then in its infancy. The royal course, where racing had been inaugurated by Queen Anne back in 1711, had staged its first National Hunt meeting on 30 April 1965, and good prize money and an excellent track were soon attracting top-class horses. Dunkirk beat Mill House there in October 1965, and the following month Arkle's brilliant stablemate Flyingbolt sauntered round to take the Black and White Gold Cup.

The SGB Chase – Scaffolding Great Britain was the company who sponsored the race – was first run in December 1965 and won by the favourite Vultrix, who carried

... but at the last fence are nowhere to be seen.

12 stone 1 pound and won by eight lengths from topweight Happy Arthur. It is a signal of how far Arkle now dominated the handicap chasing ranks that when Vultrix returned to Ascot for the 1966 race he was set to carry just 10 stone, thirty-five pounds less than Himself on 12 stone 7 pounds. The ground was heavy.

For the first time that Arkle-watchers could remember, the Dreaper star appeared in the paddock with his mane unplaited: Betty Dreaper later explained that the operation of plaiting his mane before a race had started to get him wound up in anticipation of what lay ahead, and leaving the mane hair flowing free was intended to prevent the horse expending unnecessary nervous energy: 'With 12 stone 7 pounds to carry in this deep ground he wanted all the energy that could be conserved, so it was decided on a new hair-do for him rather than me.'

There were three other runners in addition to Arkle and Vultrix: Master Mascus, who had finished fifth in the Hennessy; Sunny Bright, who had won two of his three races the previous season and was now having his first race of the 1966-67 term; and Big George, who had failed to win in three earlier races that season. Arkle opened in the betting at 2-9, but with few in the Wednesday crowd willing to bet at such odds had eased to 1-3 by the off; the other starting prices were 9-2 Vultrix, 10-1 Master Mascus, 100-6 Sunny Bright, 33-1 Big George.

Tom Nickalls in the *Sporting Life* saw normal service resumed:

Over the water.

Mighty Arkle has decisively readjusted his crown, knocked slightly awry by Stalbridge Colonist at Newbury. So many of racing's greatest heroes have won on the Royal Heath and it was most fitting that this prince of steeplechasers should add his name to the roll of honour at Ascot yesterday.

In doing so he put up one of his great weight-carrying performances in the SGB Handicap Chase, though he caused slight misgiving among his legion of fans by appearing in the paddock in rather a sweat. But he soon cooled off and went out on to the course his usual imperturbable self.

He was over the first fence in front and was never actually headed, though Big George was with him down to the water. A little later Sunny Bright and Vultrix almost jumped up to him at the second open ditch.

The champion was fairly showing off – sailing high over his fences, and he must have given Pat Taaffe the most glorious ride.

Vultrix stuck to him manfully, also jumping fabulously and giving the fences plenty of daylight.

But Arkle, unconcerned, strode right away from him along the Old Mile for the last time.

Turning for home with two to jump, Vultrix had given all he had. He was passed by Sunny Bright.

ABOVE AND NEXT SPREAD
The Ascot winner's enclosure: delight ... then concern ... then heading for home past his doting admirers.

141

*Sunny Bright, however, could make no impression on Arkle, who
raced home fifteen lengths in front of him – and conceding 35 pounds,
that was surely a champion's mark if ever there was one.*

The attendance at Ascot had increased by 35 per cent over the previous year's
running of the SGB Chase, and the enthusiastic post-race welcome was reported by
The Times:

*Rarely has Ascot witnessed such scenes near the winner's enclosure.
Heartfelt clapping, cheers, and even three cheers, greeted the great horse,
whose performance must have reassured those who doubted his unique
position in the world of steeplechasing.*

It had all been very straightforward, but when Arkle was being unsaddled it was
noticed that he had suffered a slight overreach – a small cut caused by a hind shoe
striking the heel of a foreleg – on his nearside front foot. This was a routine nick for
a chaser, and nothing was made of it at the time. Yet Pat Taaffe was uneasy, sensing
that Arkle's action that day had not been quite right: uncharacteristically, the horse
had jumped to the left over the last three fences, which could not have been due to
that cut on his near fore. When Arkle returned to Kilsallaghan he was subjected to a
careful examination by the vet, but there appeared to be nothing amiss, and all
seemed set fair for the King George, where he was due to meet Mill House for a
sixth time.

King George VI Chase, Kempton Park, 27 December 1966

In the early hours of Monday 26 December 1966 – Boxing Day – Kempton Park was attacked by frost. That day's racing programme was rescheduled for the Tuesday, and the Tuesday card abandoned. With a spare afternoon unexpectedly on their hands, the Arkle team – in the absence of Tom Dreaper, who had stayed in Ireland to supervise the stable's runners at Leopardstown – had to find ways of passing the time. Betty Dreaper went to a concert (which included *The Nutcracker Suite*) at the Royal Festival Hall, while Pat Taaffe took the Dreapers' fifteen-year-old son Jim off to Highbury to watch Arsenal (whose star players that day included George Graham and Peter Storey) beat Southampton 4-1. Johnny Lumley stayed with Arkle at Kempton.

Kempton Park racecard for the 'first day' of the Christmas meeting, which was actually run on the second day, with the second day's programme being abandoned.

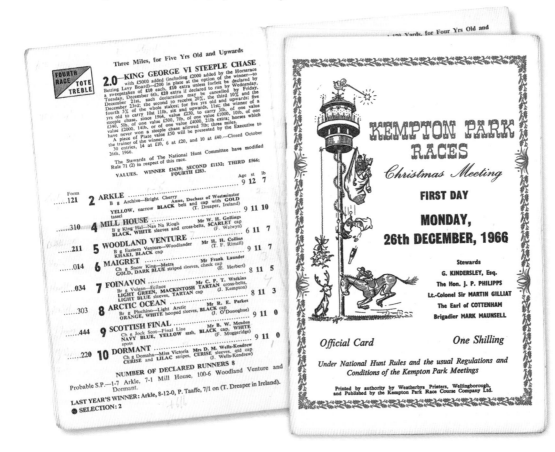

To the huge relief of the Kempton Park management, for whom the Christmas meeting was easily the most important fixture of the year, the course escaped another attack of frost, and the programme went ahead on Tuesday 27 December.

Mill House – who had not set eyes on his old rival for more than a year – was declared to run in the King George, and the announcement that The Big Horse had pulled a muscle in his quarters while exercising on Christmas Day and would not take part robbed the race of much of its edge. Without a Mill House or Dunkirk to provide a sideshow, this would surely be an exhibition round for Arkle.

Under the then conditions of the King George, Arkle, as winner since 1964 of a race with a value of over £4,000, had to carry twenty-one pounds over the base weight of 11 stone, which brought him up to his familiar mark of 12 stone 7 pounds. Carrying a stone less was the six-year-old Woodland Venture, a highly promising young horse who had won his last two races at Newbury and Cheltenham, and Maigret, who had run in the 1964 County Hurdle, the race before Arkle won his first Gold Cup, and, now trained by Arkle's biographer Ivor Herbert, was a very fair chaser: he had won over the King George course and distance in October 1966, and two Sandown Park chases the previous spring.

Foinavon, whom we last met on Easter Monday 1963, carrying the Westminster colours in a Fairyhouse hurdle, was now trained in Berkshire by John Kempton (who rode him in the King George), but the change of air seemed to have done little to improve his attitude to life: he had failed to win for his new connections, and indeed had not won since landing the Foxrock Cup at Leopardstown in February 1965. Arctic Ocean had finished a remote third (and last) to Arkle in the 1965 King George and had not run since. Scottish Final was a nine-year-old handicap chaser who rarely troubled the judge, and sharing bottom weight of 11 stone with him was Dormant, who had finished a distant second to Arkle in the 1965 King George and again in the 1966 Gold Cup.

The standard joke was that Dormant spent more time in a horsebox than in a stable, for he seemed to be for ever changing trainers. When running third in his first race, a Lingfield Park hurdle in March 1961, he was trained by Alec Kerr; when he won two novice chases in spring 1962 he was trained by Ryan Price; when he won the Holman Cup at Cheltenham a year later he was in the charge of his owner, Doris Wells-Kendrew; when he won at Doncaster in November 1963 and the Mildmay Memorial Chase at Sandown Park in January 1964 he was trained by Neville Crump; and he was still with Crump when returning to the Esher course for the Whitbread Gold Cup in April 1964, when he made himself the most unpopular horse in training by narrowly beating Mill House, who was conceding him three stone in his first race since being dethroned by Arkle at Cheltenham. Dormant had not won in nine races since playing the villain in that race, and had continued his stable-hopping, coming into the care of John Sutcliffe junior, Peter Rice-Stringer and Roy Pettit. Now he was back with the Wells-Kendrewses near Dorking. (Apologies to any trainers of Dormant inadvertently omitted.)

The last — the very last — with Dormant looming.

A King George of seven runners and only one feasible winner was reflected in the starting prices: 2-9 Arkle (shortening from an opening 1-4), 6-1 Woodland Venture, 10-1 Dormant, 100-6 Maigret, 25-1 Scottish Final, 33-1 Arctic Ocean and Foinavon.

Kempton Park was packed to the rafters with a crowd of 16,000 people, many of whom had been forced to abandon their preferred option of watching the race on television. Pay-TV, one of the earliest attempts at pay-per-view television in Britain, had acquired the rights to show the Kempton racing, denying the usual BBC audience the opportunity to see Arkle in action.

For those who made the effort to venture into deepest Sunbury-on-Thames it was a gloomy, murky afternoon, with patches of fog swirling around Kempton. Those who believed in the Hardyesque idea of 'pathetic fallacy', that the natural world reflects human moods, might have felt that something untoward was about to happen.

If so, they were proved right. For after leading uneasily for most of the race and seeing his main rival Woodland Venture fall when challenging strongly at the second last fence, Arkle jumped the last well clear of Dormant, on whom Jeff King was plugging on energetically. Nine-year-old Nicholas Clee was watching from the infield just after the fence, and over forty years later vividly captured the atmosphere of the next few seconds: 'As they galloped past, I craned my neck over the rails (did someone lift me?). The two horses' receding backsides now appeared to be level. Something was wrong. The crowd noise had that eerie, muted quality you get at a football ground when the away team scores.' Arkle had inexplicably slowed almost to a walk on the run-in, was caught near the post and beaten a length. It was clear as he hobbled back into the unsaddling enclosure that he had injured himself badly.

For a description of Arkle's darkest hour, there remains no one better than his finest contemporary chronicler, John Lawrence in *Horse and Hound*:

> *Although Arkle set off in front as usual, [Woodland Venture and Dormant] had no great difficulty staying with him and almost from the first there were grounds for suspicion that all might not be well.*
>
> *To Pat Taaffe the signs were even more ominous. His old friend reached uncharacteristically for the second fence, never really took hold of the bit and, most significant of all, soon began to hang outward away from the rails — and away from his off-fore leg.*
>
> *He had never done this before and Taaffe, who believes that the injury was probably caused by striking the guard rail of a fence, is now convinced that Arkle was feeling it for much of the greater part of the*

race. If he is right – and no one is in a position to argue – then this is a story of tremendous courage as well as tragedy.

Passing the stands after one circuit, Dormant passed Arkle to take the lead, and among the crowd an anxious buzz greeted the unaccustomed sight of the champion in second place. As Dormant went by, Arkle's ears lost, for a moment, their normal confident poise. He looked, to one sympathetic observer, 'like Samson must have looked when he found his strength gone with his hair.'

But Arkle's strength was by no means all gone yet. Soon after the water he was back in front and then, just as his supporters began to kick themselves for worrying, he made, at the fourteenth fence, the last and by far the worst of several minor blunders.

This, in fact, was not minor at all. It made even Pat Taaffe sit back, and many horses, less powerful, agile and superbly balanced, would have fallen.

No one can say how much it may have cost in terms of pain and energy, but even so Arkle would not give up his lead. Round the final bend, as Pat Taaffe began to ride, he answered heroically – but beside him on Woodland Venture, Terry Biddlecombe was sitting ominously still.

Terry believes – and I wholeheartedly agree with him – that, as they went to the second last, the younger horse had the race at his mercy.

In the light of what happened afterwards, he must surely be right, but we'll never know for sure. For now, taking off beside Arkle two from home, Woodland Venture just clipped the top foot of the fence, lost his balance and fell. He had done nothing at all to discourage my view that he is the best young chaser in England.

And now, some ten lengths clear of Dormant with only one fence to jump, Arkle's troubles were surely over. As if to make even more certain, he threw at the last one of his special grandstand leaps and, to those standing by the fence, it looked inconceivable that he could be beaten.

As Dormant landed apparently without a chance on the flat, Jeff King, to his eternal credit, had still not given up. And, as he sat down to ride, Arkle, still far ahead, must suddenly have begun to feel the full, agonising, strength-sapping effects of his injury.

Now too he had no fence ahead on which to concentrate his mind and, until Dormant appeared beside him fifty yards from the line, no visible enemy to fight.

Small wonder then, in all the circumstances – with 12st 7lb on his back and a broken bone in his foot – that even this peerless, unconquerable fighter could fight no more. And as his strength drained away it seemed, as often happens in finishes such as this, to be flowing into his rival. For Dormant, give him his due, did quicken after the last.

Returning through the gloom.

Halfway up the run-in, his prospects still looked remote, but for poor Arkle the winning post might just as well have been a million miles away.

Fifty yards from it, for only the fourth time in his steeplechasing career, he had to acknowledge defeat. That in itself was sad enough – but what is one defeat compared with our loss if we are never to see him race again?

Scarcely able to walk, Arkle was carefully loaded into the racecourse's horse ambulance and driven the short distance to the racecourse stables, where arrangements were made for a X-ray to be taken without delay.

Moments of high drama are often balanced by moments of light relief, and down in the Silver Ring that gloomy afternoon was a twentysomething former bookmaker's clerk named John McCririck, with his friend 'Shifty' Eddie, the World's Worst Loser. Shifty worked the outdoors markets, and was looking to play up Christmas takings by lumping on the horse he invariably referred to as 'Ankle'. As at most courses, there was a very restricted view of the finish from Kempton's Silver Ring, as John McCririck remembered in his *Racing Post* column 'At Large':

With the course commentary drowned out by the noise of the huge crowd all we could see was that Dormant (receiving 21 pounds) was making a race of it up the run-in, though 'obviously' that was because 'Himself', as Arkle's Irish legions called him, was simply easing down.

Eventually, though, when the premature celebrations collapsed as the dreadful outcome sank in that Dormant had sneaked back up to win by a length, Shifty was beside himself in voluble fury. Jockey Pat Taaffe 'didn't try, did he? – you saw for yourself, he went to sleep – what are the stewards doing? – this will kill the game – I'll never have another bet, that's it – look at those [expletives deleted] bookies,' etc. etc.

All total nonsense. Apart from the fact that in the Silver Ring Dormant would have been a far worse result than the unbackable favourite, save for those cunning enough to offer 6-1 and 7-1 while laying off at 10-1 inside, from what I'd seen that old-style horseman Pat Taaffe had been vigorous and alert.

But nothing could placate the enraged-to-the-point-of-apoplexy Shifty.
Always a rotten loser, this seemed to unloose the last screw that held him
together and for the rest of the day he was the boring epitome of nature's
biggest complaining pain.

By the time Shifty and his friend had got back to central London, the initial X-ray
had revealed that Arkle had broken a pedal bone – the lowest bone in the equine
leg, sitting against the wall of the hoof and roughly equivalent to the human
fingertip – in his off-fore hoof. He would be out of action for the rest of the season,
and possibly for ever.

The following weekend an article about Arkle by Jeremy Bugler in the *Sunday
Times* tried to analyse the appeal of the horse's celebrity – 'He won't have his name
taken, won't (can't) get involved in a paternity suit, won't say the Americans should
get out of Vietnam or the British into Rhodesia' – and ended:

> *The next act is waiting. If Arkle never runs again it will be tragic. If he*
> *runs again and loses, it will be dramatic tragedy. If he runs and wins, I*
> *expect half the country and three quarters of Ireland will be ill with backs*
> *cricked from too much obeisance. He will deserve much of it. He always*
> *won as a great horse should and last Tuesday, after running more than*
> *two miles with a broken bone, he lost as a great horse should.*

Exit Arkle.

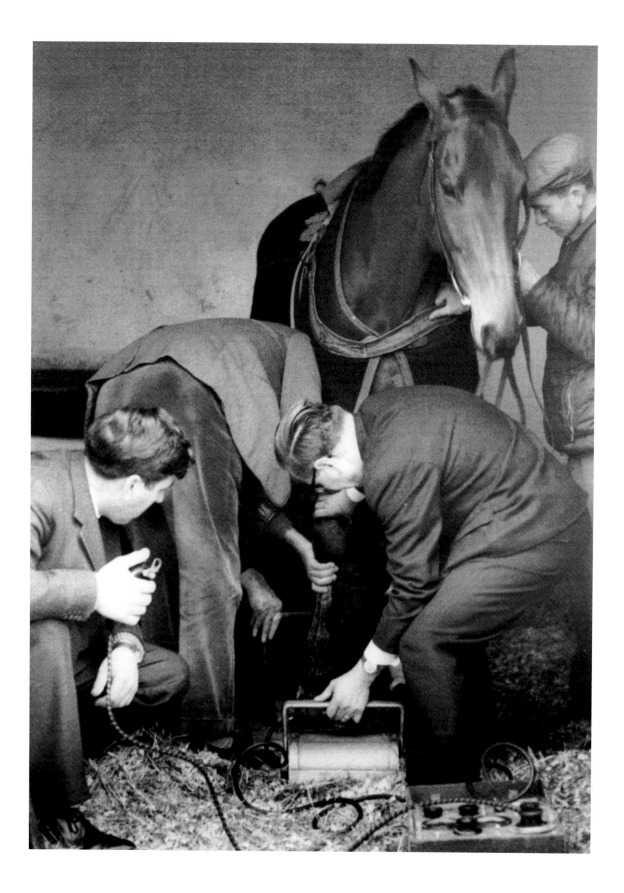

The patient

Arkle remained in confinement in the racecourse stables at Kempton Park for nearly two months.

As soon as word of the injury reached Dublin, Tom Dreaper's usual vet Maxie Cosgrove made arrangements to fly over the following day. He examined the early X-rays (one of which is now displayed in the Arkle Bar at Cheltenham racecourse), which indicated a serious break. The injured leg was encased in a plaster weighing five pounds, and Cosgrove prescribed that Arkle should remain in his Kempton box for at least six weeks. There was absolutely no question of his racing again during the 1966-67 season, and at that stage no better than an even chance that he would ever see a racecourse again.

Lads from the Dreaper yard took it in turns, two at a time per week or ten days, to travel over to Kempton and look after Arkle, and the stricken champion now became even more of a star than he had been when in action – and even more newsworthy. In the very early days of the horse's confinement, Paddy Woods, undertaking his stint of guard duty, was approached by a newspaper photographer. 'Two hundred and fifty quid for a photo' was his delicately whispered proposition, met with a rasping 'Not for two million and fifty!' The invalid Arkle was still one of the family, and not to be disturbed.

OPPOSITE
Yet another X-ray ...

BELOW
... and a visit from the Duchess.

Footnotes in the wages book at Greenogue for January 1967, in Betty Dreaper's hand, show the deployment of lads to look after Arkle at Kempton – Johnny Lumley and Sean Barker in the first week, Sean Barker and Liam McLoughlin in the second. And the cost of replying to all those 'get well soon' letters is beginning to be noticed – '(£1 postage Arkle)'. (Note that head lad Paddy Murray was earning £12 per week, Paddy Woods £10 10s., and Johnny Lumley £9.)

Both Kempton and Kilsallaghan were bombarded with gifts for the patient: the staple equine treats of carrots, apples and sugar lumps, but also plenty of Guinness and at least one Christmas cake. Get-well cards and letters flooded into both places. Many intended for Greenogue bore the two words 'Arkle, Ireland', addressed with the same conviction that they would arrive as a child painstakingly inscribing 'Father Christmas, North Pole' on an envelope. (One letter, reportedly addressed 'Arkle, Westminster Abbey', was redirected.) Most were heartfelt expressions of regret, sympathy, appreciation and hope for a speedy and complete recovery. For example, Mick Rogers, trainer of 1964 Derby winner Santa Claus, wrote to Betty Dreaper:

> It is so very, very sad. However, in this moment of grief I think one should reflect on the past, and the glorious triumphs this superb, once-in-a-lifetime horse has accomplished, and the pleasure he has given to millions of people.
>
> To Tom and yourself must go the credit for his wonderful racing record – the skill you have shown in always producing him in peak condition is admired and respected by everyone, and the worries and responsibility associated with training such a great horse must have been immense.

A slurp of restorative Guinness, courtesy of Kempton Park's managing director Henry Hyde.

Cliff Road
Waterville
Co Kerry.
12/1/67

Dear Mr Draper.
I am
indeed very sorry to
learn of Arkle's injury
I am a lover of horses.
This is a piece of
St Anthonys lily I do
hope you will put it
in Arkle's bandage.
This relic has been blessed
blessed at St Anthonys
shrine there is a cure
in it, so will you say
at least 3 hail marys

Others offered practical help:

I am now in possession, from my fatherland Lebanon, of the cure for the leg of your great horse 'Arkle'. It is a cure which has been used for thousands of years by the Arabs and before that by the Phoenicians, from which I am a descendant ... Mr Dreaper, I want you to believe me, I can cure your horse, if you give me this chance to prove that our treatment is beyond any veterinary knowledge ...

or

I was thinking: if you got a block of foam rubber about two or three inches thick and either stick or strap it on the hoof, it would help to take the jar as he walks, therefore saving him putting all his weight on the other leg. I feel sure it would be

21 Usher's Quay
Dublin 8
2·1··1967

Mr. Dreaper   Having read of the
tragic mishap to the great Arkle
a thought occured to me which
just might be of some use to you.
I was thinking if you got
a block of foam rubber about two
or three inches thick and either
stick or strap it on the hoof it
would help to take the jar as he
walks therefore saving him putting
all his weight on the other leg.
I feel sure it would be much better
than straw. I hope you can get
my meaning it is not very easy putting
ideas on paper, for me at any rate,
however it is only a simple thing which
might be useful, but no matter what
you use, get him back at it soon.

Yours

95 Sallynoggin Park.
Dun Laoghaire
Co Dublin
17 January 1967

Dear Arkle
Your injury come
as a great shock to me, and I hope
that when you are better you will
win the Gold Cup and Retire in
your greatness,
You are the greatest
horse in the world ever, greater than
golden Miller. Your greatness is
greater than that of "Cassius Clay's"
greatness, or anyone for that
matter, do you know I even named
my dog after you, I had the greatest
pleasure in seeing you running
at Leopardstown last February
you were just "Super" in that
very soft and hard going,
I hope to visit you
some time
P.S. - Running is agony I know it"

much better than straw. I hope you can get my meaning. It is not very easy putting ideas on paper, for me at any rate.

One letter had neatly attached to it small piece of lily:

Dear Mr Dreaper

I am indeed very sorry to learn of Arkle's injury. I am a lover of horses. This is a piece of St Anthony's lily. I do hope you will put it in Arkle's bandage. This relic has been blessed at St Anthony's shrine. There is a cure in it, so will you say at least three Hail Marys to St Anthony. I think he's wonderful for cures, and he was a lover of animals too. So please put this piece of lily in his bandage and I will pray that he gets well soon. This is genuine so believe me: do have faith in this relic.

Many letters were addressed not to the Dreapers but to Arkle himself

PHONE 4757.

CATHEDRAL PRESBYTERY.
WATERFORD.
28th December 1966.

Dear Mrs. Dreaper,

Please permit me to join the many thousands who so sincerely sympathise with Mr. Dreaper and yourself on the great tragedy that has befallen your hero and ours. Excuse the word 'ours' but, as you know so well, in every corner of Ireland, there are many who regard **Arkle** as their own in some way. I hope he will recover fully from this injury and will again give us the thrills and the joys that looking at him on television gives. If you will allow me, I would like to pay him a visit some time. You were good enough to give me plates of **Arkle** and **Flyingbolt** which occupy a place of honour on either side of the mantle place in my room here. There are no others.

You are the greatest horse in the world ever, greater than Golden Miller. Your greatness is greater than that of Cassius Clay's greatness, or anyone for that matter. Do you know, I even named my dog after you. I had the greatest pleasure in seeing you running at Leopardstown last February. You were just super in that very soft and hard going.

I hope to visit you some time.
Billy Murphy
PS. Running is agony. I know it!

A blind girl sent a Braille message to Arkle at Kempton:

155

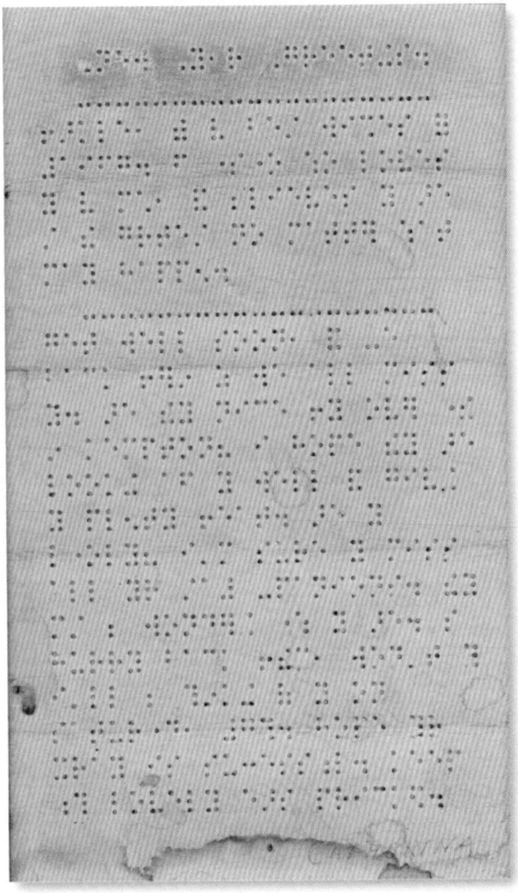

New Year Greetings.

To Arkle, with very best wishes for 1967.
    From someone who loves you very much, and believes you are still the greatest no matter what may happen.
    Get well soon, and come back to Erin as we all miss you. Are they nice to you over there in Kempton? I hope they are looking after you well and giving you plenty to eat. Are you lonely? I'm sure you will miss all your stable companions. They must all be wondering where you are. So hurry back to them, won't you. I'll be thinking of you on Saturday 7th [when Arkle was scheduled to have another X-ray]. Hope your X-ray is successful. Keep those lovely ears pricked.

    Catherina

And an old friend wrote:

Dear Arkle

I was so sorry to hear about your recent injury at Kempton Park.
    Ironically, I have only just recovered from a series of injuries, and I am only now back at my best. I was so looking forward to racing against you at Cheltenham and I think, with all due respect, I might have beaten you, as I am in tip-top condition now.
    Wishing you a very speedy recovery, and looking forward to seeing you up and about and racing soon,

    Yours faithfully
    Mill House

Whether The Big Horse licked the stamp himself has not been recorded, but it was good of him to write.

'An easy end'

'An easy end'

Retirement, death and after

In the final scene of Owen McCafferty's 2005 version of *Days of Wine and Roses*, Donal muses on 'What it's like to be Arkle'.

Arkle – What is it like to be Arkle? – Does he know he's Arkle? – Does he know how brave he is? – Coming up to a fence – With the rain beating against his face – And the mud flying about the place – Does he know that he could hit the fence? – Fall arse over hoof and his neck snap like a twig – Coming up to a fence does he say to himself – I must be brave – Is that what happens? – Does he say to himself, I'm a hero? – I'm a hero and I have to be brave even thought I'm frightened – Or is it just a horse jumping fences because he doesn't know any different? – A dumb animal doing something for no other reason than it's there to do – Isn't something you could ever know, is it? – What it's like to be Arkle.

It is indeed something you could never know, but to a degree the issue of Arkle's self-awareness is beside the point. Human relationships with any animal are constructed more by what the human side brings than by the contribution, however magnificent, of the animal, and while it is natural for followers of racing to attribute human characteristics to horses – both positive (courage, intelligence, generosity, etc.) and negative (cowardice, lack of resolution, etc.) – Arkle really did seem to be different. Plenty of racehorses inspire awe, respect, admiration and affection in their associates and followers, but Arkle was simply – and genuinely – loved as well as revered more than any other racehorse before or since. Probably the nearest equivalent was Brown Jack, the famous stayer of the 1930s who won at Royal Ascot seven years running. At the height of his fame Brown Jack was the recipient of regular parcels of fruit and other comestibles – he was especially fond of cheese – from all over the world and, like Arkle, continued to receive them, along with letters and cards, after his retirement.

And in the devotional stakes Arkle had one huge advantage over Brown Jack: television. For Himself was the first really great racehorse of the television age, the first equine superstar whose mass of fans could witness his mighty deeds as they happened, and follow his career as if it were some sort of ongoing sporting serial.

Arkle appeared regularly on the news pages in the months following the 1966 King George – through reports first of his recovery at Kempton, then his return to Ireland, then the 'will-he-won't-he race again?' question – and much of the coverage in the non-racing press is written as if of a human celebrity. He 'generously flashed around his toothy smile', he 'downed his pint of stout', he might well 'write something nice' about Clement Freud, he is asked for his autograph.

More recent equine heroes such as Red Rum and Desert Orchid confirm that the racehorses whose fame spreads beyond the racing pages are quickly given a startling range of human characteristics, but with Arkle the distinction between human and equine became so blurred as to become almost invisible.

Red Rum was the scrapper who fought his way out of the boondocks and posted a unique and probably unbeatable record in the world's most famous steeplechase. Desert Orchid was the mythical white horse who clearly revelled in galloping and jumping.

But Arkle operated at a higher level. He was a national hero, in the way that Red Rum or Desert Orchid never quite achieved. That much is apparent from the Dominic Behan song which celebrated the great Gold Cup victory of 1964, from his appearance on Irish stamps, from the display cases of memorabilia in Arkle Bars all over Ireland, and from the triptych in a west of Ireland pub which has John F. Kennedy on the left-hand side, Pope John XXIII in the centre and Arkle on the right.

Arkle – as one whose contribution to human happiness was unalloyed, and as the only Irishman of the three – should surely be in the centre.

PREVIOUS SPREAD
Tom Dreaper welcomes Arkle back to Greenogue, October 1967.

Recuperation and retirement

Two months after the King George VI Chase, the fracture in the off-fore pedal bone had healed well enough to allow Arkle to return to Ireland. On Sunday 26 February 1967 he boarded a plane at Heathrow, and the following morning the *Irish Times* reported:

> A big crowd assembled at Dublin Airport yesterday morning to see him when he arrived by BKS aircraft from London. He was very nervous and excited and for a time refused to go into the horse ambulance ...

The sight of a reluctant Arkle being goaded up the ramp alarmed one of his fans, who swiftly wrote to Betty Dreaper with yet more practical advice:

> After watching Arkle's reluctance to enter the horsebox yesterday, it struck me that if you had a recording of Pat Taaffe's voice in the van, it should have done the trick.
>
> As an ardent admirer of Arkle, I felt that all that pushing and shoving was an affront to his dignity.
>
> Please try the record to see if it works.

Dublin Airport, 26 February 1967: Johnny Lumley leads Arkle down the ramp.

Arkle,
Ireland.

'Arkle' Ireland.

TO ARKLE IRELAND

Arkle Ireland.

"ARKLE" WILL SPARKLE AGAIN

REMEMBER POST CODE

THE 4 LEGGED WONDER

IRELAND

a Little Prayer-To Jesus Say For Arkle & Pat Taff.

Jesus of Lazarath King of the Jews grant Arkle + Pat a complete & speedy recovery.

10 Heath
From Drumcondra
anxious and believes in This Prayer

Berkshire.
27th February, 1967

Dear Mr. Dreaper,

It may perhaps interest and surprise you to know that Arkle listened to the broadcast of the Leopardstown Chase on Saturday!

I saw Arkle run his last two races here, at Ascot when I walked across the Heath with my dogs to the start and watched his wonderful jumping all the way round, he made the fences look like hurdles; and I was in the enclosure at Kempton on that fatal December 27th, when he walked round the paddock alone before the start acknowledging the applause like a king, and I saw that he was lame when he was led away from the unsaddling enclosure after the race. I also saw his great dual with Mill House at Sandown the previous year.

Having passed Kempton many times during the last two months I have always thought of Arkle confined there so far from home, but never thought that I should be allowed to see him, but Saturday being the last day before he returned I thought I would try.

Having left my car outside the main gates I saw no one so set off on foot, but the hour's return journey was well worth while. I found Arkle just as the B.B.C. was about to broadcast the Leopardstown Chase (having backed Fort Leney I was particularly interest to hear the race and therefore took my wireless with me!) Having had a horse of my own I naturally would not have taken the wireless anywhere near Arkle

---

ve been the slightest bit nervous
but he seemed delighted to see me
r we listened to his stable companion
onderful race on going that sounded
Please accept my congratulations.

was amazed at Arkle's wonderful
ter beeing cooped up for two months,
eyes were bright and intelligent and
ked. I was also delighted with his
My only regret was that I had not
a with me, but then I had never
ld be allowed to see him.

now you must get a lot of silly
Know how busy you are, but I would
ul if you could spare the time to
re I could get a really good
(about 9" or 10" by 7" or 8") as
to have this framed; he is such
rse and such a great character.
think I am asking you to send me
ld be awfully grateful if you
photo a photo.

ly may I express my very sincere
will be able to get Arkle racing
ou will find that the accident
ne any permanent damage.
you the greatest possible
t Leney both at Cheltenham and
nd with all your other horses.

Yours sincerely,

LOT OF PICTURES OF ARK
TAAFEE
ME YOUR OTHER ADDRESS
TO ENGLAND.

Dear Mrs. Dreaper,

After watching Arkle's reluctance to enter horse-box yesterday, it struck me that if you had a recording of Pat Taffe's voice in the van, it should have done the trick.

As an ardent admirer of Arkle, I felt all that pushing & shoving was an affront to his dignity.

Please try the record to see if it works.

Sincerely,
Kitty Austin

ENGLAND

Good Luck
You 4 Legged Wonder.
Rise And Shine Again
Thrill Us With Your
"Sparkle"

Our Dear "Arkle"

"Up And Over" Fence By Fence

J.S.K

Berks.
19/9/67

Dear Arkle or Sir

(supporters) I am one of your greatest fans. and I have made two pictures of you on a frame.
I am a deaf boy and I am 13.
My birthday is on March 24th.
This is the first time I ever wrote to you. and I want to

---

you are better
ought a book about Arkle
will be very excited if
ou wrote back with Arkle
ntograph somehow perhaps a
e of his trimmings

m in the world's only gramm
ool for the Deaf. and I am
the Second Form after
nding one years in the
Form.

e Arkle's mother okays.
So long.
Hope you will write back.
Love from

The same post had brought news of an unusual encounter on Arkle's final day in the Kempton Park racecourse stables, when the patient was visited by a fan who lived not far away in Sunningdale. She had been so excited by her meeting with Himself that she wrote to Tom Dreaper:

> *It may perhaps interest and surprise you to know that Arkle listened to the broadcast of the Leopardstown Chase on Saturday! ...*
>
> *Having passed Kempton many times during the last two months I have always thought of Arkle confined there so far from home, but never thought that I should be allowed to see him, but Saturday being the last day before he returned I thought I would try.*
>
> *Having left my car outside the main gates I saw no one so set off on foot, but the hour's return journey was well worth while. I found Arkle just as the BBC was about to broadcast the Leopardstown Chase. (Having backed Fort Leney I was particularly interested to hear the race and therefor took my wireless with me!) Having had a horse of my own, I naturally would not have taken the wireless anywhere near Arkle should he have been the slightest bit nervous or excited, but he seemed delighted to see me and together we listened to his stable companion winning a wonderful race on going that sounded like a bog. Please accept my congratulations.*
>
> *I was amazed at Arkle's wonderful condition after being cooped up for two months: as ever his eyes were bright and intelligent and his ears were pricked. I was also delighted with his friendliness.*

Bryanstown: Arkle and Nellie visited by the Duchess and Pat Taaffe.

Arkle was back in Ireland, but it would be months before there could be any possibility of his returning to training at Greenogue. His convalescence continued at Bryanstown, and the letters kept coming. When in early February a terrible fall at Haydock Park put Pat Taaffe out for the rest of the season, the Dreapers received

> *A little prayer to Jesus say for Arkle and Pat Taaffe: Jesus of Nazareth, King of the Jews, grant Arkle and Pat a complete and speedy recovery to health.*

Another letter was from a thirteen-year-old boy in England ('I am in the world's only grammar school for the deaf'):

I will be very excited if you wrote back with Arkle's autograph somehow, perhaps a piece of his trimmings.

At Bryanstown, a cattle barn was converted for Arkle's use, with straw bales piled around the walls for protection. Nellie the donkey became his constant companion, and stud groom Johnny Kelly his principal carer.

After the initial shock of the injury, prognosis for complete recovery had been favourable. Examination had shown no deterioration in the condition of the pedal bone, and early in February, after the plaster had been removed for good, vet Maxie Cosgrove announced that there was 'a little further encouragement that Arkle may go into training again. The X-rays show that the break is healing satisfactorily.' An operation was ruled out. Time and rest would be the principal forms of treatment, with Arkle's equable temperament a vital contributor to a successful outcome.

The affected bone continued to heal well through the spring and summer, and a return to Greenogue in the autumn became increasingly likely.

Arkle finally reached home in October 1967, though when (and of course whether) he would run again was far from clear. Come the spring, racecourses were lining up to provide suitable races for the greatest comeback since Lazarus: Leopardstown, for example, proposed staging a welter-weight Flat race for him and Pat Taaffe (who had returned to action at the beginning of the 1967-68 season). Eventually it was decided that the Mosney Hurdle at Fairyhouse on Tuesday 16 April – the day after the Irish Grand National on Easter Monday – would fit the bill: a two and a half mile hurdle with conditions specifically framed to suit Arkle.

ABOVE
Arkle and the Duchess.

BELOW
Norah Pearson, mother-in-law of legendary jockey and trainer Fred Winter, being shown round Bryanstown by Himself.

Arkle and Tom Dreaper on his return to Greenogue.

Early in March *The Times* carried on its news pages the headline 'ARKLE IS READY TO RACE AGAIN', over a report which began:

> On a bright March morning at Greenogue, near Dublin, in a field where the sun has lifted a silvering of frost and softened the ground, Arkle, the world's most famous steeplechaser, canters before the critical watch of his trainer, lithe chestnut [sic] body superbly trim, and relishing the exercise ...
>
> He still likes Guinness and he still cocks his ears photogenically when a camera is pointed at him, and drops them when the shutter has clicked. He still rolls on his back with his legs in the air. He did this yesterday and generously flashed around his toothy smile.

It is a measure of how Arkle's fame had spread around the globe that the Greenogue occasion found its way into places as distant from County Dublin as Norman, Oklahoma, where the *Oklahoma Daily* wrote:

> Arkle, Ireland's wonder horse, downed his pint of stout Thursday, flashed a toothy grin and announced by way of a twitch of his ears that all is well.

Meanwhile the role of winning the Gold Cup for the Dreaper yard had passed to Arkle's contemporary Fort Leney. A year younger than Himself, Fort Leney had been bred by Colonel John Thomson, chairman of Barclays Bank, from his remarkably successful mare Leney Princess, and had been steadily climbing the ranks. He had

Arkle strides back, but easy does it !

By
CLIVE GRAHAM (The Scout)
Pictures by
HARRY MacMONAGLE

After his spin—Arkle is still like a playful colt

AT LAST the picture that Arkle's fans feared they might never see—tuning up now for his public reappearance (probably over hurdles) at the Irish Grand National meeting at Fairyhouse in April).

Here, he strides out freely in a brisk canter over Co. Dublin parkland.

The attitude of exercise rider Paddy Woods in the saddle, and the position of his hands show that Arkle, the champion belonging to Anne, Duchess of Westminster, is taking an exuberant hold of his bit.

It is noticeable, too, that his trainer Tom Dreaper had fitted him with a bit-martingale, a precautionary device to make it more difficult for him to overpower his rider and run away.

It is now nearly a full year since the injured Arkle returned home from Kempton Park.

Light exercise

He had spent two months there confined to a box in the racecourse stables after fracturing the pedal bone in his off fore-foot during the running for the King George VI Steeplechase on December 27, 1966.

Almost miraculously for a horse of his age—he is now 11 years old—the damaged bone began to knit.

Early in December Maxie Cosgrove, his veterinary consultant, after examining yet another series of X-ray plates considered it safe for Arkle to take light trotting exercise.

It was decided, though, that it would be impossible to have him fit for next month's Cheltenham Gold Cup, the steeplechasing blue riband which he won in the three successive years from 1964-66.

Plans for Arkle's future still depend on the verdict from Mr Cosgrove when he makes an inspection on returning from his holiday later this month.

Arkle appears to have little doubt about the favourable outcome, judging by the joyous way he bucked over in the deep stride of this box-shore into a playful roll than a fully formal jauntily steeplechaser—when his training spin was over. Past 34 races he has won 26 and been placed in five. To judge by his present liveliness, it seems highly premature to draw any line under these figures.

With Paddy Woods in the saddle, Arkle moves with all his old eagerness. It won't be long before he's carrying punters

February 1968: Arkle's imminent return is headline news.

started favourite for the 1967 Gold Cup, having taken the Arkle path of winning the Leopardstown Chase on his pre-Cheltenham outing, but ran disappointingly at Cheltenham to finish sixth behind Woodland Venture (who had been challenging the injured Arkle when falling in the 1966 King George); Stalbridge Colonist, who had beaten Arkle half a length when receiving thirty-five pounds in the 1966 Hennessy, was second, beaten three quarters of a length. (Some facts bear repetition.) In the betting for the 1968 Gold Cup, Fort Leney (who had again won the Leopardstown Chase on the way to Cheltenham) was fourth fancied of the five runners – Mill House started 2-1 favourite – but battled on to win by a neck from second favourite The Laird; this time Stalbridge Colonist was third, one length behind The Laird. (Fort Leney's sire was the 1947 Gold Cup winner Fortina, making the Dreaper horse the only Gold Cup winner in the race's history by a Gold Cup winner.)

Thus Fort Leney gave Tom Dreaper his fourth Gold Cup in five runnings. When it became known that Colonel Thomson had been unable to see his horse's moment of glory as he was detained in London by a meeting with the Monopolies Commission, one racegoer observed that 'It's Tom who should be had up for monopolising.'

March 1968: Fort Leney asks Arkle (in box 7) for last-minute hints on how to win the Gold Cup.

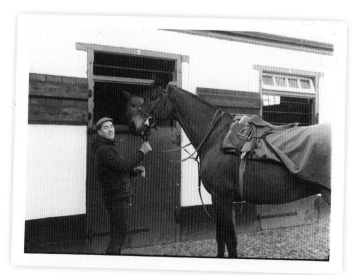

Peter Biegel's card to Colonel John Thomson, 1968: 'The Immortals', with an additional hero added in ink.

Arkle did not, after all, run in the Mosney Hurdle. For some reason the story took hold in later years that the crowds had flocked to Fairyhouse and were eagerly awaiting the appearance of their hero in the paddock when the commentator was handed a slip of paper which read, 'Horse does not run', and had to make the announcement which in an instant would fling thousands at the racecourse and millions around the world into the depths of disappointment.

The truth is more prosaic. As part of his preparation for the race, Arkle was taken to Naas racecourse to be ridden by Pat Taaffe in a school over hurdles with his stable companion Splash. As the horses pulled up after jumping the hurdles, Tom Dreaper asked his jockey:

'All right, Pat?'

'No, sir.'

'When do you think he'll be right?'

'I think he'll never be right, sir.'

On 10 April, six days before Arkle's Fairyhouse date, it was announced that he would not run there, and that a decision about his racing future would be put off until the autumn, by which time he would be rising twelve years old. Few were optimistic about ever seeing him race again.

Arkle returned to Bryanstown, where during the summer he was regularly ridden round the estate by the Duchess or her friends. Visitors – including on one occasion Julie Andrews – made their way along the leafy road from Maynooth to pay their respects to the most fabled horse in the world, and most of the time he was turned out in his paddock with Meg, an old grey hunter.

There was vague speculation regarding whether he might be able to race before the end of the year, but an announcement on 8 October 1968 put paid to any hope of a resumption. The Duchess issued a statement:

*Arkle is sound and very well, but although his comeback had been
planned for Leopardstown after Christmas, that would be only just short
of his twelfth birthday. After a great deal of thought and discussions with
Tom Dreaper and Mr Cosgrove, we have decided
to retire him. Not even Arkle, with his immense
courage, could be expected to reproduce his old
brilliance.*

In the *Sun* the following day, Clement Freud, who
had 'interviewed' Arkle years earlier, saluted 'the
best-known Guinness swiller of all':

*For this equine knight in a shining brown coat
the competitive life is over, and while we shall
miss his prowess and his humour, I'm glad
that his most humane of owners has taken
this decision and saved him from possible
humiliation.*

*Now he deserves all the good Irish clover
hay that he will get, and if, in years to come,
I see him again in the green fields of Co.
Kildare, I shall bring him a Guinness and
remind him of the day we met when we were
both starting in our chosen careers.*

*Perhaps, one day, Arkle will write
something nice about me. There is no telling
what that horse might do in his retirement.*

BELOW
*Arkle: The
Wonder Horse*,
published in
1968 as no. 1 in
the series
'Portrait of a
Star'. The
photograph on
the front was
taken before the
start of the SGB
Chase at Ascot in
December 1966,
the last race
Arkle won.

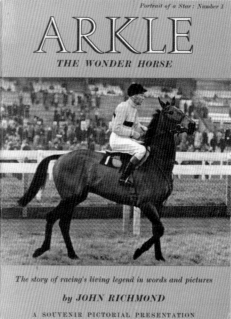

Portrait of a Star: Number 1

ARKLE
THE WONDER HORSE

The story of racing's living legend in words and pictures

by JOHN RICHMOND

A SOUVENIR PICTORIAL PRESENTATION

169

Horse of the Year Show, October 1969

Arkle continued to enjoy a happy retirement at Bryanstown, but his doting public had by no means forgotten him, and he was invited to travel to London to appear at the Horse of the Year Show at the Empire Pool, Wembley in October 1969.

Arkle appeared at the show on six consecutive nights, beginning on Monday 6 October with the Royal Gala Performance in aid of three charities: the Army Benevolent Fund, Riding for the Disabled, and the Injured National Hunt Jockeys' Fund (later the Injured Jockeys' Fund). The early part of the entertainment included the Stoke Mandeville Championship, in which several leading jump jockeys (including Terry Biddlecombe, Josh Gifford, Richard Pitman, Stan Mellor and Bob Davies, as well as the top amateur John Lawrence) competed in a show-jumping class. Just before the interval, which preceded the Butlin Championship in which such famous horses as Beethoven, Mister Softee, Vibart, Merely-A-Monarch and O'Malley were due to compete, came the parade of 'Horse Personalities of 1969'. First into the arena, to the strains of the Grand March from Verdi's *Aïda*, walked the State Trumpeters from the Blues and Royals; then a police horse from Birmingham City Police (to the theme tune from *Z Cars*); then two Dartmoor ponies (music: 'Widecombe Fair'); two black geldings from the Household Cavalry; leading point-to-pointer Musk Orchid and various other notable horses; then, pulling behind him a costermonger's cart stacked with fruit, a twenty-three-year-old grey donkey named Blinkers, who had been bought at Barnet Fair for £9 and had appeared in the film *Doctor Doolittle*. Following behind Blinkers came the retired show jumper Pegasus, and finally, to a rapturous welcome from the audience, Arkle, with Pat Taaffe in the saddle. The Duchess had been asked which tune she wished the band to strike up as he entered, and it had not taken her long to request the Harry Warren song, 'There Will Never Be Another You'. The programme noted:

> No horse ever crossed a steeplechase fence much faster or more safely, no horse ever produced a more deadly turn of speed at the finish of a three-mile chase, and no horse ever had a bigger heart.
>
> Perhaps, one day, there will be another like him, but we who watched Arkle in his prime will believe it when we see it.

For part of the week Paddy Woods came over to subsitute for Pat Taaffe. He remembers how on the final night Jennie Loriston-Clarke, the top three-day eventer who was riding the mare Desert Storm in the parade, asked, before they made their entrance, whether she could sit on Arkle. Paddy happily agreed, and in turn had a sit on Desert Storm.

Each evening Arkle entered the arena directly behind the donkey Blinkers and his cart piled with apples pears, and oranges, and Paddy recalls how the horse 'never got his eyes off it.' Towards the end of the week temptation proved too much, and with Paddy letting the reins go loose, Arkle moved up to the back of the cart and started helping himself – much to the delight of the crowd and the alarm of the Duchess. She subsequently wrote to the donkey's owner to apologise, and received a reply declaring that it was an honour to have Arkle scoff his fruit.

Arkle (Johnny Kelly leading him) at the Horse of the Year Show, October 1969.

The end

Arkle had revelled in his appearances the Horse of the Year Show, but throughout 1969 his general physical condition had been slowly deteriorating, and for reasons nothing directly to do with the Kempton injury. He had started to show signs of increasing stiffness in his hind legs, and it was suspected that he might have arthritis in his hip. The eminent vet Sir Charles Strong came from London to work on his muscles, but as the months passed the horse became increasingly stiff, and in early 1970 it was noticed that when turned out in his field, he would frequently lie down.

Towards the end of May 1970, not long after the Duchess had returned to Cheshire after one of her trips to Bryanstown, she was phoned by Pat Taaffe, who regularly stopped by to see his former comrade-in-arms. Pat had found Arkle more stiff than ever, and suggested she come back over. Then Maxie Cosgrove phoned her, with the same suggestion: he had examined Arkle, and a decision needed to be made quickly.

On the afternoon of Sunday 31 May 1970, the Duchess entered Arkle's box to find him lying down and clearly uncomfortable. There was only one kind course of action, and James Kavanagh, partner in Maxie Cosgrove's veterinary practice, promptly gave the injection which ended Arkle's life.

There had been no alternative, and the Duchess stated: 'Over a period of the last month Arkle has had progressive lesions developing in both hind feet. During the last few weeks these these became worse and he was in a certain amount of pain.' Pat Taaffe said: 'It was best for him to be put down so that he would not suffer. I am glad that he had an easy end.'

Paddy Woods was in England with his wife, unaware of what was going on in Ireland. 'We visited Kempton so that I could show Phyllis where Arkle had been convalescing for all those weeks following the King George,' he remembered, 'and afterwards went into Sunbury for a coffee. I bought a *Sporting Life*, and there was the headline. That was a very emotional cup of coffee.'

Arkle's death reverberated around the racing world and far beyond. This was an event important enough to be front-page news in *The Times* and the subject of a lengthy editorial in the *Irish Times*, and in the next weekend's *Horse and Hound* John Lawrence, who had found the perfect words to celebrate Arkle's racing life, now found the perfect words with which to mark his death. Arkle was put down three days

Leader column in the *Irish Times*, 1 June 1970. ('The dilemma of the British World Cup captain' refers to Bobby Moore's arrest in Colombia.)

Arkle

How often has the death of a horse—and at a time of political excitement at home and abroad—been accorded the distinction of front-page news? And the horse in question was not a favourite for a big race; he was retired, out on grass, no longer of any interest to those whose livelihoods depend on the various aspects of the business of horses. Nor had he any pecuniary value; a gelding, as most steeplechasers are, he had pride of ancestry divorced from hope of posterity. No money, it may reasonably be said, could have bought him from his owner. Such was the measure of this animal.

Enthusiasts have their heroes. And it is not simply a matter of admiring their skilled performances or taking a vicarious thrill from their triumphs: the relationship is more personal than that. A fan takes a close interest in everything that has to do with his champion. The champion does not know of his existence, and can only guess at the pleasure he gives. He has plenty of evidence of interest and enthusiasm. The dilemma of the British World Cup captain was probably as agonising for a great many people as would be a similar *contretemps* in which one of their own family had the misfortune to get involved.

Arkle, then, won the regard that a human champion inspires; but he had something else. Many people have a special feeling for horses. It is not rational: they will eat some animals and enjoy the experience, but the idea of eating a horse, they feel, is repellent—a kind of cannibalism.

* * *

This may be irrational, but so are most of the sentiments that reconcile mankind to the anxious business of existing. Horses are associated with people since the beginning of history. Nowhere does a man feel so proud as astride a fine horse. His head is that much nearer the clouds.

"Only a horse" is the dismissive remark of the rationalist who may not always analyse closely the value in eternity of some of his own favourite preoccupations.

It was not an accident that Swift, in the greatest of all satires on the human condition, made his superior beings in the likeness of horses. Admittedly, these were somewhat priggish if noble beasts, enforcing a homely view that a horse is at its best when performing as horses have always performed in their long, sometimes much-abused, faithful and gallant association with man.

Were any bard to sing the praises of Arkle, there would be nothing unfitting in the exercise. That horse added to the lives of thousands. His instinct, which allowed him to put his power under human control—men are suffered by horses—had about it something that did honour to horses and to man.

before the 1970 Derby – which would produce, in Nijinsky, another great Irish-trained horse winning a famous victory in England – and the contrast between the riches of Flat racing and the comparative deprivation of jumping gave Lawrence pause for thought:

> It is a slightly sobering thought that, in under three minutes this week, a three-year-old colt will, by galloping 12 furlongs on the flat, have earned nearly as much (£60,000) as the total (£75,000) Arkle won by galloping almost 100 miles and jumping 500 fences and hurdles.
>
> Such are the topsy-turvy values of modern racing. But it wasn't for money that Arkle ran his heart out. He did it because he had been bred for the job and taught to do it well by kindly men whose kindness and skill he was glad to repay.
>
> He did it because he loved his own speed and strength and agility – and perhaps because he loved the cheers they brought him. He was, more certainly than any other Thoroughbred I can think of, a happy horse who enjoyed every minute of his life.
>
> In that sense perhaps the human race did repay some small part of the debt it owed him and at least when his life ceased being a pleasure it was quickly and humanely ended.
>
> But mostly the debt remains unpaid. We can only try to pay it by remembering Arkle as he was – brave in defeat, magnificent in victory, and gentle in repose.
>
> Now he is gone and we must search for others to warm our blood on winter afternoons, to fill the stands and set the crowds on fire. No doubt we shall find them – but they will be pale shadows of the real thing. For those who saw Arkle will never forget the sight and, until they see another like him, will never believe that two such miracles can happen in a lifetime.

Tommy Bracken, the famous Dublin character who plied a good trade peddling his ballads around the pubs of the capital, promptly penned an elegy which ended:

> But never again on a racecourse if for centuries we wait
> Will we see your equal, Bold Arkle the Great.
> So, from all of us now who loved you so well,
> We'll remember you always, Arkle – farewell.

Letters of condolence poured in to the Duchess and the Dreapers, among them another message from the company which brewed Arkle's favoured tipple, Guinness: 'We were very sorry to see that Arkle had to be put down. We were very proud to be associated with such a wonderful horse, and hope that he enjoyed his bottles of Guinness during his lifetime.'

Arkle was buried in his field near the main house at Bryanstown, where his body was soon joined by that of Meg. His grave simply bore his name and dates (inscribed erroneously '1958-1970'), and hers read 'Meg, a good hunter'.

After Arkle

Tom Dreaper, having trained his fifth Gold Cup winner in 1968, when Fort Leney added another victory to those of Prince Regent (one) and Arkle (three), retired on 31 January 1972. The following day his son Jim – who had been beaten a neck when riding Black Secret in the 1971 Grand National as a twenty-year-old amateur – took over the licence, and maintained the flow of big-race winners, becoming leading jumps trainer in Ireland for the first five years of his career. He has won the Gold Cup in 1975 with Anne, Duchess of Westminster's gelding Ten Up (ridden by Tommy Carberry); the Irish National four times in five years with Colebridge (1974) and Brown Lad (1975, 1976 and 1978); and the Welsh National in 2008 with Notre Pere. Tom Dreaper died in 1975, and after his death his widow Betty married the widower Colonel Sir John Thomson, owner of Fort Leney and several other Greenogue horses. Betty Dreaper died in 1993.

Anne, Duchess of Westminster owned several good horses after Arkle. She won a fourth Gold Cup in 1975 with Ten Up, and although she had sold Foinavon before his bizarre moment of Grand National glory in 1967, she saw her colours swept to the fore up the Aintree run-in when the enigmatic Last Suspect, trained by Tim Forster, won the National in 1985. Her other good horses included Kinloch Brae, Sea Brief, Sub Rosa, Ballyross, Cherrykino, Wandering Light and Carbury Cross. She died in September 2003 at the age of eighty-eight.

Members of the Dreaper team gathered at the launch of Bryony Fuller's book *Tom Dreaper and his Horses*, Keadeen Hotel, Kildare, 1991. Left to right: Peter McLoughlin, Sean Barker, Pat Taaffe, Ken Morgan, Paddy Woods, Val O'Brien and Liam McLoughlin.

Pat Taaffe retired from the saddle in 1970, after riding three winners at the Cheltenham National Hunt Meeting and landing a second Grand National on Gay Trip. His record of twenty-five winners at the Cheltenham Festival (including four Gold Cups: three on Arkle and one on Fort Leney) has not been surpassed. After hanging up his saddle he took out a trainer's licence, and in his new role handled one of the very few postwar chasers fit to be mentioned in the same breath as Arkle – Captain Christy, who won the Gold Cup in 1974 and the King George VI Chase in 1974 and 1975. Pat Taaffe died in July 1992 at the age of only sixty-two. In the homily at his funeral, the priest quoted the tribute of Irish trainer and former amateur jockey Ted Walsh: 'As gentle as a lamb off a horse, a lion in the saddle.' His son Tom trained Kicking King to win the 2005 Cheltenham Gold Cup.

Mill House, whose signal piece of bad fortune was to be foaled in the same year as Arkle, ran eleven times after his fifth and final race against Himself in the Gallaher Gold Cup in November 1965. He was plagued by injury and training problems, but still had his moment of glory when winning the 1967 Whitbread Gold Cup at Sandown Park to trigger widespread blubbing on the slopes of Esher. He had fallen in that season's Gold Cup (won by Woodland Venture) and fell again when favourite for the 1968 Gold Cup (won by Fort Leney). In autumn 1968 he won a small race at Wincanton then fell at Ludlow, after which he was retired. He died in October 1975 at the age of eighteen, destined to be remembered as Arkle's main rival, but certainly a great horse in his own right.

Flyingbolt was never the same horse after winning the 1966 Irish Grand National. Moved to Britain to be trained by Ken Oliver following training problems, he ran second to Titus Oates in the 1969 King George VI Chase but he was afflicted by brucellosis and never showed form remotely like his best. He was then moved again, to Roddy Armytage at East Ilsley in Berkshire, where John Oaksey regularly rode out:

> Having no idea of the arrival in the yard of a famous new inmate, I arrived (a little late) one morning – to be told, a bit sharply: 'Get on that chestnut over there.' It seemed rather a long way up, but neither the height of the horse nor the distinctive white face – a broad white blaze from above his eyes to the tip of his muzzle – made me register that this was the great Flyingbolt.
>
> There was, in those days, a gallop above East Ilsley which ran for five or six furlongs uphill to a small circular wood, around which you could continue as many times as you were instructed. 'Up and once round' were my orders that morning – but my trusty steed did not appear to hear them. I held him, more or less, up the hill – but then ...
>
> Oh dear, maybe he was looking for Arkle. Round and round and round that wood we went – four times in all, I think – with Flyingbolt not exactly running away but me not exactly in control either! It was only after I had eventually got him to pull up that I learned of the identity of my partner.

Flyingbolt died in 1983 at the age of twenty-four.

Comparisons

Arkle was cursed by comparisons from a very early stage in his career. No sooner had he established himself as a young chaser of immense promise than he was being compared with another in the same category, Mill House (who himself had had to contend with being labelled 'the best since Golden Miller' as soon as he won the 1963 Gold Cup at the age of six). Once Arkle had established himself as indisputably the best of his generation and of recent memory, the key comparison was inevitably with Golden Miller, who had won five Gold Cups and a Grand National.

Golden Miller raced before the age of television, and with each passing year there are fewer people left to make a case for him based on the evidence of their own eyes. Gregory Blaxland, whose excellent book *Golden Miller* was published in 1972, while Arkle was still very fresh in the memory, undertook a lengthy and detailed comparison, bringing in such factors as their respective styles of jumping and how their performance would be affected by the going, before wisely concluding:

Arkle was rarely compared with fellow residents of Bryanstown, but this extraordinary photograph – given to royal photographer Bernard Parkin, but of unknown provenance beyond that – shows Himself being short-headed at level weights.

Arkle in the ratings

The magic of Arkle has nothing to do with arid figures or rankings, but none the less it is instructive to see how he would compare with other horses in some Universal All-Time Handicap. He raced before the days of official ratings – each handicap was then assessed individually – but a reasonably accurate and impartial ranking of the greatest chasers can be taken from Timeform ratings, expressed in pounds. The annual *Chasers and Hurdlers* was first published for the 1975-76 season, but the jumping edition of the Timeform Black Book supplied National Hunt ratings from the early 1960s. Merging these Timeform ratings with pre-Timeform figures calculated for the book *A Century of Champions* by John Randall and Tony Morris, published in 1999, the top ten steeplechasers since the start of the twentieth century are:

212	Arkle (for the season 1965-66)
210	Flyingbolt (1965-66)
192p	Sprinter Sacre (2012-13): *the 'p' indicates that the horse is likely to improve from that mark*
191	Mill House (1963-64), Kauto Star (2009-10)
190	Easter Hero (1928-29)
188	Golden Miller (1933-34)
187	Desert Orchid (1989-90)
186	Dunkirk (1965-66)
184+	Moscow Flyer (2004-05): *the '+' indicates that the horse may be better than this rating*

It is his superiority to his rivals that earns a horse fame, and maybe it is as well that there can be no conclusive means of gauging the exact measure of the superiority or the exact merits of the rivals, for no one who loved either Golden Miller or Arkle could bear to see his glory dimmed – which is why the bland assertion that Arkle was the greatest ever caused a certain amount of pain.

Arkle aficionados themselves felt a sharp stab of pain when Best Mate started prompting comparisons with Himself, first by winning his second Gold Cup in 2003, and then matching Arkle's tally by winning a third in 2004. Hitherto the acclamation of yet another fine young steeplechaser as 'The New Arkle' had been easy enough to laugh off: given time – not too long, usually – that horse's record would founder in comparison with Arkle's. But in strict numerical terms Best Mate equalled Arkle's Gold Cup record, and that was not a matter for debate. (Pain turned to downright outrage when the late Terry Biddlecombe, husband of Best Mate's trainer Henrietta Knight, made a provocative contribution to the discussion after Best Mate's second Gold Cup by observing that Arkle had been 'just a galloper who beat old boats' – though as he had first-hand knowledge of Arkle through having ridden against him, in the 1966 Gold Cup as well as the fateful King George VI Chase, it is fair to assume that the remark was not made entirely seriously.)

As so often, it fell to the Clever Men at Timeform to dowse an inflammatory issue with reason and intelligence. *Chasers and Hurdlers 2002-03*, having noted that 'tiresome references to Arkle have dogged Best Mate's career', proceeded to show with forensic skill that Best Mate's achievements were not remotely in the same league as those of Arkle, whose measure should be taken not from the number of Gold Cups he won, but from his astonishing performances in handicap chases – a category of race which Best Mate had tended to avoid. *Chasers and Hurdlers 2002-03* rests its case with the words:

> If these reminiscences about Arkle conjure up strains of the theme from a brown bread commercial, we apologise – but if comparisons with Arkle had not been made we should not have had to refute them. Arkle's feats were extraordinary by the standards of his day, and nothing short of staggering by those of the present day.

By the time that Timeform's jumps annual for the following year was published, Best Mate had won his third Gold Cup, but beyond repeating that references to Arkle in the context of Best Mate's achievements are 'tiresome', *Chasers and Hurdlers 2003-04* had nothing to add to the persuasive case made a year earlier. Nor did Timeform take kindly to Phil Smith, Head of Handicapping at the British Horseracing Authority, declaring in 2009 that awarding Arkle a rating of 212 pounds was 'a nonsense'. In the essay on Kauto Star in *Chasers and Hurdlers 2008-09*, they briskly direct Smith and fellow agnostics who 'don't have the time to come up with a figure of their own' towards where the Timeform position has been carefully rehearsed in previous essays: on Desert Orchid in the 1988-89 volume, Best Mate in 2002-03, and Denman in 2007-08. Kauto Star himself registered his highest Timeform rating of 191 at the end of the 2009-10 term – the same season that his fourth King George VI Chase victory prompted serious comparisons with Himself. And the exploits of the outstanding Nicky Henderson-trained chaser Sprinter Sacre in the 2012-13 season earned him a Timeform rating of 192p, the highest ranking ever, apart from Tom Dreaper's two great champions – and still twenty pounds short of Arkle.

In any case, comparisons, as Dogberry says when misquoting John Donne in *Much Ado About Nothing*, are odorous. Better to acknowledge that Arkle was matchless, and leave it at that.

Lest we forget

Arkle's fame and name have lived on in all sorts of ways, in addition to the books, paintings, songs, plates, tea towels, sculptures, etc. etc.

Appropriately, Cheltenham racecourse is home to three permanent memorials.

The Arkle statue at Cheltenham racecourse: *top left*, unveiled by the Duchess in March 1972; *bottom left*, en route to its present position; *top right*, saluted in April 1982 on the twenty-fifth anniversary of Arkle's birth by Philip Arkwright (then Clerk of the Course) and Edward Gillespie (then managing director of Cheltenham racecourse) on the left, and Lord Oaksey on the right; *bottom right*, as it is today.

ABOVE
**The original
Arkle Bar.**

The Cotswold Chase, championship event for two-mile novice chasers at the Cheltenham National Hunt Meeting, was renamed the Arkle Trophy in 1969. Tom Dreaper sent two horses across for the inaugural running, with both Straight Fort, ridden by Paddy Woods, and Garrynagree, ridden by Pat Taaffe, going to post. Garrynagree fell when leading at the second last fence, and Straight Fort finished second behind Chatham, trained by Fred Rimell and ridden by Terry Biddlecombe. Dreaper won the third running of the race in 1971 with Alpheus, and the list of subsequent winners features some familiar names, among them Pendil, Alverton, Anaglogs Daughter, Bobsline, Waterloo Boy, Remittance Man, Flagship Uberalles, Moscow Flyer, Azertyioup, Well Chief and Sprinter Sacre. The Arkle Trophy, which was sponsored (appropriately) by Guinness from 1994 to 1999 and now enjoys the support of the *Racing Post*, remains the chasing highlight of the first day of the Cheltenham Festival.

RIGHT
**'The Arkle Bar'
by Tod Ramos.
The painting is
of the old bar.**

Arkle's skeleton
at the Irish
National Stud
at Tully.

Cheltenham is also the home of the statue of Arkle, by Doris Lindner, unveiled in 1972 to overlook the old paddock and subsequently relocated to its position above the current parade ring. The Arkle statue is the favourite meeting place for racegoers, though the less savvy have been confused in recent years by the addition of three other statues at the course: Dawn Run, Golden Miller and Best Mate.

The Arkle Bar at Cheltenham is the most famous, and most atmospheric, racecourse bar in the British Isles. Weeks before the Festival, racegoers start working out their strategy for (a) getting to the counter, (b) getting served with pints of Guinness, and (c) returning said pints to their companions on the other side of the room. The special atmosphere of the Arkle Bar derives from its doubling as an informal Arkle Museum. In display cases and around the walls are preserved cuttings, photographs, letters and other memorabilia: of special interest are one of the X-rays of the broken hoof; the Cheltenham number board entry for 'P. TAAFFE'; the Braille letter to Arkle reproduced on page 156; and two snapshots of Arkle at Sandown Park for the 1965 Whitbread Gold Cup, taken by one of his legion of young fans, twelve-year-old Edward Gillespie – later managing director of the course and the brains behind the pre-eminent racing event of the calendar.

But not all Arkle memorials have met with universal approval, and the decision taken in 1976 to exhume his body from his grave of six and a half years, clean off his bones and display his skeleton in the new museum at the Irish National Stud at

Tully, not far from The Curragh in County Kildare, remains controversial. Michael Osborne, then manager of the stud, approached the Duchess, received her permission, and the grave was opened. The details of how Arkle was dug up and his remains transported to Tully in three plastic sacks in the back of a Mini Minor are not for the squeamish – one of the staff at the Museum remembers how 'they took on a good deal of whiskey' while the reassembly work was being carried out – and certainly not pleasant reading for Arkle fans. While the *Irish Independent* was surely over-egging the pudding when writing that the skeleton would be, 'For devotees and necrophiles alike, a unique insight into mighty Arkle – an irresistible peek, as it were, beneath the bonnet of a very special racing machine', the display does at least

---

Arkle, painted by Wendy Walsh, appeared on the 18 pence stamp issued by the Irish Post Office in October 1981 in a set of five stamps, part of a series depicting the flora and fauna of Ireland. Arkle was one of two Thoroughbreds in the set; the other was Ballymoss, who appeared on the 24 pence stamp. The other three stamps showed the show jumper Boomerang, the Irish Draught stallion King Of Diamonds, and the Connemara Pony stallion Coosheen Finn.

leave the visitor with an immediate and lasting impression of the depth of Arkle's rib cage, suggesting the unusual size of the heart and other vital organs which those ribs protected. The museum, with Arkle its centrepiece, was formally opened in February 1977.

Michael Osborne had few doubts about the rectitude of displaying the great horse in this way:

> We still get letters for Arkle and most people agree we have done the right thing by making a focal point for all the songs and poems about him. But we have had one or two letters saying we should have let the dead rest in peace.

The latter view was shared by Pat Taaffe, who remarked: 'I hated seeing his frame up there. I couldn't look at him for long.'

Arkle's image has become pervasive in Ireland. More than once he has appeared on stamps: in October 1981, in a series celebrating the flora and fauna of his native country, and again in 2002, in a set marking the 250th anniversary of the birth of steeplechasing, when Arkle was one of a quartet of famous Irish jumpers, along with L'Escargot, Dawn Run and Istabraq. There are displays of photographs, cuttings and other memorabilia at Leopardstown racecourse and in countless pubs around the country. Arkle and Pat Taaffe adorn the weathervane on the building which Tattersalls Ireland occupied at Ballsbridge before the company moved to Fairyhouse.

And the beat goes on. In 2006 the principal exhibition at the National Horseracing Museum in Newmarket was 'Arkle and the Duchess', billed as 'the story of one of Britain's wealthiest women and the greatest steeplechaser the world has ever seen, a story of coincidences, good fortune and equine courage.' A wide array of memorabilia, paintings and photographs were brought together to form a Tutankhamun's tomb of delights for Arkle fans, and the exhibition was opened by the irrepressible Paddy Woods, who rode the horse every day and whose infectious joy in having been so close to Arkle burned as brightly as ever.

The following year the *Racing Post* marked the fiftieth anniversary of Arkle's birth with a double-page spread celebrating the horse and his legacy, and the same day Cheltenham racecourse paid appropriate homage by placing a laurel wreath on the Doris Lindner statue and selling racegoers fizz in plastic champagne flutes bearing the simple inscription 'Arkle: 19 April 1957 – 19 April 2007'.

Later in 2007 Bernard Parkin, who had recently retired as official photographer at Cheltenham racecourse, put together a framed montage of his famed Arkle photographs, signed by every jockey who had ridden Himself in a race: Pat Taaffe (whose signature Parkin had secured twenty-five years earlier), Paddy Woods, Mark Hely-Hutchinson, Liam McLoughlin and T. P. Burns. This unique and unrepeatable item was auctioned at the annual lunch of the Sir Peter O'Sullevan Charitable Trust in November 2007 and fetched £9,000, while further evidence of the desirability of Arkle collectables came in November 2010 with the Graham Budd Auctions sale of sporting items at Sotheby's in London.

Star turn was the saddle on which Pat Taaffe had ridden Himself in every one of his twenty-six steeplechases, and had been originally auctioned at the Anglo-American Sporting Club dinner held to honour Arkle in 1966. No doubt about it: this was a holy relic, and after Nick O'Toole of Naas, doyen of Arkle memorabilia collectors, had secured it for £11,000, it was returning to Ireland. At the time of writing the saddle has pride of place in a display of Arkle memorabilia at Straffan Antiques in Straffan, County Kildare, in the very heart of Arkle country and only a couple of miles from Bryanstown.

The continuing importance of Arkle as an Irish icon was underlined when the Queen paid a visit to Ireland in May 2011. Given the monarch's love of horseracing, it was natural that she should spend some time at the Irish National Stud at Tully, and while there she was introduced to a group of people who had played their parts in the Arkle story, including Peter Reynolds of Ballymacoll Stud; Alison Baker, who had given the young horse his early education; Jim Dreaper, who took over from his father at Greenogue; Paddy Woods, who rode Arkle every day; T. P. Burns, who partnered Arkle in the horse's only Flat race; and Willie Robinson, veteran of those memorable duels with Mill House.

The same group of people featured on the itinerary for 'The Arkle

RACING POST

Friday, February 20, 2004 · WWW.RACINGPOST.CO.UK · £1.20
Issue No. 5,717

EVERYONE OUT FOR HIMSELF

The waiting's over. Arkle, the best steeplechaser of all time, is also the most popular horse of all time, as voted for by you. Appreciation, pages 11-17

OPPOSITE PAGE

On 21 September 2004 a quantity of Arkle memorabilia, previously the property of the late Anne, Duchess of Westminster, was auctioned by Christie's at Woburn Abbey, Bedfordshire. Lots included the Duchess's binoculars; a post-Arkle set of her racing colours; assorted books, paintings and sculptures; a bottle of vintage cognac bottled in memory of Arkle and presented with the 1970 Hennessy Gold Cup; and this lot of miscellaneous memorabilia including six tea-towels, a tee-shirt and a sweatshirt. The collection was expected to sell for around £20,000 but fetched nearly £52,000 for charities which the Duchess had supported. Top earner was a Lionel Edwards painting of Arkle at Cheltenham, which went for nearly £15,000.

The Arkle Pilgrims outside box 7 at Greenogue in October 2013, presenting a framed portrait of Himself to Jim Dreaper. Behind the picture is the Dreapers' daughter Lynsey, with Johnny Lumley directly behind Jim, and Paddy Woods on the extreme right.

Pilgrimage' in October 2013, when – in return for substantial donations to the O'Sullevan Trust, and thanks to the generosity of Michael O'Leary of Ryanair and Tom Egan of the Horse and Jockey Hotel in Tipperary – a small team of devotees was taken by the author of this book, accompanied by Nick O'Toole, to visit the major Arkle shrines.

At Ballymacoll Stud the pilgrims stood in the foaling box where Arkle had first drawn breath, then repaired to the house for a perusal of various Arkle-related documents which Peter Reynolds had unearthed. Among these was the menu for a dinner at the Shelbourne Hotel held to celebrate Tom Dreaper's seventy-fifth birthday, which included 'Petite Marmite à l'Arkle' (note: not the Marmite which you either love or hate) and 'Flyingbolt Gateaux', the recipe for which one pilgrim vowed to spend the rest of his life researching.

At Malahow they defied the rain and the heavy going to retrace Arkle's hoofprints in Quarry Field, and were treated royally by Alison Baker and her family – as they were by Jim Dreaper and family at Greenogue, where they were joined for lunch by Paddy Woods and Johnny Lumley. Then to Straffan Antiques to view the display of Arkle memorabilia.

The next two days included visits to Bryanstown, to see where Himself retired, died and was buried; to The Curragh, to visit T. P. Burns; to the Irish National Stud, to view Arkle's skeleton and talk to Sally Carroll, who has graphic memories of how she and INS colleagues scrubbed the bones with hydrogen peroxide, then reassembled the horse's infrastructure 'like the pieces of a jigsaw'; and to Navan,

186

where Arkle registered his first win in January 1962, and where T. P. rode him to win the Donoughmore Plate.

In addition to those key Arkle shrines, the pilgrims were taken to the Bronze Art Foundry in north Dublin, and thereby hangs a tale.

For some years Jim Dreaper and a group of similarly committed individuals have been working towards establishing in the centre of Ashbourne, close to Greenogue, a major work of public art: a larger-than-life-size bronze of Arkle and Pat Taaffe, by the renowned equine sculptor Emma MacDermott. Various fund-raising initiatives were put in place – including in 2011 a memorable evening at Bellewstown races, with none other than Lester Piggott as the guest of honour – and eventually the project got the go-ahead. By late 2013 the statue was essentially finished, but bureaucratic hold-ups were delaying its installation, and the bronze itself was put into a siding – or rather, into the Bronze Art Foundry, where the Arkle Pilgrims were able to gaze upon this wonder as it sheltered amid the hustle and bustle.

Arkle in waiting: the Emma MacDermott bronze of Himself and Pat Taaffe in the Bronze Art Foundry, October 2013.

As this book goes to press the expectation is that the bronze will be installed in Ashbourne on 19 April 2014 – fifty-seven years to the day since Himself was born, and a fitting celebration of Arkle's place in the history of this area.

But it has not all been good news. A representation to Cambridge University Press that Arkle should be included in the *Dictionary of Irish Biography* which that estimable institution was in the process of compiling has fallen on deaf ears thus far, as has the suggestion that Ascot racecourse should rectify the shocking omission of Arkle from the list of distinguished winners on the royal heath who have had their names enshrined in bars in the new grandstand.

A perfect encapsulation of the spirit of Arkle occurs in the video *Arkle: The legend*. The eccentrically coiffed Twinny Byrne, one of the great characters of Irish racecourses in the 1960s, is being interviewed by a plummy-voiced English television journalist about the effect of Arkle's success:

'What does it mean to the local people here?'
'Sure, they think there's no horse in the world like him.'
'But you've had good horses in Ireland before.'
'No, you hadn't one as good as him, but – hadn't one as good as Arkle.'
'Tell us what the conversation's like in the evening here, in the pub.'
'It's only ArkleArkleArkleArkleArkle – Arkle, that's all – Arkle the whole way.'

The Racing Record

Arkle's racing career in summary

1961/62

Date	Course	Race	Weight	Jockey	Result	Odds
Dec 9	Mullingar	Lough Ennel Maiden (NH Flat)	11-4	Mr M Hely-Hutchinson	3rd	5-1
Dec 26	Leopardstown	Greystones Maiden (NH Flat)	10-11	Mr M Hely-Hutchinson	4th	5-1
Jan 20	Navan	Bective Novice Hurdle	11-5	L McLoughlin	WON	20-1
Mar 10	Naas	Rathconnel Handicap Hurdle	11-2	P Taaffe	WON	2-1F
Apr 14	Baldoyle	Balbriggan Handicap Hurdle	10-1	L McLoughlin	unpl	6-1
Apr 24	Fairyhouse	New Handicap Hurdle	10-5	L McLoughlin	4th	8-1

1962/63

Date	Course	Race	Weight	Jockey	Result	Odds
Oct 17	Dundalk	Wee County Handicap Hurdle	11-13	P Taaffe	WON	6-1
Oct 24	Gowran Park	President's Handicap Hurdle	10-5	P Woods	WON	9-2JF
Nov 17	Cheltenham	Honeybourne Chase	11-11	P Taaffe	WON	11-8F
Feb 23	Leopardstown	Milltown Chase	12-11	P Taaffe	WON	1-2F
Mar 12	Cheltenham	Broadway Novices' Chase	12-4	P Taaffe	WON	4-9F
Apr 15	Fairyhouse	Power Gold Cup	12-5	P Taaffe	WON	2-7F
May 1	Punchestown	John Jameson Gold Cup	12-4	P Taaffe	WON	4-7F

1963/64

Date	Course	Race	Weight	Jockey	Result	Odds
Oct 9	Navan	Donoughmore Maiden (Flat)	9-6	T P Burns	WON	4-6F
Oct 24	Gowran Park	Carey's Cottage H'cap Chase	11-13	P Taaffe	WON	4-7F
Nov 30	Newbury	Hennessy Gold Cup	11-9	P Taaffe	3rd	5-2
Dec 26	Leopardstown	Christmas Handicap Chase	12-0	P Taaffe	WON	4-7F
Jan 30	Gowran Park	Thyestes Handicap Chase	12-0	P Taaffe	WON	4-6F
Feb 15	Leopardstown	Leopardstown Handicap Chase	12-0	P Taaffe	WON	4-7F
Mar 7	Cheltenham	Cheltenham Gold Cup	12-0	P Taaffe	WON	7-4
Mar 30	Fairyhouse	Irish Grand National	12-0	P Taaffe	WON	1-2F

1964/65

Date	Course	Race	Weight	Jockey	Result	Odds
Oct 29	Gowran Park	Carey's Cottage H'cap Chase	12-0	P Taaffe	WON	1-5F
Dec 5	Newbury	Hennessy Gold Cup	12-7	P Taaffe	WON	5-4F
Dec 12	Cheltenham	Massey-Ferguson Gold Cup	12-10	P Taaffe	3rd	8-11F
Feb 27	Leopardstown	Leopardstown Handicap Chase	12-7	P Taaffe	WON	8-11F
Mar 11	Cheltenham	Cheltenham Gold Cup	12-0	P Taaffe	WON	30-100F
Apr 24	Sandown	Whitbread Gold Cup	12-7	P Taaffe	WON	4-9F

1965/66

Date	Course	Race	Weight	Jockey	Result	Odds
Nov 6	Sandown	Gallaher Gold Cup	12-7	P Taaffe	WON	4-9F
Nov 27	Newbury	Hennessy Gold Cup	12-7	P Taaffe	WON	1-6F
Dec 27	Kempton	King George VI Chase	12-0	P Taaffe	WON	1-7F
Mar 1	Leopardstown	Leopardstown Handicap Chase	12-7	P Taaffe	WON	1-5F
Mar 17	Cheltenham	Cheltenham Gold Cup	12-0	P Taaffe	WON	1-10F

1966/67

Date	Course	Race	Weight	Jockey	Result	Odds
Nov 26	Newbury	Hennessy Gold Cup	12-7	P Taaffe	2nd	4-6F
Dec 14	Ascot	SGB Handicap Chase	12-7	P Taaffe	WON	1-3F
Dec 27	Kempton	King George VI Chase	12-0	P Taaffe	2nd	2-9F

The main statistics

Arkle

- ■ ran in 35 races, winning 27

- ■ finished second twice, third three times, fourth twice and unplaced once

- ■ won £78,464 5s. 6d. in prize money

- ■ was ridden in races by five different jockeys:
  Pat Taaffe (28 rides: won 24, second twice, third twice)
  Liam McLoughlin (three rides: one win)
  Paddy Woods (one ride: one win)
  T. P. Burns (one ride: one win)
  Mark Hely-Hutchinson (two rides: no wins; one third; one fourth)

- ■ ran in 26 steeplechases, 6 hurdle races, two National Hunt Flat Races ('bumpers') and one regular Flat race

- ■ was beaten in his 26 steeplechases by only six horses: Mill House and Happy Spring in the 1963 Hennessy Gold Cup; Flying Wild and Buona Notte in the 1964 Massey-Ferguson Gold Cup; Stalbridge Colonist in the 1966 Hennessy Gold Cup; and Dormant in the 1966 King George VI Chase

- ■ never fell in a race

- ■ was unbeaten in eleven steeplechases in Ireland

- ■ ran 20 races in Ireland and 15 in England

- ■ raced at 14 separate courses: Cheltenham (6 races), Leopardstown (6), Newbury (4), Gowran Park (4), Fairyhouse (3), Kempton Park (2), Sandown Park (2), Navan (2), Ascot (1), Mullingar (1), Dundalk (1), Naas (1), Punchestown (1) and Baldoyle (1)

- ■ started odds on in 22 of his 26 steeplechases

- ■ carried an average weight of approximately 12st 4lb in the 16 handicap steeplechases he contested

- ■ returned his longest starting price when winning the Bective Novice Hurdle at Navan on 20 January 1962, his first victory, at 20-1

- ■ returned his shortest starting price when winning his third Gold Cup at Cheltenham on 17 March 1966 at 1-10

- ■ recorded his longest winning distance when beating Dormant 'a distance' in the King George VI Chase at Kempton Park, 27 December 1965

- ■ recorded his shortest winning distance when beating Height O' Fashion a neck in the Leopardstown Chase, 1 March 1966

The complete record

Reproduced here are the entries for each of Arkle's races in *Chaseform* – and, in one case, *Raceform* – the formal record of racing in Britain and Ireland.

Those unfamiliar with the arcane mysteries of the form book might need a brief word of explanation:

The top line of each entry provides: reference number of race within the form book (thus the first race listed was 968b); title and nature of race (in the first entry, the Lough Ennel Plate for maidens – horses who had not yet won a race – to be ridden by amateur jockeys); prize money to winner; distance of race; scheduled time of race (and actual time of 'off' in parentheses if the race started late).

The name of each runner is preceded as appropriate by the form book reference number of the last race in which that horse took part that season (race 688b in the case of Lady Flame: she came third); the horse's age and weight (in the Lough Ennel Plate, Arkle was a four-year-old carrying 11 stone 4 pounds, with a five-pound allowance granted in view of the inexperience of his jockey); the name of the jockey; for the leading finishers, the distance between the horse and the horse who finished immediately in front of him (Arkle was eight lengths behind Kilspindie at Mullingar) and his finishing position.

Beneath the list of runners come the starting prices ('SP'). In the Lough Ennel Plate winner Lady Flame started 4-1 joint favourite with Hal's Son; Arkle was fourth market choice on 5-1. Then are given the Tote returns, which for Irish races include a 2s. 6d, stake, and for English races a four-shilling stake.

Next comes the name of the owner (Mrs C. Ronaldson in the case of Lady Flame) and trainer (C. Ronaldson), the number of runners (17 at Mullingar) and the time of the race (5 minutes 3 seconds).

The record of the races run in England provide additional information, notably comments about the individual horse's appearance and performance: thus in Arkle's first steeplechase, the Honeybourne Chase at Cheltenham – race 9 below – the comment about him is: 'j.w.: led 10th: led 3 out: sn clr: smoothly', which translates as 'jumped well; led 10th [fence]; led 3 out; soon clear; smoothly'. In the entries below, translations are provided for Arkle.

The English entries also note fluctuations in the betting (in the Honeybourne Chase, Arkle returned a starting price of 11-8 but in the racecourse betting ring his price had been as long as 6-4 and as short as evens), and relate the winning time to the average for that course and distance (in the Honeybourne Chase, Arkle's time of 5 minutes 17 2/5 seconds was 4 3/5 seconds under average).

In the going descriptions, 'yielding' is equivalent to the current 'good to soft'.

1961-62 season

1

Mullingar

Saturday 9 December 1961

going: heavy

Lough Ennel Maiden Plate
(National
Hunt Flat Race)

2 miles 1 furlong 160 yards

*Arkle started at 5-1 and finished 3rd
behind Lady Flame and Kilspindie,
beaten 1 length and 8 lengths.*

```
968b  LOUGH ENNEL PTE (Mdn) (Amateurs) £133 2m 1f 160y 3.30
688b³ LADY FLAME 6-12-0 ... C Ronaldson ...............——1
      Kilspindie 4-11-9 ........ J R Bryce-Smith ..........1.2
      Arkle 4-11-4‡5 ........... M Hely-Hutchinson ........8.3
661   Why Worry 8-11-9‡5 ... J C Ford ..................2.4
664b  King Desmond 5-12-0        907 b Cypriot 6-12-0
      A Cameron                         K Prendergast
829b  Serving Line 4-11-9        186b³ Frenchman 5-12-0
      K Woods                           E D Delany
      Prudent Gertle 7-11-9‡5    664b Soldropina 4-11-9‡5
      P M O'Roarke                      D J Hayes
688b⁴ Hal's Son 5-11-9‡5         688b Painter's Cottage 5-11-9‡5
      P D McCreery                      F J Lacy
688b  Mother Courage 5-12-0            Carbury Castle 4-11-5‡5
                                        S Kirk
      First of the Cheyneys II   827 Deerstalker II 6-11-9‡5
          6-11-9‡5 N Hanley             J P Daly(p.u)
611b  Oleins Nut 6-12-0 P J Stokes
S.P.: 4 LADY FLAME, Hal's Son, 9/2 Kilspindie, 5 Arkle, 6 Mother
Courage, 13/2 King Desmond, 8 Cypriot, 10 Serving Line. 100/7 Ors.
Tote 11/6: 5/- 5/- 6/6. Mrs C Ronaldson (C Ronaldson) 17 Rn 5m 3
```

2

Leopardstown

Tuesday 26 December 1961

going: good

Greystones Flat Race (National
Hunt Flat Race for maidens)

2 miles

Arkle started at 5-1 and finished 4th.

```
1038b    GREYSTONES FLAT RACE (Mdn) £202   2m   3.40
493b² ARTIST'S TREASURE 4-11-2 Mr K Prendergast ..........——1
      Glyndebourne 6-11-7 .... Mr C Ronaldson ............5.2
      Flying Wild 5-11-2† ... Mr J Gilsenon .............2.3
968b³ Arkle 4-10-7† ......... Mr M Hely Hutchinson .......4
829b³ One Seven Seven 5-11-7       Holy Mackerel 4-11-2
      Mr A Lillingstone                Mr A Cameron
                                 Fursey 4-11-9‡   T P Burns
968b  Cypriot 6-12-0‡ ...D Page     1000b Gosley 4-10-11†
968b² Kilspindie 4-11-2                 Mr H de Bromhead
      Mr J R Bryce-Smith
            ‡ 7lb Rider's penalty added
            † 5lb Rider's allowance deducted
S.P.: 6/4 Glyndebourne, 2 ARTIST'S TREASURE, 5 Arkle, 7 One Seven
Seven, Kilspindie, 10 Gosley, 100/7 Ors. Tote 11/6: 4/6 4/6 36/6.
Mr J Wood (C Magnier) 10 Rn                            3m 57
```

3

Navan

Saturday 20 January 1962

going: heavy

Bective Novice Hurdle

3 miles

*Arkle started at 20-1 and won by 1½
lengths from Blunts Cross.*

```
1176     BECTIVE NOVICE HURDLE £133   3m   3.45
1038b⁴ ARKLE 5-11-5 ........ L McLoughlin ...............——1
1055* Blunts Cross 9-11-12‡5 .. Lord P Beresford ........1.2.2
1065* Kerforo 8-12-3 ......... P Taaffe .................8.3
1125  Sharptapa 9-11-13‡5 .... Mr G Gault ...............4
1065  Brittas 9-11-12‡5 J Hogan   1050b Solsboro 6-11-4‡5 D Burke
 999  Grand Princess 7-11-12‡5        Grand Destiny a-11-9 J Cash
      Mr J H Agnew   1063 Moment's Thoughts 7-11-9
      Shangraloo 7-11-4‡5               T P Burns
          B Hannon   827 Blazes Kate 10-11-4‡5
1122  Jungle Folly 6-11-9              M Cunningham
      R Coonan   1122 Irish Day 6-11-9  A Redmond
 557b Bright Endeavour 5-11-5    998 Beau Bear 7-11-12‡5
      Mr G Rooney                      Mr J Stinson
1066b Bidale 6-11-9 ...T E Hvde  1034 Lord Snottle 6-12-3 A Duff
 73²  Another Fort 8-11-12‡5           Priscilla's Choice 9-11-4‡5
      Mr J G Bredin                        J McKennan
1044b⁴ Sea Swallow 5-11-13       1034 Irish Drake 8-11-4‡5
      J Magee                          P Coates
1125  Irish Reel 9-12-3         1062⁴ Snow Finch 8-12-3
      C Finnegan                       Mr G Dunwoody(p.u)
1051  Tim Frazer 5-11-13        1040³ Hal Baythorn 8-11-9
      W J Brennan                      T Taaffe(p.u)
1056b Captain Moonlight 7-12-3   1000b My Gift 6-11-4‡5
      Mr A Cameron                     L O'Brien(p.u)
S.P.: Evens Kerforo, 4 Tim Frazer, 8 Sea Swallow, 100/8 Blunts Cross,
Brittas, Hal Baythorn, 100/7 Sharptapa, 100/6 Moment's Thoughts, Snow
Finch, 20 ARKLE & Ors. Tote 124/6: 13/- 8/- 3/6. Duchess of
Westminster (T Dreaper) 27 Rn                         6m 40
```

```
1571      RATHCONNEL H'CAP HURDLE £202     2m        3.30
1176* ARKLE  5-11-2  ...........  PTaaffe  .........................—1
1299 Soltest  6-9-4‡5  ..........  MJHogan  .....................4.2
1230* Gainstown  8-10-6  ......  TTaaffe  ......................6.3
1475⁴ Mariner's View 7-9-10 ..  GWRobinson  ..................4
                                 12992 Fawcett's Bridge
          MrEDDelany               12-11-0‡5  MrJGBrowne
10413 SanMarco 9-10-8 RCoonnan 14814 Silverhill  4-9-5!‡5  MEnnis
14713 Speckled Curtains 8-9-9    1441 Packed Home 7-10-9
          FShortt                                   PPowell
S.P.: 2 ARKLE. 4 Mariner'sView.PackedHome. 5 Fawcett'sBridge.
7 SanMarco.Gainstown. 8 Oou-de-Bee,SpeckledCurtains, 100/8 Ors.
Tote 11/6: 5/- 10/6 9/-. Duchess of Westminster (T Dreaper) 10
Rn                                              4m 21.8
```

4

Naas

Saturday 10 March 1962

going: soft

Rathconnel Handicap Hurdle

2 miles

Arkle started 2-1 favourite and won by 4 lengths from Soltest.

```
1878      BALBRIGGAN H'CAP HURDLE £387 1〕s   2m        4.0
1749 STORMING  5-10-8  ......  ARedmond  ......................—1
1042* Snow Trix 7-10-5  .......  FCarroll  .................1⅝.2
1604 Rainlough 6-11-10  ........  TTaaffe  ................hd.3
1749⁴ Moonsun 5-10-12  .........  RWilliams  ................4
1648 Soltest 6-9-2‡5 ..MJHogan 1767 Gun Smoke 6-10-6‡5
14712 Arbeamar 7-9-7 TCarberry              MMurphy
14852 Narcotic Nora 8-10-11  1472* K.O. 5-9-91 CFinnegan
          TRegan     1600 High Tempo 6-10-0
16022 Fortria 10-12-7 ..PTaaffe              GWRobinson
15723 Last Link 6-9-3‡5 PWoods 1646 Snow Finch 8-9-8 THyde
1410 Supersede 4-9-9 ..ADuff 1475 Trench House 9-9-9‡5
1571* Arkle 5-10-1 LMcLoughlin              PCoates
1285b* Fair Gina 6-9-7 CKinane 1533 GoldenAli 8-9-10 TPBurns
S.P.: 9/2 Moonsun. 6 Arkle. 7 HighTempo. 10 STORMING. K.O.
100/8   NarcoticNora.Fortria.SnowTrix.  100/7  LastLink,GoldenAli.
100/6 FairGina, 20 Ors. Tote 34/6: 11/6 24/- 37/-. Mr J Brady
(P Norris) 18 Rn                                 3m 52.9
```

5

Baldoyle

Saturday 14 April 1962

going: good

Balbriggan Handicap Hurdle

2 miles

Arkle started 6-1 second favourite and finished unplaced.

```
2060        NEW H'CAP HURDLE £742     2m        3.40
17493 ANTHONY  6-10-10  ......  FCarroll  ...................—1
18783 Rainlough 6-12-0  .......  PTaaffe  ..................2.2
      Quita Que 13-10-2  ......  GWRobinson  ..............2.3
1878 Arkle  5-10-5  ..........  LMcLoughlin  ...............4
1603 Ferry Boat 5-9-7 CFinnegan 1589* Tripacer 4-10-5 TCarberry
1878 Gun Smoke 6-10-6‡5      1749 Gainstown 8-9-7 RCoonan
          MJMurphy      1878 Supersede 4-9-13 ...ADuff
S.P.: 11/4 ANTHONY. 4 Rainlough. 5 FerryBoat. 8 Arkle,Tripacer.
10 QuitaQue.GunSmoke. 100/7 Ors. Tote 7/6: 3/6 5/- 5/-. Ld
Fingall (J Brogan) 9 Rn                          4m 9.2
```

6

Fairyhouse

Tuesday 24 April 1962

going: good

New Handicap Hurdle

2 miles

Arkle started at 8-1 and finished fourth.

1962-63 season

7

Dundalk

Wednesday 16 October 1962

going: good

Wee County Handicap Hurdle

2 miles 216 yards

Arkle started at 6-1 and won by 6 lengths from Killykeen Star.

```
460    WEE COUNTY H'CAP HURDLE £163    2m 216y    3.30
       ARKLE 5-11-13 .......... PTaaffe ..................—1
2814 Killykeen Star 6-10-8 ... JRafferty ...............6.2
3914 Gosley  5-9-12 .......... THyde ...................1.3
     Inniskeen 7-10-4 ........ TRegan ..................10.4
       Gainstown 8-10-7 RCoonan    391 The Drummer 10-9-8
391 Panther Ledge  14-9-6‡‡5                          JMagee
           MrJStinson            Hindu Word 7-9-13‡5
                                              TO'Sullivan
       High Tempo 6-11-3‡5      Jungle Trix 8-12-1 FCarroll
           MMurphy
S.P.: 6/4 Gosley, 3 KillykeenStar. 6 ARKLE. 8 JungleTrix. 10 Innis-
keen. 100/8 Ors. Tote 15/-: 3/- 3/- 3/-. Duchess of Westminster (T
Dreaper) 10 Rn                                        4m 7.5
```

8

Gowran Park

Wedensday 24 October 1962

going: good

President's Handicap Hurdle

2 miles

Arkle started 9-2 joint-favourite and won by 5 lengths from Silver Green.

```
525      PRESIDENT'S H'CAP HURDLE £432    2m      4.0
460* ARKLE 5-10-5 (4x) ...... PWoods ................—1
     Silver Green 6-11-3 ..... RCoonan ...............5.2
483 Soltest 6-9-7 ........... JFlannery ...........4.3
412* The Shining One 7-9-11 (4x) CKinane .............1.4
334* Height o' Fashion 5-12-0    391 Rainlough 6-11-12 TTaaffe
           TLacy              434 Narcotic Nora 8-10-9
3912 Tripacer  4-10-13 MEnnis                         TRegan
483* Prince Hatton 10-10-3   1612 K.O.  5-9-12 ...CFinnegan
       (7x)      PPowell       Coniston 6-11-2 ..TPBurns
328 Jungle Folly 6-9-7  THyde    Coloured Cowboy  7-10-9
     FitzForest 5-9-10 JRafferty              LMcLoughlin
3314 Buckaroo 5-9-7 ARedmond   483 Tina Berg 6-9-7
4833 Breakers Hill 6-10-0                     MrPO'Donnell
           JBrabston          Ballygowan 8-10-0 ADuff
     Owen'sSedge9-11-1 JMagee 3344 Ross Sea 6-11-3
     Fredith's Son 11-11-2                   MrWMcLernon
           FShortt
S.P.: 9/2 ARKLE, RossSea. 5 HeightO'Fashion, 9 Tripacer. 10 Conis-
ton. 100/8 K.O. Buckaroo 100/7 PrinceHatton. 20 Ors. Tote 10/6:
7/- 18/- 49/-. Duchess of Westminster (T Dreaper) 21 Rn    4m 2
```

9

Cheltenham (Old Course)

Saturday 17 November 1962

going: good

Honeybourne Chase

about 2 miles 4 furlongs

Arkle 'jumped well; led 10th; led 3 out; soon clear; smoothly'; started 11-8 favourite and won by 20 lengths from Billy Bumps.

```
715    HONEYBOURNE CHASE £680   abt 2m 4f    1.0  (1.1)
525* ARKLE 5-11-11 ..PTaaffe j.w: led 10th: led 3 out: sn
                        alr: smoothly .................—1
674 BillyBumps 8-12-0 Beasley j.w: hdwy fr 8th: led 12th to
                         3 out: mo ch w wnr .........20.2
5433 Milo 7-12-0 ...MrIBalding bhd whn mstk 8th: hdwy fr
                         3 out: nvr nrr .............4.3
5162 Kilvara6-11-9‡5 LWalthew prom to 12th: grad wknd ...11½.4
    Time 7-12-0 MScudamore nt trble ldrs ..............6.5
    Tim Frazer 5-11-11 Mellor led to 10th: bhd fr 12th ...8.6
5862 Trews 11-12-0 Brookshaw prom to 10th ..............7
642 Border Ring 5-11-11  SHayhurst  t.o whn p.u bef
                        last .......................0
6804 Fan Tan 5-11-8‡3 Richards prom to 10th: t.o whn p.u bef
                        last .......................0
5763 Hop On 5-11-11 EHarty blnd 5th: bhd whn fell 3 out ...0
650 Dargent 6-12-0 ...WRees w ldrs whn fell 6th ..........0
645* Jomsviking 5-11-11 JKing fell 3rd .................0
S.P.: 11/8 ARKLE (6/4—evens). 11/2 Jomsviking(op4/1). 6 Milo
(op10/1). 8 Dargent(op5/1). 100/8 BillyBumps(op8/1). 100/6 Tim
Frazer. 25 Ors. Tote 8/10: 6/- 19/8 6/4. Duchess of Westminster
(T Dreaper. in Ireland) 12 Rn    5m 17 2/5 (4 3/5 under av)
```

10

Leopardstown
Saturday 23 February 1963
going: yielding
Milltown Chase
2 miles

Arkle 'jumped well; slight lead 3 out; quickened flat; very easily'; started 1-2 favourite and won by 8 lengths from Rubor.

```
1104    MILLTOWN CHASE £461 10s    2m         4.25
 715* ARKLE    6-12-11  PTaaffe j.w: slt ld 3 out: qcknd flat: v
                                 easily ....................—1
9203 Rubor   5-11-3  ...DWeeden jnd ldr 6th: disp ld 3 out: w
                                 wnr last: one pce ........8.2
 947² Moonsun 6-11-11 JRafferty prom fr 7th: cl up 2 out: no
                                 imprssn .................5.3
10572 D'YouMind 6-11-11 THyde cl up 7th: effrt 3 out: wknd
                                 next ....................3.4
 568* ChelseaSet 7-11-11 FShortt w ldr 1st: cl up to 6th: sme
                                 late hdwy ...............3.5
 678 Flamecap 6-11-11 FCarroll nrst fin ................2.6
 949 Rue de Paris 6-11-11
                      SMellor w ldrs tl wknd fr 3 out ...
1057* One Seven Seven 7-12-7
                      TCarberry j.w: led to 7th: wknd qckly next 0
1079 Fortinbras7-11-6‡5 SBarker mstks 1st: n.d aftr .........0
1079* Hyland Patrol 8-12-2‡5  in rear to 6th: w ldrs wknd
                      BHannon    2nd & ev ch whn fell 2 out 0
10843 High Tempo 7-11-6‡5
                      MMurphy in rear whn fell 5th ........0
 912 Fernbank 5-10-12‡3
                      JMalone in rear whn fell 2nd ........0
  Also ran:—             1088 Hartlands 6-11-11 CKinane
 7723 Ferry Boat 6-11-11  10742 Rainbow Battle 7-11-11
                      RCoonan                  CFinnegan
S.P.: 1/2 ARKLE, 7 ChelseaSet, 100/9 OneSevenSeven, 100/8 D'You
Mind.Moonsun, 100/7 HighTempo, 100/6 Rubor, 20 Ors. Tote 4/6:
4/- 16/- 5/-. Duchess of Westminster (T Dreaper) 15 Rn    4m 16.2
```

11

Cheltenham (New Course)
Tuesday 12 March 1963
going: very soft
Broadway Chase
3 miles and a few yards

Arkle 'led 2 out; very easily'; started 4-9 favourite and won by 20 lengths from Jomsviking.

```
1184    BROADWAY CHASE £1360   3m & few yds   4.40 (4.41)
1104* ARKLE 6-12-4 ...PTaaffe led 2 out: v easily ........—1
 950* Jomsviking 6-11-8 JKing mstks 5th & 17th: chasd wnr
                             fr 2 out: no imprssn ......20.2
 961 Brasher 7-11-8 JFitzGerald led 10th to 17th: r.o one pce
                             fr 2 out ....................4.3
1152⁴ Border Flight 8-12-1
                      DNicholson no hdwy fr 17th .........6.4
933² Red Tide 6-11-8 ...WRees prom to 16th: stdly wknd ...2.5
 759 Uncle Coke 5-11-0
                      MScudamore nvr nrr .............bad.6
  97 Boutinskino 7-11-8 WFisher led to 9th: wknd qckly ......0
2013 Badreddine 6-11-8 Bassett a.in rear: t.o .............0
7152 BillyBumps 9-11-8 Beasley t.o ......................0
8783 Legion Star 9-11-8
                      PBroderick t.o ....................0
 716 Givus Light 7-11-8
                      TBrookshaw blnd 2nd: a.bhd: t.o ....0
 938 Darien 5-11-0 ....DMould prom to 10th: t.o whn p.u bef
                             17th .......................0
1152 BorderRing 6-11-8 Hayhurst prom to 15th: sn wknd: p.u ...0
11453 Just My Mark 10-11-8
                      EKelly fell 5th ...................0
 950 Lowe II 9-11-8 ...SRooney fell 5th .................0
S.P.: 4/9 ARKLE (1/2—2/5), 11/2 Jomsviking(9/2—6/1), 100/7 Billy
Bumps(op10/1), 100/6 BorderFlight(op100/7), Brasher(op100/8), 20
GivusLight, 33 JustMyMark.BorderRing, 50 Ors. Tote 6/6: 5/10 8/-
14/10. Duchess of Westminster (T Dreaper, In Ireland) 15 Rn
                                           6m 32 1/5
```

12

Fairyhouse
Monday 15 April 1963
going: heavy
Power Gold Cup (steeplechase)
2 miles 2 furlongs

Arkle started 2-7 favourite and won by 3 lengths from Willie Wagtail III.

```
1635    POWER GOLD CUP (Chase) £1137 10s  2m 2f   4.10
1184* ARKLE 6-12-5 ...... PTaaffe ....................—1
1079 Willie Wagtail III 6-11-2‡5 BHannon ...........3.2
1186 Chelsea Set 7-11-7 ...... FShortt ............25.3
1392 Ballygowan 9-11-11 ADuff(fell) 11223 D'You Mind 5-11-7
                                           THyde(fell)
S.P.: 2/7 ARKLE, 7 WillieWagtail III. 100/9 D'YouMind,ChelseaSet,
100/6 Ballygowan. Tote 3/-: 3/- 4/6 (9/-). Anne Duchess of West-
minster (T Dreaper) 5 Rn                    5m 12
```

13

Punchestown

Wednesday 1 May 1963

going: good

John Jameson Cup (steeplechase)

2 miles 4 furlongs

```
1765     JOHN JAMESON CUP (Chase) £852 15s    2m 4f    4.25
1635*  ARKLE  6-12-4 ........... PTaaffe ...................—1
1357   Silver Green  7-11-10 ... MrALillingston .........15.2
17413  Chelsea Set  7-11-6 ...... FShortt ..............dist.3
S.P.: 4/7 ARKLE, 7/4 SilverGreen, 100/7 ChelseaSet. Tote: 4/- (4/6).
Anne Duchess of Westminster (T Dreaper) 3 Rn       5m 31.1
```

Arkle started 4-7 favourite and won by 15 lengths from Silver Green.

1963-64 season

14

Navan

Wednesday 9 October 1963

going: good

Donoughmore Plate (for maidens on the Flat)

1 mile 6 furlongs

```
2918     DONOUGHMORE PTE (Mdn) £287      1m 6f    5.0
       ARKLE 6-9-6 ............. TPBurns  ...............—1
27913 Descador  3-8-9 ......... JRoe(h) ................5.2
25863 Pearl Lady  6-9-3 ....... TKinane ...............1⅔.3
2791  Reynard's Heir  3-8-9 ...... JWright ...............4.4
1800  Mary Kate Muldoon  5-9-63      Keenogue 3-8-6 ...TRegan
             FCarroll 2504  Fur Coat 3-7-13⅔7
2791  Interosian  4-9-6  LBrowne                    PMangan
2791  Bright Water  3-8-6       2810  Michael E 3-8-4⅓5 TEnright
             MKennedy 2791  Black Brandy 3-8-6 PCanty
      Aussie  6-9-6  ...... FShortt 1528  Shelbert 3-9-05 JJRafferty
S.P.: 4/6 ARKLE, 9/2 Descador, 7 MichaelE, 9 Aussie, 100/8 Ors.
Tote 4/-: 3/- 3/- 8/6. Anne Duchess of Westminster (T Dreaper)
13 Rn. T/Dble: Cool Air & Arkle £1 15s (372 Tckts)   3m 17.4
```

Arkle started 4-6 favourite and won by 5 lengths from Descador.

15

Gowran Park

Thursday 24 October 1963

going: yielding

Carey's Cottage Handicap Chase

2 miles 4 furlongs

```
540     CAREY'S COTTAGE H'CAP CHASE £519    2f 4f    3.30
      ARKLE  6-11-13 ........... PTaaffe ...............—1
4414  Greatrakes  8-9-7 ...... MrPKiely ..............10.2
383*  Corrigadillisk  6-10-2 ... TTaaffe ...............4.3
3824  San Marco  10-9-7 ...... BHannon ..............3.4
      Silver Green  7-10-10      440  Flamecap 6-9-7 FCarroll
             RCoonan  257*  One Seven Seven 7-9-9
456   Free Frolic 7-9-10 FShortt              TCarberry(fell)
477   Limeking  6-10-2        496* Cloncahir 12-9-81
             THyde(fell)                    JBrabston(p.u)
S.P.: 4/7 ARKLE, 6 Corrigadillisk, 9 Limeking, 100/8 SilverGreen,
OneSevenSeven, 100/7 Greatrakes, 100/6 FreeFrolic, 20 Ors. Tote
3/6: 3/6 5/6 5/-. Duchess of Westminster (T Dreaper) 10 Rn 5m25
```

Arkle started 4-7 favourite and won by 10 lengths from Greatrakes.

16

```
899   HENNESSY GOLD CUP £5020 10s   3m 2f 82y   2.10 (2.11)
                         (H'cap Chase)
      MILL HOUSE 6-12-0
                         GRobinson l.w: led 1st: led 4th: easily ...—1
7472 HappySpring 7-10-0 ...Vibert gd hdwy fr 18th: nvr nrr ...8.2
540* Arkle 6-11-9 ...PTaaffe hdwy fr 17th. 2nd whn slippd
                                  landg 19th: hdwy flat ...³₄.3
4212 John O'Groats 9-10-0
                         PKelleway no hdwy fr 18th ...........15.4
6863 King's Nephew 9-10-6
                         SMellor blnd 14th: nvr trbld ldrs ...3.5
645* Hamanet 8-10-0  JGifford nvr nrr ..................5.6
755 Soilmyth 7-10-0 ...WRees led 2nd & 3rd: prom tl wknd
                                  fr 19th ..................0
4594 Springbok 9-10-1 PBuckley prom to 17th ...........0
747 DukeOfYork8-10-10 Winter hit 14th: p.u bef 19th ........0
459 Pappageno's Cottage
                       8-10-52 TBrookshaw h: fell 2nd ...........0
S.P.: 15/8 MILL HOUSE (op2/1), 3/2 Arkle(tchd11/4), 8 Duke of
York(op10/1), 9 Springbok(op10/1), 100/9 HappySpring(tchd100/7),
100/7 Hamanet(tchd100/6), King'sNephew(tchd100/6), 100/6 Pappa-
geno'sCottage. 50 Ors. Tote 11/4. 7/6 10/4 9/-. Mr W H Gollings
(Fulke Walwyn, Lambourn) 10 Rn          7m 1 (9)
```

Newbury

Saturday 30 November 1963

going: very soft

Hennessy Gold Cup (handicap steeplechase)

3 miles 2 furlongs 82 yards

Arkle 'headway from 17th; second when slipped landing 19th; headway flat'; started 5-2 second favourite and finished third, beaten 8 lengths and ¾ of a length by Mill House and Happy Spring.

17

```
1122        CHRISTMAS H'CAP CHASE £846      3m       3.10
8993  ARKLE 6-12-0 ........... PTaaffe ..................—1
9132  Loving Record 9-9-13 ... TTaaffe ..................2.2
980   Willow King 8-9-103 ... LMcLoughlin ..............15.3
1031  San Marco 10-9-7 ...... RCoonan ..................5.4
      Fredith's Son 12-9-7      980  New Year's Eve 9-9-7
                     FShortt                    JRafferty
S.P.: 4/7 ARKLE, 11/4 LovingRecord, 10 WillowKing, 100/8 New
Year'sEve, 100/7 Fredith'sSon. 25 SanMarco. Tote 4/-: 3/6 4/-
(6/6) Anne, Duchess of Westminster (T Dreaper) 6 Rn  6m 16.2
```

Leopardstown

Thursday 26 December 1963

going: yielding

Christmas Handicap Chase

3 miles

Arkle started 4-7 favourite and won by 2 lengths from Loving Record.

18

```
1331     THYESTES H'CAP CHASE £899  15s   3m 170y   3.20
1122*  ARKLE 7-12-0 ........... PTaaffe ..................—1
11222  Loving Record 10-9-11 ... TTaaffe ................10.2
1257*  Springtime Lad II 9-9-7 WSlattery ...............1.3
11913  Kilspindie 7-9-81 ........ BHannon ................1.4
1257   My Baby 9-9-7 ...FShortt 1257  Kerforo 10-10-3
11574  Blunt's Cross 11-9-7            LMcLoughlin(p.u)
                        RCoonan 1254  Jungle Folly 8-9-7
1304   Cloncahin13-9-7 Brabston            DHughes(fell)
S.P.: 4/6 ARKLE, 4 LovingRecord, 11/2 Blunt'sCross, 100/8 Kerforo,
20 Ors. Tote 5/-: 3/6 4/6 6/-. Anne Duchess of Westminster (T
Dreaper) 9 Rn                              7m 7.1
```

Gowran Park

Thursday 30 January 1964

going: heavy

Thyestes Handicap Chase

3 miles 170 yards

Arkle started 4-6 favourite and won by 10 lengths from Loving Record.

19

Leopardstown

Saturday 15 February 1964

going: yielding

Leopardstown Handicap Chase

3 miles

Arkle started 4-7 favourite and won by 12 lengths from Greatrakes.

```
1492    LEOPARDSTOWN H'CAP CHASE £1671 5s    3m    3.40
1331*  ARKLE  7-12-0  .........  PTaaffe  ...................—1
 633³  Greatrakes 9-9-7 .........  MrPKiely  ...................12.2
1304   Vulsea 9-10-0 ..........  TTaaffe  ...................20.3
1369*  Aussie  7-10-3 (10x) ... FShortt  ...................4.4
1235*  Flying Wild  8-10-2       1331³ Springtime Lad II 9-9-7
                   TCarberry(fell)              WSlattery(fell)
S.P.: 4/7 ARKLE, 7/2 Vulsea, 11/2 FlyingWild, 20 Aussie, 28
SpringtimeLad II, 66 Greatrakes. Tote 3/-: 3/- 16/6 (88/6). Anne
Duchess of Westminster (T Dreaper) 6 Rn              6m 25.2
```

20

Cheltenham (Old Course)

Saturday 7 March 1964

going: good

Gold Cup (steeplechase)

about 3 miles 2 furlongs 130 yards

Arkle 'jumped well; held up; led between last two; shaken up last; quickened; smoothly'; started 7-4 second favourite and won by 5 lengths from Mill House.

```
1683    GOLD CUP (Chase) £8004   abt 3m 2f 130y   3.50 (3.53)
1492*  ARKLE  7-12-0  ...PTaaffe  j.w: hld up; led btwn last 2; shkn
                                  up last: qcknd: smoothly ...—1
1506*  Mill House 7-12-0          led to 2 out: hrd drvn: unable
                   GRobinson      qckn  flat  ...................5.2
1516 Pas Seul 11-12-0 ...DDick    one pce fr 17th ...............25.3
1349* King's  Nephew  10-12-0
                   SMellor        no ch fr 17th ..................15.4
S.P.: 8/13 MillHouse(op4/5), 7/4 ARKLE (op6/4), 20 King'sNephew
(tchd25/1), 50 PasSeul. Tote: 11/10 (21/8) Anne. Duchess of West-
minster (T Dreaper, in Ireland) 4 Rn
            6m 45 3/5 (4 under best time; 9 2/5 under av)
```

21

Fairyhouse

Monday 30 March 1964

going: soft

Irish Grand National (handicap steeplechase)

3 miles 2 furlongs

Arkle started 1-2 favourite and won by 1¼ lengths from Height O' Fashion.

```
2024 IRISH GRAND NATIONAL (H'cap Chase) £2630 3m 2f 3.20
1683*  ARKLE  7-12-0 .........  PTaaffe  ...................—1
1676   Height O' Fashion 7-9-12 TLacy  ...................1¼.2
1774²  Ferry Boat 7-9-7 .........  FShortt  ...................8.3
1684³  Loving  Record 10-9-7 .. TTaaffe  ...................2½.4
1848   Flying Wild  8-10-0       1848  Baxier  8-9-7 ...RCoonan
                   TCarberry 1645  Greatrakes 9-9-7 FCarroll
S.P.: 1/2 ARKLE, 13/2 HeightO'Fashion, 15/2 FlyingWild, 17/2
LovingRecord, 20 FerryBoat, 25 Ors. Tote 4/-: 4/6 5/-. Anne.
Duchess of Westminster (T Dreaper) 7 Rn              7m 5
```

22

```
617    CAREY'S COTTAGE H'CAP CHASE £741    2m 4f    2.30
       ARKLE 7-12-0 ........... PTaaffe    .........................—1
479²   Greatrakes 9-9-7 ......... PKiely   ..........................5.2
555    Gosley 7-9-7 ........... TCarberry  .....................dist.3
S.P.: 1/5 ARKLE, 5 Greatrakes, 20 Gosley. Tote: 3/- (3/6). Anne
Duchess of Westminster (T Dreaper) 3 Rn                  5m 16.4
```

Gowran Park
Thursday 29 October 1964
going: good
Carey's Cottage Handicap Chase
2 miles 4 furlongs

Arkle started 1-5 favourite and won by 5 lengths from Greatrakes.

23

```
1007 HENNESSY GOLD CUP £5516 2s 6d 3m 2f 82y 2.10 (2.11)
                          (H'cap Chase)
617* ARKLE 7-12-7 ...PTaaffe j.w: led 3rd: led 12th: hit 2 out:
                           rdn  out  .........................—1
825⁴ FerryBoat 7-10-0 TMJones chasd ldr fr 17th: hrd rdn fr
                           18th: unable qckn fr 2 out 10.2
705² The Rip 9-10-2² ...WRees v late hdwy: nvr nrr ........12.3
     Mill House 7-12-4         led 2nd: led 10th & 11th: hit
           GRobinson           16th: wknd fr next: fin v
                               tired   ........................6.4
509* Pappageno's Cottage
              9-10-4 ABiddlecombe h: nvr nr to chall ...........10.5
     Happy Spring 8-10-0
              SDavenport nvr  nrr  ..........................6.6
844¹ Hoodwinked9-10-5 Buckley a.bhd:  bind 11th ...........7
825  Vultrix 6-10-0 ...SMellor led 1st: t.o whn p.u bef 19th ...0
705* John O'Groats 10-10-6
          (6x) DNicholson t.o whn p.u bef 18th ...........0
S.P.: 5/4 ARKLE (op evens), 13/8 MillHouse(tchd7/4), 8 TheRip(op
100/8), 20 Pappageno'sCottage, 25 JohnO'Groats,HappySpring, 33
Ors. Tote 9/10: 7/- 17/8 7/- (109/-). Duchess of Westminster (T
Dreaper, Ireland) 9 Rn                  6m 34.5 (17.5 under av)
```

Newbury
Saturday 5 December 1964
going: good
Hennessy Gold Cup (handicap
steeplechase)
3 miles 2 furlongs 82 yards

*Arkle 'jumped well; led 3rd; led 12th;
hit 2 out; ridden out'; started 5-4
favourite and won by 10 lengths
from Ferry Boat.*

24

```
1082   MASSEY-FERGUSON GOLD CUP  abt 2m 5f  2.15 (2.21)
                          (H'cap Chase) £3,989
778¹ FLYING WILD 8-10-6     j.w: w ldrs fr 11th: led appr
            TCarberry       last: hdd: sn led: jst led appr —1
     Buona notte 7-10-12 Haine ! & j.w: hdwy fr 10th: slt ld
                            last: blnd on landg: r.o wl
                            flat  ........................s.h.2
1007* Arkle 7-12-10 (3x)    j.w: a.prom: led appr 6th: led
            PTaaffe         13th tl appr last: rallied nr
                            fin  .........................1.3
     Scottish Memories 10-10-5 hdwy fr 10th: r.o wl fr 3 out:
            CFinnegan         nvr nr to chall ..............2.4
928* Wilmington II 8-10-6 (6x)
            WRees         prom tl wknd qckly fr 3 out 15.5
1007 Happy Spring 8-10-5
            SDavenport   no ch whn fell last ..............0
968  The O'Malley 6-10-0     led tl appr 6th: sn led agn to
            PBroderick        13th: wkng whn hmpd &
                             slippd up flat bef 2 out ......0
S.P.: 8/11 Arkle(tchd4/7), 4 Buona notte(tchd11/2), 8 Scottish
Memories(tchd9/1), 100/8 FLYING WILD (op10/1), 100/7 Wilming-
ton II, 33 Ors. Tote 31/-: 11/6 12/2 (105/10). Mr R R Guest (D
Moore, Ireland) 7 Rn                  5m 21
```

Cheltenham (New Course)
Saturday 12 December 1964
going: good
Massey-Ferguson Gold Cup
(handicap steeplechase)
about 2 miles 5 furlongs

*Arkle 'jumped well; always
prominent; led approaching 6th; led
13th until approaching last; rallied
near finish'; started 8-11 favourite
and finished third behind Flying
Wild and Buona Notte, beaten a
short head and 1 length.*

25

Leopardstown

Saturday 27 February 1965

going: good

Leopardstown Handicap Chase

3 miles

Arkle started 8-11 favourite and won by 1 length from Scottish Memories.

```
1670    LEOPARDSTOWN H'CAP CHASE £2583 15s    3m    3.40
10823   ARKLE 8-12-7 .......... PTaaffe ............................—1
14044   Scottish  Memories  11-10-0 FCarroll .................1.2
1358*   Persian  Signal  8-9-7 ... ARedmond ...............10.3
14302   Greek Vulgan 8-9-7 ...... BHannon .................1½.4
1430    Anonymous  6-9-7        14613  Zonda 14-9-7    PWoods
                     TCarberry  1461   Cavendish 9-9-9 RCoonan
15744   Brown Diamond 10-9-2    14303  Greatrakes 10-9-7 PKielv
                     CFinnegan
S.P.: 8/11 ARKLE, 5 ScottishMemories, 8 PersianSignal,GreekVulgan,
100/8 Cavendish, 28 BrownDiamond, 40 Ors. Tote 5/6: 3/- 4/6 4/-.
Anne. Duchess of Westminster (T Dreaper) 9 Rn    6m 14.6
```

26

Cheltenham (New Course)

Thursday 11 March 1965

going: firm

Gold Cup (steeplechase)

about 3 miles 2 furlongs 76 yards

Arkle 'jumped well; made all; quickened approaching last; very easily'; started 30-100 favourite and won by 20 lengths from Mill House.

```
1723    CHELTENHAM  GOLD CUP (Chase) £7986 10s  4.5 (4.10)
                     abt 3m 2f 76y
1670*   ARKLE 8-12-0 ...PTaaffe j.w: mde all: qcknd appr last:
                     v easily ................—1
1487*   Mill  House 8-12-0       hit 16th: ev ch whn pckd 19th:
                     GRobinson  hrd rdn 2 out: one pce ...20.2
        Stoney Crossing 7-12-0
                     MrWRoycroft l.w: no ch fr 19th ...........30.3
        Caduval 10-12-0 OMcNally a.wl  bhd ..................bad.4
S.P.: 30/100 ARKLE (2/7—1/3), 100/30 MillHouse(tchd7/2), 33
Caduval(op25/1), 100 StoneyCrossing(op200/1,blow). Tote: 5/- (5/8).
Anne. Duchess of Westminster (T Dreaper, in Ireland) 4 Rn 6m 41.2
```

27

Sandown Park

Saturday 24 April 1965

going: good

Whitbread Gold Cup (handicap steeplechase)

3 miles 5 furlongs 18 yards

Arkle 'jumped well; hit 4th; led to 16th; led 21st; quickened flat'; started 4-9 favourite and won by 5 lengths from Brasher.

```
2208    WHITBBREAD GOLD CUP £8.230  3m 5f 18y  3.10 (3.11)
                     (H'cap Chase)
1723*   ARKLE  8-12-7 ...PTaaffe j.w: hit 4th: led to 16th: led
                     21st: qcknd flat ..............—1
1994*   Brasher 9-10-0 (7x)       led 17th to 20th: one pce fr
                     JFitzGerald  21st ..........................5.2
2143    Willow KKing 10-9-7 Mellor hdwy 16th: nvr nrr ..........20.3
15072   Rough Tweed 11-9-7
                     LMajor mstks: wknd fr 22nd ...........5.4
18264   Persian Signal 8-9-7
                     CChapman no hdwy fr 20th ..............8.5
1897    SignPost 9-9-103 OMcNally wknd fr 18th .............20.6
1994    Over Court 9-10-0 (7x)
                     KBWhite mstks: bhd fr 15th ...............7
S.P.: 4/9 ARKLE (op1/2), 5 RoughTweed(op9/2), 8 Brasher(op7/1),
25 OverCourt,WillowKing,PersianSignal, 33 SignPost. Tote 6/6: 5/2
9/2 (14/2). Anne. Duchess of Westminster (T Dreaper, in Ireland)
7 Rn. T/Dble: Arkle & Toffee Nose £4 5s. T/Trble: Nearside, Ulster
Prince & Philanderer £4 18s          7m 31.8 (15.2 under av)  T
```

```
792  GALLAHER GOLD CUP (H'cap Chase)  3m 118y  2.40 (2.44)
                                £5,165
(Previous best time recorded by Mill House over 3m 118y—Feb. '65.
6m 16; the record for 3m 125y was clocked by Gold Wire in '62—see
                          Front Section)
     ARKLE 8-12-7 ....PTaaffe led 9th to 15th: led 20th ...—1
     Rondetto 9-10-9 ...JKing hdwy 19th: nvr nrr ...........20.2
619* Mill House 8-11-5        led 5th to 8th: led 16th to 19th:
            DNicholson     tired fr 20th ..................4.3
7012 The Rip 10-10-0 ...WRees no hdwy fr 16th .............15.4
4962 Lira 7-10-0 ..JBuckingham prom to 16th ..............10.5
     John o' Groats 11-10-0
            PKelleway t.o whn p.u bef 20th ..................0
654 Candy 10-10-3(3) ..PJones h: led to 4th: t.o whn p.u aftr
                          13th
                       ..................................0
S.P.: 4/9 ARKLE (op4/7), 7/2 MillHouse(op9/4), 9 Rondetto(op10/1).
20 TheRip(op33/1), 33 John o'Groats, 100 Ors. Tote 6/6: 4/10 7/6
(14/8). Anne, Duchess of Westminster (T Dreaper, in Ireland) 7 Rn
            5m 59 (17 under best time; 35 under av)
```

28

Sandown Park

Saturday 6 November 1965

going: good

Gallaher Gold Cup (handicap
steeplechase)

3 miles 118 yards

*Arkle 'led 9th to 15th; led 20th';
started 4-9 favourite and won by 20
lengths from Rondetto.*

```
1013 HENNESSY GOLD CUP (H'cap Chase) 3m 2f 82y 2.5 (2.9)
                                £7,099 6s
792* ARKLE 8-12-7 ...PTaaffe led 5th, 7th & 14th: hit 19th:
                          rdn out ...................—1
816¹ Freddie 8-10-3  McCarron gd hdwy fr 20th: fin wl ......15.2
816  Brasher 9-10-0 JFitzGerald led to 4th: led 6th: led 8th to
                          13th: wknd 18th ...........3.3
916* Wayward Queen 7-10-6
            (6x) JCook late hdwy: nvr nrr ...........4.4
9212 John o' Groats 11-10-0
            PKelleway t.o whn p.u bef 2 out ...........0
629¹ Norther 8-10-0  TNorman t.o whn p.u bef 19th ...........0
717¹ GamePurston7-10-0 Cowley t.o whn p.u bef 19th ...........0
885 Happy Arthur 8-10-4(3)
            GMilburn fell 13th ...........................0
S.P.: 1/6 ARKLE (op 1/8, blow), 9 Freddie(tchd100/8), 20 Wayward
Queen(op100/8), 25 HappyArthur(op20/1),Brasher(op33/1.blow),John
o'Groats(op33/1.blow), 50 Norther, 100 GamePurston. Spl pl btg:
1/2 Freddie, 4/5 Wayward Queen, 3 Brasher, Happy Arthur, John
o'Groats, 6 Norther, 100/8 Game Purston, Arkle in proportion. Tote
4/10: 4/4 5/2 7/10 (12/4). Anne, Duchess of Westminster (T
Dreaper in Ireland) 8 Rn            6m 49.2 (5.8 under av)
```

29

Newbury

Saturday 27 November 1965

going: good

Hennessy Gold Cup (handicap
steeplechase)

3 miles 2 furlongs 82 yards

*Arkle 'led 5th, 7th and 14th; hit
19th; ridden out'; started 1-6
favourite and won by 15 lengths
from Freddie.*

```
1177    KING GEORGE VI CHASE £4634    3m      2.0 (2.0)
1013* ARKLE 8-12-0 ...PTaaffe lw: hdwy 9th: led 15th .........—1
9953 Dormant 8-12-0 ...SMellor nvr nr to chall .............dist.2
1078 Arctic Ocean 7-11-3
            RWalker a.in rear .....................dist.3
871* Dunkirk 8-12-0 ...WRees led to 14th: fell 15th: killd ......0
S.P.: 1/7 ARKLE (1/8—1/6.blow), 7 Dunkirk(op8/1), 25 Dormant,
100 ArcticOcean. Tote: 4/4 (8/6). Anne, Duchess of Westminster
(T Dreaper, in Ireland) 4 Rn            6m 9.2 (13.8 under av)
```

30

Kempton Park

Monday 27 December 1965

going: good

King George VI Chase

3 miles

*Arkle 'looked well; headway 9th; led
15th'; started 1-7 favourite and won by a distance from Dormant.*

31

Leopardstown

Tuesday 1 March 1966

going: heavy

Leopardstown Handicap Chase

3 miles

```
1585        LEOPARDSTOWN  CHASE  £2475      3m           3.40
1177* ARKLE 9-12-7 ........ FTaaffe ........................—1
1504   Height O' Fashion 9-9-7 .. JPSullivan .............nk.2
1504   Splash 8-9-7 ........... PWoods ..................15.3
774* Packed Home 11-9-7 .. TCarberry ...................6.4
S.P.: 1/5 ARKLE, 7 Splash, 10 PackedHome, 100/8 HeightO'Fashion.
Tote: 3/- (9/6). Anne, Duchess of Westminster (T W Dreaper) 4 Rn
                                                        7m 2.3
```

Arkle started 1-5 favourite and won by a neck from Height O' Fashion.

32

Cheltenham (Old Course)

Thursday 17 March 1966

going: good

Gold Cup (steeplechase)

about 3 miles 2 furlongs 76 yards

*Arkle 'led 8th; blundered 11th;
canter'; started 1-10 favourite and
won by 30 lengths from Dormant.*

```
1779  CHELTENHAM  GOLD  CUP  (Chase) abt 3m 2f 76y  4.5 (4.9)
                                          £7674 10s
1585* ARKLE 9-12-0 ......PTaaffe led 8th: blnd 11th: canter ......—1
1556  Dormant 9-12-0 Scudamore led 2nd to 7th: wknd fr 18th 30.2
1530* Snaigow 7-12-0 DNicholson led 1st: 2nd & no ch whn blnd
                                         18th ........................10.3
1720  Sartorius 11-12-0
                    TBiddlecombe h: a.bhd .......................8 4
1766  Hunch 9-12-0 ......SMellor in rear 6th tl fell 18th: destroyd 0
S.P.: 1/10 ARKLE (tchd8/100.blow), 100/7 Snaigow(op100/8), 20 Dor-
mant(op100/6), 33 Hunch(op25/1), 50 Sartorius(op200/1.blow). Tote:
4/6 (12/-). Anne, Duchess of Westminster (T W Dreaper. In Ireland)
5 Rn                                                     6m 54.2
```

1966-67 season

33

Newbury

Saturday 26 November 1966

going: yielding

Hennessy Gold Cup (handicap
steeplechase)

3 miles 2 furlongs 82 yards

*Arkle 'led to last; every chance near
finish; ran on very gamely'; started
4-6 favourite and finished second, beaten half a length by Stalbridge Colonist.*

```
1035 HENNESSY GOLD CUP (H'cap Chase) £5713 10s 3m 2f 82y 2.5 (2.7)
955 STALBRIDGE COLONIST 7-10-0
                    Mellor hdwy 18th: led flat: all out ........—1
   Arkle 9-12-7 ..............Taaffe led to last: ev ch nr fin: r.o v
                                       game .......................1½.2
743* What a Myth 9-10-2 Kelleway hit 4th, 5th & 14th: hrd drvn 18th:
                                       r.o wl fr last ...............1½.3
8042 Kellsboro' Wood 6-10-0 ...Haine ev ch 18th: one pce fr 2 out ..6.4
804  Master Mascus 7-10-0 ...JKing no hdwy fr 18th ...............4.5
804* Freddie 9-10-7(7x) ...McCarron prom to 15th: in rear fr 16th ...20.6
S.P.: 4/6 Arkle(tchd8/11), 7/2 What a Myth(op9/2), 13/2 Freddie(op7/1), 10
MasterMascus(op100/7), 22 Kellsboro'Wood, 25 STALBRIDGE COLONIST. Tote
99/4: 18/6 5/4 (360/10). Mr R J R Blindell (K Cundell, Compton) 6 Rn
                                                 6m 48 (6 under av)
```

34

```
1194        S.G.B. H'CAP CHASE £2823  8s     abt 3m        2.15 (2.15)
10352 ARKLE  9-12-7 ...........Taaffe mde all: v easily .................—1
       Sunny Bright 9-10-0 ...Pitman chasd wnr fr 18th: no imp .........15.2
10803 Vultrix  8-10-0 ...........Mellor chasd wnr to 17th: one pce .........3.3
11311 Big  George 11-10-0 Morrissey hit 6th: no ch fr 14th ...............15.4
1035 Master Mascus  7-10-3 ...JKing in rear fr 11th ................12.5
S.P.: 1/3 ARKLE (op2/9), 9/2 Vultrix(tchd5/1), 10 MasterMascus(op8/1), 100/6
SunnyBright, 33 BigGeorge. Tote: 5/- (26/2). Anne, Duchess of Westminster
(T W Dreaper, in Ireland) 5 Rn                              6m 32.6
```

Ascot
Wednesday 14 December 1966
going: heavy
SGB Handicap Chase
about 3 miles

Arkle 'made all; very easily'; started 1-3 favourite and won by 15 lengths from Sunny Bright.

35

```
1249        KING GEORGE VI CHASE £3689      3m          2.0 (2.3)
1212 DORMANT 9-11-0 ........JKing lw: hit 6th: led 10th: hit 13th: str
                            rn flat: led cl hme ................—1
1194* Arkle 9-12-7 .............Taaffe led to 9th: led 11th tl blnd 14th:
                            led 16th: led 2 out: r.o wl: v
                            lame aftr r ...............1.2
7951 Maigret 9-11-7 ..........Haine no ch fr 14th ...............bad.3
5004 Foinavon  8-11-5 ......Kempton h: bhd fr 7th ..............5.4
12124 Scottish Final 9-11-0 ...TJones a.bhd
       Arctic Ocean 8-11-5(2) RWalker bhd tl fell last ...............0
1030* Woodland Venture 6-11-7   lw: led 15th: led 17th: 2nd & ev
       (Biddlecombe  ch whn fell 2 out ...............0
S.P.: 2/9 Arkle(op1/4),  6 WoodlandVenture(op7/1), 10 DORMANT (op8/1),
100/6 Maigret, 25 ScottishFinal, 33 Ors. Tote 50/-: 7/8 4/10 (10/6). Mrs D M
Wells-Kendrew (Wells-Kendrew, Dorking) 7 Rn            6m 22.2 (0.2)
```

Kempton Park
Tuesday 27 December 1966
going: good
King George VI Chase
3 miles

Arkle 'led to 9th; led 11th until blundered 14th; led 16th; led 2 out; ran on well; very lame after race'; started 2-9 favourite and finished second, beaten 1 length by Dormant.

OPPOSITE

Arkle and Pat Taaffe going to post for the 1965 Whitbread Gold Cup.

The Mighty Arkle

bay gelding by Archive out of Bright Cherry

That horse bought fridges, TVs, motor cars.
It was no wonder thousands gripped the rails
when the hero hunted Mill House down again,
pulling back the earth with each great stride,

the pride of England frothing, broken, bate.
If I had a cap, I'd throw it in the air.
This was how the Irish won the war,
everything riding on every whipping boy

to face the white man down against the odds.
I have my grandda's photo of the god,
an icon, like good Pope John and JFK,
Pat Taaffe up, who, he used to say,

needed that horse 'for he couldn't sit on a stool'.
But the beefcake underneath is Cassius Clay,
the footwork perfect, the arrogance a joy,
the sucker punch a lucky horseshoe in each glove.

Damian Smyth, from *Downpatrick Races* (2000)

Index

Page numbers in *italics* refer to illustrations.

adulation 122, *122*, 124-127, *126*, *127*, 130, 131, 160-161, *163*, 164-165 *see also* convalescence; fame
Airborne 116
Allez France 42
Alpheus 180
Alverton 180
American Grand National 87
Anaglogs Daughter 180
Ancil, Derek 88
Andrews, Julie 169
Anglo 119
Anglo-American Chewing Gum Company 127, *127*
Anthony 33
Anthony, Jack 24
Archive 10, 12, 13-14, 15, 16, 17, 20, 27
Arctic Ocean 106, 107, 108, 145, 146
Arkle (mountain), name adopted 20, *21*, *22*, 23
'Arkle' (ballad) 50, 65-67, *66*
'Arkle and Mill House – Cheltenham' (painting) *86*
'Arkle Bar, The' (painting) *180*
Arkle: The legend (video) 135, *184*
Arkle: The story of a champion 126-127, *126*
Arkle: The Wonder Horse 169
Arkloin 27
Arkwright, Philip *179*
Army Benevolent Fund 170
Armytage, Roddy 175
Arsenal FC 144
Artist's Treasure 30
Ascot 116, 133, 139, 187
  SGB Handicap Chase 138-140, *138*, *139*, 140-141, *140*, *141*, *142*, 143, 169
Astor, Lord 14
Azertyuiop 180

Bailey, David 94
Baker, Alison 16, 17, 90, 184
Baker, Henry 14
Baker, Mary 10, 16, 17, 90, 112
Balding, Ian 36
Baldoyle *13*, 22, 31-32
Ballymacoll Stud, Co. Meath 15-16, *15*, 118, 184, 186

Ballymoss 19, *182*
Ballynonty, Co. Tipperary 23
Ballyross 174
Ballysway 16
Barker, Sean 96, *152*
BBC television 51, 61, 119-120
Beatles, The 51, 94, 126, 130
Beethoven 170
Behan, Brendan 50, 65
Behan, Dominic 50, 65, 66, 161
Ben Stack 22, 27
Ben Stack (mountain) *21*, 22-23
Bend Or 14, 18-19, *32*
Benson, Charles 112, 114
Beresford, Lord Patrick 31
Best Mate 10, 65, 124, 177-178, 180
Bicester, Lord 14, 24
Biddlecombe, Terry 130, 147, 170, 178, 180
Biddlecombe, Tony *68-69*
Biegel, Peter *55*, *168*
Big George 140, 141
Billy Bumps 36, *37*, 38
birth 10, 15-16, *15*
Black, Cilla 51
Black Secret 174
Blaxland, Gregory 176
Blessington Esquire 106
Blinkers (donkey) 170
Blunts Cross 31
Bobsline 180
Book Law 12, 14
Boomerang *182*
Border Flight 38
Box of Pin-Ups 94
Bracken, Tommy 173
Brasher 38, 88, *88*, 102, *102*, 103, 104, 105
Bray Flame 20, 23
Brigadier Gerard 13, 34, 63
Bright Cherry 10, 12, *13*, 14, 15, 16, 17, 18, 20, 23
Brown Jack 34, 160
Brown Lad 174
Bryanstown *18*, 19, 33, 40, 70-71, 90, *90*, 121, 122, 130, 164, *164*, 165, *165*, 169, 170
  Arkle's grave *173*, 181, *182*
Buckley, Pat *68-69*
Bugler, Jeremy 149
Buona Notte 80-81
Burns, T. P. 40, *40*, 184, 186, 187
Byles, A. J. *89*
Byrne, Twinny 187

Caduval 85, 87
Cambridge University Press 187
Candy 97, 98, 99
Captain Christy 175
Carberry, Tommy 81, 174
Carbury Cross 174

Carey's Cottage 40
Carrickbeg 37, 38
Carroll, Frank *84*
Carroll, Sally 186
Carter, Rubin 'Hurricane' 58
Cashel View 19
Catherina (blind girl) 155-156, *156*
Cazalet, Peter 36, 106, 108, 109
Century of Champions, A 10, 177
Chasers and Hurdlers 177, 178
Chelsea Set 39
Cheltenham 175
  Arkle Bar 151, *180*, 181
  Arkle memorials 179-181, *179*, *180*
  Arkle Trophy Chase (formerly Cotswold Chase) 22, 27, 180
  Broadway Chase 38, 42, 50
  Cathcart Challenge Cup 24
  Champion Hurdle 116
  Honeybourne Chase 36-37, *37*
  Mackeson Gold Cup 27, 36
  Massey-Ferguson Gold Cup 80-81, *80*, *81*
  National Hunt Chase 19, 27, 116, *116*
Cheltenham Gold Cup 24, 118, 133, 136, 167, 174, 177-178
  1963: 38-39, *41*, 42, 50
  1964: 50-54, *53*, *54*, *55*, 56-57, *56*, *57*, *61*, *62*, 63-64
    the race *48-49*, *58*, 59-62, *60*
  1965: 71, 84-85, *84*, *85*, 86, 87, *87*
  1966: 95, 118-121, *118*, *119*, *120*, *121*
Cherry Bud 16
Cherry Tang 16
Cherry Wine 16
Cherrykino 174
Child '66: *132*
Clay, Cassius 51, 77, 155
Clee, Nicholas 130, 146
Colebridge 16, 174
Common Market 10
comparisons 176-178
convalescence 151, *151*-159, *153*-156, 160-161, *162*, *162*-167, 164-169
Cook, Robin 22-23
Coosheen Finn *182*
Cosgrove, Maxie 151, 165, 169, 172
Cottage Rake 26, 118
Crobeg 96
Croker, Boss 15-16
Crump, Neville 145
Cundell, Frank 54
Cundell, Ken 133

Daily Express 52, 63, 96, 100, 112, 114

Daily Sketch 120-121
Daily Telegraph 19, 100
Dale, Syd 41
Dargent 36
Davenport, Steve 68-69
Dawn Run 42, 65, 181, 183
Days of Wine and Roses (film, 1962) 59
Days of Wine and Roses (play, 2005) 50, 59-60, 64, 160
Dean Swift 24
death 172-173
Denman 178
Descador 40
Desert Orchid 124, 130, 161, 177
Desert Storm 170
Dick, Dave 106
Dicky May 27, 133
Different Class 119
Doctor Doolittle 170
Doncaster, Great Yorkshire Chase 54-55
Donegan, Lonnie 10
Donoghue, Steve 34
Donoughmore, Lord 29
Dormant 46, 75, 85, 106, 107, 108, 109, 119, 120
　　King George VI Chase 145, 146, *146*, 147, 148
Down Royal 16
Doyle, Jack 41
Dreaper, Betty 22, 24, 39, 45, *62*, *82*, 174
　　1964-65 season 70, *82*, 83, *92-93*
　　1965-66 season 110, 122, 124
　　1966-67 season 137, 140, 144, *152*, 153, 155
Dreaper, Jim 16, 34, 144, 174, 184, *185*
Dreaper, Tom 14, 17, 19, 20, 22, 24, *25*, 26, 27-28, 35, 38, 39, 46, 186
　　and Arkle 11, 23, 31, 33, 36, 39, 40, 45, 46, 67
　　　　1964-65 season 79, 83, 87
　　　　1965-66 season *92-93*, 105, 114, 117, *124*
　　　　1966-67 season 132, 136, 144, 153, 154, 155
　　　　convalescence *158-159*, *166*, 168
　　　　retirement and after 169, 174, 180
　　and Fort Leney 166, 167
Dreaper, Valerie 83
Dreaper family 29, 110, 166
Dublin, Tolka Park stadium 124-125, *125*
Dublin Horse Show 90, *91*, 124
Duck, Donald 42
Duke of York 44
Dundalk, Wee County Hurdle 33
Dunkirk 65, 95, 96, 106-108, 109, 139, 177
Dylan, Bob 58

Easter Hero 10, 78, *168*, 177
Eaton Hall, Cheshire 19, 20, 28, 80
Eclipse 130
Eddie, 'Shifty' 148-149
Edwards, Lionel *86*
Egan, Tom 186
Eldorado 85
Elizabeth II, Queen 184
Elizabeth, Queen, the Queen Mother 76, 96, 130
England football team 130
Evening Press 169
Evening Standard 94

Fairyhouse 32-33, 39, *39*, 165, 168, 169 see also Irish Grand National
fame 130, 131, 179-184 see also adulation; convalescence
Ferry Boat 32, 68-69, 77, 85
Finney, Tom 10
FitzGerald, Jimmy 38, *88*, 103, 104
Flagship Uberalles 180
Flamenco 40
Flying Fox 19, 63
Flying Wild 30, 46, 72, 80, 81, *81*
Flyingbolt 24, 46, 83, 116-117, *116*, *117*, 121, 139, 175, 177
Foinaven (mountain) 20, *21*
Foinavon 20, 22, 27, 39, 145, 146, 174
Folktrax (record) label 109
Forster, Tim 174
Fort Leney 46, 80, 83, 88, 96, 117, *117*, 164, 166-167, *167*, 168, 174, 175
Fortina 167
Fortria 24, 27, 31-32, 35, 36, 38-39, 42
Foster and Allen 65
'Four great chasers: Gold Cup runners, 7 Mar '64' (painting) 55
Freddie 53, 102, 103, 104, 132, 133
Frenchman's Cove 37
Freud, Clement 161, 169
Fuller, Bryony 27-28, 174

Gallaher 96
Game Purston 103
Garrynagree 180
Gilbey, Quintin ('Kettledrum') 63, 100, 103-105, 107-108
Giles cartoon *118*
Gillespie, Edward *179*, 181
Glyndebourne 30
Goff's Bloodstock Sales, Dublin 11, 17, *17*, 20
Golan 15
Golden Miller 10, 15, 42, 52, 118, 130, 155, *168*, 176, 177, 181
Golden Miller 176
Golden Sparkle 16
Gollings, Bill 41, 42
Gosley 33, 75
Gowran Park 32, 33, 39, 40, 46, 47, 75
Graham, Clive 63

Grand National 20, 22, 26, 35, 75
Greatrakes 40, 46, 75
Greenogue, Co. Dublin 8-9, 24, 26-28, 26, 38, 40, 71, 83, 88, *92-93*, 110, *111*, 116, *152* see also Kilsallaghan, Co. Dublin
　　Arkle's convalescence *158-159*, 164, 165, 166, *166*
Greenogue Princess 12, 14, 23
Guest, Raymond 80
Guinness 110, *123*, 124, 126, 153, *153*, 166, 169, 173, 180, 181

Haine, Johnny 81
Hal's Son 29
Halloween 106
Happy Arthur 103, 140
Happy Spring 44, 45, 68-69, 76
Hatton's Grace 26
Height O' Fashion 33, 46, 70, 72, 73, 112, 114, 121
Hely-Hutchinson, Hon. Mark 29, *29*, 30, 184
Herbert, Ivor 33, 110, 126-127, 126, 145
Hislop, John 63, 79
Holland, Anne 20
Honour Bound 38
Hoodwinked 68-69
Horse and Hound 36, 38, 45, 52, 56-57, 64, 71, 77, 98-99, 146-148, 172-173
Horse of the Year Show 170-171, *171*, 172
Horses in Training 27, *28*
Hunch 119, 120
Hunter, Tab 10
Hyde, Henry 153

Injured National Hunt Jockeys' Fund 170
injury 148-149, *150* see also convalescence
Interco 42
Ireland Sings: An anthology of modern and ancient Irish songs and ballads 65
Irish Field 46, 112
Irish Folk Collection, The, volume 2: 66
Irish Grand National 24, 27, 31, 35, 39, 70, 72-73, *72*, 116, 121, 174
Irish Horse Museum, Tully *181*, 182-183
Irish Independent 180, 182-183
Irish National Stud 181-2, 184, 186
Irish Racing Calendar 23, 30
Irish Times 113, 162, 172, *172*, 173
Istabraq 183

Jay Trump 102
John O'Groats 44, 68-69, 96, 97, 99, 103
Jomsviking 36, 38
Jones, Tim 68-69
Joseph, Nathan 65

Kauto Star 177, 178
Kavanagh, James 172

Kelleway, Paul 132
Kellsboro Wood 133
Kelly, Johnny 165, *171*
Kempton, John 22, 145
Kempton Park 54, 55, 151, 153, *153*, 157, 160-161, 164
    King George VI Chase 53, 65, 95, 106-109, *106*, 130-1, 143, 144-149, *146*
'Kempton Park' (song) 65, 109
Kerforo 24, 27, 30, 31, 46
Kerr, Alexander 145
Kicking King 175
Killykeen Star 33
Kilmore 106
Kilsallaghan, Co. Dublin 23, 70, 110, *111*, 122, 132, 143, 153 *see also* Greenogue, Co. Dublin
Kilsallaghan athletic club 124-125, *125*
Kilspindie 29
King, Jeff 146, *146*, 147
King Of Diamonds *182*
King Pin 38
King's Nephew 42, 44, 54-55, *55*, 58, 59, 60, 62
Kinloch Brae 174

L'Escargot 80, 183
Lady Flame 29
Lake, Des 125
Lambert Simnel 19
Larkspur 80
Last Link 24, 27, 39
Last Suspect 174
Lawlor family 41
Lawrence, John ('Audax') 11, 36, 38, 45, 52, 56-57, 64, 71, 77-8, 81, 98-99, 146-148, 172-173 *see also* Oaksey, John, Lord
Lemmon, Jack 59
Leney Princess 166
Leopardstown 23, 30, 37, 38, 45-46, 96-97, 165, 183
Leopardstown Chase 27, 37, 38, 46, 47, 84, 95, 112, *113*, 114, *115*, 133, 164, 167
Lewis, Geoff 34
Limeking 80
Lindner, Doris 181
Lira 97, 99
Liston, Sonny 51
Lochroe 55
Loriston-Clarke, Jenny 170
Lottery 73
Loving Record 45-46
Lumley, Johnny 27, 75, *101*, 116, *120*, 144, 152, *162*, 186

MacDermott, Emma 187
Maigret 53, 145, 146
Malahow, Co. Dublin 10, *13*, 16, 17, 186
Mandarin 27, 31, 43, 55, 100, 105, 106, 110
Mariner's Log 14
Master Mascus 133, 140

Mattie's Dream 24
McCabe, Charles 125-126
McCafferty, Owen 59, 64, 160
McCarron, Pat 103
McCririck, John 148-149
McGill, Angus 94
MacGinty, Tom 138-139
McIlvanney, Hugh 134-135
McLoughlin, Liam 31-33, 39, *117*, 152, 184
Macmillan, Harold 10
Meg 169, 173
Mellor, Stan 55, *68-69*, 133, 135, 170
Mercer, Joe 34
Merely-A-Monarch 170
Merry Coon 34
'Mighty Arkle, The' (poem) 203
Miles, Graeme 65, 109
Mill House 38, 40, 41-42, *43-44*, *44*, 45, 46, 55, 118, 130, 139, 156, 175, 176, 177
    1964-65 season *68-69*, 75, 76, *76*, 77, 84-85, 145
    1965-66 season 95, 96, 97, 98, 99, *99*, 100
    1966-67 season 143, 145, 175
    Gold Cup *41*, 84, *85*, *85*, 86, 87, 167
    Gold Cup (1964) 50, 51, 52, 54, *55*, 56-57, *56*, 58, 63, 64, 66, 67, 70, 75, 76
        the race *48-49*, 59, 60, *60*, 61-62
Mill Reef 34
Miller, J. P. 59
Milo 36
Mister Softee 170
Moore, Bobby 130
Moore, Dan 36
Morris, Tony 10, 177
Morse Code 118
Moscow Flyer 177, 180
Mott, Sue 19
Mountcashel King 27
Mr What 34
Muhammad Ali 51, 125 *see also* Clay,   Cassius
Mullingar, Lough Ennel Plate maiden race 29-30, *30*
Murphy, Billy 155
Murray, Paddy *25*, 27, 96, 97, 123, 152
Musk Orchid 170
Mustang 10, 16
My Life and Arkle's 31

Naas 31, 34, 41, 168
Nas Na Riogh 41
Navan 30-31, 40, *40*
Nearco 12, 14
Nellie (donkey) *164*, 165
New English Broadsides: Songs of our time from the English folk scene 65, 66
Newbury 42, 84-85
    Hennessy Gold Cup

1963: 40, 43-45, *43*, *44*, 55
1964: *68-69*, 71, 75-78, *75-79*
1965: 95, 96, 102-105, *102*, *103*, *105*
1966: *128-129*, 132-137, *134*, *135*, *137*
Newry nurse 136-137, *137*
News of the World 63
Nicholson, David *68-69*, 97, 99
Nickalls, Tom 38, 63, 100, 105, 140-141, 143
Nicolaus Silver 56, 106
Nijinsky 34, 42, 172-173
North Light 15
Norther 103

Oaksey, John, Lord 175, *179* see also Lawrence, John
O'Brien, Vincent 26, 35, 118
Observer 134-135
O'Grady, Willie 23
Oklahoma Daily 166
O'Leary, Michael 186
Oliver, Ken 175
Olympia 24, 27, 29
O'Malley 170
Ormonde 19, *32*, 63
Osberstown Squire 38
Osborne, Michael 182, 183
O'Sullevan, Peter (later Sir Peter) 52, 61, 62, 87, 119-120, 133-134, 136, 184
O'Toole, Nick 184, 186
Our Solo 85
Over Court 88
Owen's Sedge 27, 33, 38

Packed Home 112
Paget, Dorothy 15, 16, 118
Panorama 65
Pappageno's Cottage *44*, *68-69*
Paris, Auteuil, Grand Steeplechase de Paris 105, 132
Parkin, Bernard 183
Pas Seul 55-56, *55*, 58, 59, 60, 62, 75, 106
Pearson, Norah 165
Peck, Gregory 27, 33, 38, 119
pedigree 12-14
Pegasus 170
Pendil 180
Persian Signal 88
Peter, Paul and Mary 65
Pettit, Roy 108, 145
Phar Lap 65
Piggott, Lester 34, 35, 187
Pilsudski 15
Politician 42
Power, Bobby 24
Prendergast, Paddy 125
Price, Ryan 132, 145
Prince Regent 24, 78, 174
Punchestown, John Jameson Cup 39

Quare Times 26, 35
Queen's Hussar 13
Quita Que 32
Quorum 13

Racing Post 19, 117, 148, 184
Radio Times 52
Rainlough 32
Ramos, Tod *180*
Randall, John 10, 19, 177
Rank, J. V. 24
ratings 177
Reay Forest 97
Red Rum 13, 42, 65, 124, 130, 161
Rees, Bill *68-69*, 106, 108
Remick, Lee 59
Remittance Man *180*
Reynolds, Peter 184, 186
retirement 169-172
Revolver 130, 131
Reynoldstown 10
Rhodes Scholar 14
Riding for the Disabled 170
Rimell, Fred 38, *180*
Robinson, Willie *41*, 42, 52, *56*, 60, 62, 63, 67, *68-69*, 75, 97, 184
Rogers, Mick 153
Rondetto 97, 99, *99*
Ross Sea 33
Rough Tweed 88, *88*
Royal Approach 24, 35
Roycroft, Bill 86

Sabhal Beag (mountain) 23
Saffron Tartan 55, 106
Salmon Spray 116
San Francisco Chronicle 125-126
Sandown Park 46, 96
    Gallaher Gold Cup 95, 96, *96-101*, 97-100
    Whitbread Gold Cup 55-56, 75, 88, *88, 89*, 106, 145, 175
Santa Claus 153
Sartorius 53, 119, 120
Saval Beg 16, 23
Scott, Brough 36-37, 63, 136
Scott, Len 105
Scottish Final 145, 146
Scottish Memories 38, 81, 84
Sea Brief 174
Sea-Bird 94
Seattle Slew 42
Sempervivum 116
Sentina 19
Shagreen 24
Sign Post 88
Silver Green 33, 39, 40
Sir Ivor 80
skeleton 181-183, *181*
Sleator, Paddy 36
Smith, Phil 178
Smyth, Damian 203
Snaigow 119, 120
Sobell, Sir Michael 15, 16
Solimyth 44
Soltest 31
Songs of Sport and Play 109
Splash 24, 27, 112, 114, 168
Sporting Chronicle 63, 100, 103-105, 107-108

Sporting Life 38, 54, 63, 83, 97, 100, 103, 105, 107, 140-141, 143
Springbok 44
Springtime Lad II 46
Sprinter Sacre 177, 178
Stalbridge Colonist 97, *128-129*, 133, 134-136, *134, 135*, 141, 167
'Stewball Was A Racehorse' (song) 65
Stoney Crossing 85, 87
Straight Deal 16
Straight Fort *180*
Strong, Sir Charles 172
Sub Rosa 174
Sullivan, J. P. 112
Sun Princess 15
Sunday Independent (Irish) 138-139
Sunday Telegraph 37
Sunday Times 149
Sunny Bright 140, 141, 143
Sutherland 20, *21*

Taaffe, Pat 22, 29, 31, 32, 34-35, 144, 175, 180, 183, *183*
    and Arkle 27, 33, 34, *34*, 37, 38, *39*, 43, 45, 46, 74
        1964-65 season *68-69*, 77, *77*, 88, *88, 89*
        1965-66 season 96, 97, *97*, 98, 99, 100, 106, 109, 114, *115*, 116-117, *119*, *120*, 121
        1966-67 season 135, 136, 138, 141, 143, 146-147, *146*, 148
        convalescence *164*, 168
        Gold Cup (1964) 52, *56*, 57, 59, 60, 61, *61*, 62, 63, 67, 75
        Hennessy Gold Cup (1965) *102*, 103, 104, 105, *105*
        public appearances 90, *91*, *124*, 125, *125*
        retirement 170, *171*, 172
    and Bright Cherry *13*, 14
    and Flyingbolt 116, 117
    and Foinavon 20, 22
    and Fortria 36, 39
    injury and return *164*, 165
    and Mill House *41*, 42
Taaffe, Tom 32, 33, 40, 41, 80
Taaffe, Tos 23
Tattersalls Ireland 183, *183*
Taxidermist *43*, 106
Team Spirit 75
Temple Gwathmey Steeplechase 87
Ten Up 174
The Laird 167
The Rip *68-69*, 76, 77-78, 96, 97, 99
'There Will Never Be Another You' (song) 170
Thomond II 52
Thomson, Colonel Sir John *80*, 83, 166, 167, *168*, 174

Throughway 96-97
Timeform Ratings 177
Times, The 36, 52-54, 60-61, 63-64, 136, 166
Tingle Creek 42
Titus Oates 175
Togo 42
Tom Dreaper and his Horses 27-28, 174
Troutbeck 19
Troy 15
TV Times 130

UNICEF *132*

Veal, Bill 20
Vibart 17
Voy Por Ustedes *180*
Vulgan 20, 27
Vultrix *68-69*, 139-140, 141
Vulture 16

Walsh, Ted 175
Walsh, Wendy *182*
Walwyn, Fulke 42, 43, 63, 75
Wandering Light 174
Waterloo Bay *180*
Watkins, Cyril 22
Wayward Queen 102, 103, *104*
Weinstock, Lord 15
Welcome, John 50
Well Chief *180*
Wells, G. 16
Wells-Kendrew, Doris 145
Westminster, Anne, Duchess of 18-19, *18*, 22, 23, *32*, *47*, 174
    and Arkle 11, 17, 20, 24, 64
        1964-65 season 70, 78, *78*, 80, 90
        1965-66 season 101, 105, *105*, *121*, 124-125, *124*
        1966-67 season *132*, 141, *142*
        convalescence and retirement *151*, *157*, *164*, *165*, 169, 170, *171*, 172
        death and after 172, 173, 174, *179*, *182*, *185*
Westminster, first and second Dukes of 14, 18-19
What A Myth 106, 132, 133, 134
Whitbread, Colonel Bill 106
Wild Irish Rose: Popular Irish ballads 66
Willie Wagtail III 39
Willow King 38, 39, 88
Winning Fair 46
Winter, Eric 65
Winter, Fred 56, 105
Wogan, Terry 126
Woodland Venture 145, 146, 147, 167, 175
Woods, Paddy 27, *32*, 33, 39, 92-93, 97, 112, 117, *117*, 124-125, *151*, *152*, 170, *180*, 183
World Cup 130

Yeats, W. B. 130-131

Acknowledgements

Many people helped me with the earlier versions of this book. Jim Dreaper indulged my eccentric wish to go and stand in box number 7 at Greenogue (just checking on the ley lines, you understand) and lent me invaluable material. Paddy Woods and Alison Baker were likewise magnanimous with their time and information during my visits to Kilsallaghan and Malahow, while Nick O'Toole let me loose in his wondrous collection of Arkle memorabilia and generously allowed me to remove a good quantity for reproduction. Edward Gillespie at Cheltenham racecourse not only offered encouragement through his own enthusiasm for all things to do with Arkle, but allowed me access to the Arkle Bar during the close season: as usual, I could not get a drink in there, but the collection of material provided intoxication enough. Tim Cox was characteristically generous with the supply of information from his wonderful racing library. I am also indebted to Julian Brown and James de Wesselow at Racing Post Books; to the indefatigable Chris Pitt for all manner of fresh information; to Tony Byles for access to his wonderful photos of Arkle; to Geoff Greetham at Timeform; to Bob and Pam Sutton, custodians of the flame at the Arkle Bookshop at Cheltenham racecourse.

Many of the people named above have been involved in the current edition, published to mark the fiftieth anniversary of the 1964 Cheltenham Gold Cup, and I renew my thanks to them – and also acknowledge the particular help of Tony Murray, Bernard Parkin and David Owen.

It is also appropriate to thank all involved in the unforgettable Arkle Pilgrimage of October 2013. The pilgrims themselves – David Ashforth, Tim Cox, Richard Fisher, Tim Hailstone, David Heighway and Rebecca Mundy – are saluted for their generosity, constant good humour, and enthusiasm for a highly eccentric venture, while the ubiquitous Nick O'Toole enhanced the experience immeasurably. The munificence of Michael O'Leary and Tom Egan made the trip possible, and the hospitality we encountered all along the way was quite extraordinary. Grateful thanks to Peter and Wendy Reynolds at Ballymacoll Stud; to Alison Baker and her family; to Jim, Trish and Lynsey Dreaper; to Paddy Woods and Johnny Lumley; to Willie and Susan Robinson; to Anthony and Mary-Rose Mooney at Bryanstown; to T. P. Burns and his son James; to Sinead Hyland and Sally Carroll at the Irish National Stud; to Tom Gallagher at Kildangan Stud and Tim Corballis at Coolmore; and to Navan racecourse. You made some old men (and one young lady) very happy.

I am also extremely grateful to readers of the first edition who took the trouble to share with me their own reminiscences, and particularly so to Patricia Stewart, who wrote to unmask herself as the sender of the envelope reproduced on page 122: 'I can't remember if it was just a Valentines card in the envelope or whether I sent a letter as well at that time, but I did get a reply from Mr Dreaper and a cutting of Arkle's tail. I thought you would be interested to know this, although I don't know if it's wise admitting it! I have taken some stick for this from my husband!'

Taking stick on account of an obsession with Arkle? Join the club, Patricia ...

S.M.

Extracts from the writings of John Lawrence (John Oaksey) in *Horse and Hound* are reproduced by kind permission of Lord Oaksey. Extracts from Owen McCafferty's *Days of Wine and Roses*, published by Nick Hern Books in 2005, are reproduced by kind permission of the publisher. The words of 'Arkle' by Dominic Behan are reproduced by kind permission of Essex Music. The poem 'The Mighty Arkle' by Damian Smyth is published by kind permission of Lagan Press, Belfast. Extracts from *Chaseform* and *Raceform* are reproduced by kind permission of Raceform Ltd.